LIFE OF SPICE

LIFE OF SPICE

THE AUTOBIOGRAPHY OF GORDON SPICE

Gordon Spice

Compiled by **Jeremy Walton**

Haynes Publishing

First published in March 2009

A catalogue record for this book is
available from the British Library

ISBN 978 1 84425 568 9

Library of Congress catalog card no.
2008926369

Published by Haynes Publishing,
Sparkford, Yeovil, Somerset BA22 7JJ, UK
Tel: 01963 442030 Fax: 01963 440001
Int. tel: +44 1963 442030
Int. fax: +44 1963 440001
E-mail: sales@haynes.co.uk
Website: www.haynes.co.uk

Haynes North America, Inc.,
861 Lawrence Drive, Newbury Park,
California 91320, USA

Page layout by G&M Designs Limited,
Raunds, Northamptonshire

All photographs appearing in this book are
courtesy of the author unless otherwise
credited

Front jacket images courtesy of Graham
Robson (top) and LAT (bottom)

While the publisher has made every effort
to trace the copyright ownership of
photographs, this has not proved possible
in every case. If a copyright owner has
inadvertently been offended, please contact
the Editorial Director of the Book Division
at Haynes Publishing.

Printed and bound in Britain by
J. H. Haynes & Co. Ltd, Sparkford

Contents

Introduction

'Work as if you will live forever, live as if you will die tomorrow.'

I've tried to live by that motto, and as you get older you have time to reflect on life. We remember the good times with pleasure and tend to forget the bad times, that were so real at the time. We think our lives have been unique, which of course they have, and wonder how we'll be remembered.

I started writing my memoirs ten years ago, thinking that friends and family would enjoy reading them. Of course, it had nothing to do with ego: or had it?

After five years I hadn't got very far. There were always more enjoyable things to do: it could wait. It was late in 2007 that I decided to finish my autobiography. The decision was kick-started after being diagnosed with oesophageal cancer and old age seemed unlikely.

I again asked myself: why do it? This time the answer became clear: do it for yourself! I make no apology for this indulgence – writing it has been enormously therapeutic.

With Mandy's full support, I enlisted the help of an old friend, Jeremy Walton, partly to introduce some self-discipline and partly to finish it as a biography if I wasn't around. It has been enormous fun working with him.

You never get these things quite right. I've not mentioned many friends and colleagues who've given great help and support over the years, whether in private life, business or motor racing. But they know who they are and their omission in no way diminishes my gratitude.

Gordon Spice
Old Windsor, Spring 2009

March 1975 F5000 Gold Cup meeting. A surprise win at a snowy Oulton Park. (LAT)

Chapter 1

A wheezy start

April 1940 was not the most promising start in life, for I was born just seven months after World War 2 began. Apparently I was a sickly and underweight baby, wheezing with asthma and bothered by eczema. My early existence centred on life in an incubator, a total contrast to the sports, social and business activities that were to dominate most of my life.

I was born in Enfield, Middlesex, and christened Gordon Edward George Spice. It was only when I needed a passport that I found I was registered at Somerset House as George Gordon Spice – 'Gordon' being after Gordon Gill, who had been my father's boss in the City at the time.

I went through school as G.E.G. Spice, but my second name of Gordon stuck though my public life, although family simply called me 'Ga'. Nicknames abounded in our house: my mother Irene was known as Renee, whilst my elder sister Maureen was known as Noo, and my brother Derek simply as Dee. My younger brother Martyn John was called MJ, and my sister Andrea – the youngest of the five kids – was known as Zani. Our Nanny was with the family for over 50 years in multiple roles from nurse to peacekeeper and mentor. She was also my Godmother and I loved her enormously.

My father, George Spice, was an East London boy, genuinely 'born within the sound of Bow bells' – to qualify as a proper Cockney – in 1910. He started work as a messenger boy (aka a runner) in the City at 14. He was extremely bright and noted that successful city businessmen, 'toffs' to the runners, spoke the King's English. So he took himself to night school and lost his Cockney accent. This must have demanded acute perception and single-minded courage to withstand the inevitable teasing by his peers.

Dad rapidly rose through the City ranks. At just 21, Gordon Gill of Gill & Duffus, who were edible nut brokers, gave him the opportunity to start a cocoa broking department. The brief was: 'Make a profit in your first year, otherwise look for a new job.' Within five years, G&D were out of the nut business and, with Dad at the helm, became the world's largest cocoa brokers.

Father's vision and dealing skills were legendary. He changed the whole structure of the cocoa business by building processing plants in the countries of origin. Countries like the Gold Coast, Brazil and the East and West Indies benefited from this new approach. With Dad's success came wealth, which he generously shared.

Post-war Dad travelled extensively to the Americas, Africa and the Far East and in 1958 became Chairman of the Cocoa Association of London. High living and heavy drinking led to his early death in 1962 at the age of 52. He'd lived life to the full and succeeded in raising his family from working to middle class. He always put the family first and gave his five kids the very best education – something he had not enjoyed. I was a competitive and strong-willed child and never showed him due respect, and it is a source of regret that we didn't have a better relationship.

Born in 1912, my mother came from a middle-class background, but became very much the Grande Dame. Her maiden name was Hagon and she claimed to be distantly related to the Norwegian royal family, the Haakons – a source of much merriment to us all.

Mum was a wonderfully warm lady. Totally devoted to Dad and at his beck and call 24 hours a day, she put up with his outrageous behaviour. Whenever he called her, whether to catch the next flight to New York, or to join him (and his entourage of hostesses) in the early hours of the morning in a London night-club, she'd join him without question. If Dad brought a so called 'secretary' or 'lady buyer' home for the weekend, she accepted it with good grace and would never embarrass them.

When we asked Mum why she put up with him, the answer was always the same: 'For the sake of the children.' At that time, the stigma of divorce, particularly for women, was very much greater than it is today.

In 1965, after my father's death, she married Colonel Henry Henchman. 'Theo', as he was known. lived in Guernsey and was the total opposite of Dad. He was your original upright Colonel Blimp and a pillar of society. After tea planting in India he'd retired to Guernsey, where he became High Sheriff. He made Mum very happy for the last 20 years of her life.

In 1940 Dad moved the family to Hook in Hampshire and a house called Oakfield. It was a safe distance from wartime bombs and close to G&D's cocoa processing factory near Reading.

One of my earliest memories dates from 1945, just after the war, when we had a celebration VE party at Oakfield. We celebrated with a huge bonfire, topped by Hitler as Guy Fawkes. RAF Odiham was nearby, and some of their Canadian pilots were invited. The excite-ment of clinging to their backs as they leapt through the flames of that enormous fire was awesome.

Oakfield had a large garden with plenty of driveways and at Christmas in 1946 Dad bought us a two-seater Atco trainer car. It had a 50cc motor mower engine, clutch and mechanical brakes, plus forward and reverse gears. It could reach all of 10mph, but it was the ultimate contemporary toy. It had been in the window of Giffords hardware shop in Basingstoke for the duration of the war but, due to petrol rationing they had not been allowed to sell it. It was typical of Dad that he had put a deposit on it, told nobody – and then produced the best gift that any kid could dream of. Dee and Noo, eight and ten years old respectively, could drive it, but I was too short to reach the pedals. My frustrated anger at not being allowed to drive this device, which we called the Atom, was huge.

Whilst at Oakfield we attended a pre-prep school which was just behind the White Hart pub in Hook. Miss Cracknell was the head-mistress, so the school was nicknamed 'Cracky Nells'. Discipline was strong and the penalty for misdemeanours was to have the palm of your hand struck with a ruler. Extremely painful, but effective.

At eight, I followed Dee to the Old Malthouse (OMH), a preparatory school near Swanage in Dorset. The discipline was strict here too, but we were always treated fairly and

The Spice family in Shanklin, Isle of Wight, in 1948: (left to right) Nanny, MJ, Dee, Noo, Mum, GS, Zani and Dad.

you knew exactly where you stood. Never a term went by without being beaten at least twice, trousers down, by the headmaster, Victor Haggard. The result was a black and blue bottom for weeks but the kudos of a striped bottom in the plunge pool after games made the pain worthwhile – and guaranteed you were not seen as a wimp!

I thrived at the OMH and actually looked forward to school. The teaching was superb and learning was challenging and fun. Most of the masters were eccentric and everyone's favourite was Peter Mattinson, the games master, who also taught French. How do you teach young boys which French nouns ending in 'ou' demand an x in the plural? Even today I remember bijou, caillou, genou, chou… hibou, jou-jou, poo-poo-poo. It was the poo that made it scan and, being slightly rude, you remembered the words!

Sunday afternoons were devoted to pitched battles between teams on opposite sides of an old quarry, using balls of clay which were fired at the opposition using willow 'mud-switchers'. It was aggressive but harmless sport – unsupervised – and developed teamwork and leadership in a way that would not be allowed today.

Music played a major part in our school lives under the tutelage of Lobbo Lowe, the music master. I chose to play the cello on the basis that should I ever be stranded on a desert island, I had a better chance of boating away than a violinist.

Carpentry, a lifelong hobby, began for me in Mr Rideout's workshop at the OMH. The wooden stool that took a term to make was hardly a masterpiece, but it gave me immense pride to show it off at home. Although I did not achieve the carpentry skills of Dad, who's father had been a shipwright in the London docks, I still take great pleasure from a hobby learnt at an early age.

Despite my slight build (back then) I was a good rugby player. I played scrum half in the school's First XV, and captained it for two unbeaten seasons. I was also Captain of hockey and, in my last year, Head Boy.

Academically I was pretty average and there was never any question of a scholarship to Public school, so, because it was a rugger school, I was sent to Sherborne, which I simply hated.

From being a sports star and head of everything, I became a very small fish in a very big pond: I never really adjusted to what was a complete comedown after OMH. I rebelled,

became badly behaved, and took every opportunity to buck the system.

I had always won my weight boxing at the OMH, so I volunteered to join Sherborne's boxing team – anything to make a name for myself. For my first contest I had to lose weight to be eligible for the flyweight division against Clifton School. I was weak with hunger and up against a 16-year-old, roughly my size but stronger and a better boxer. I survived the first round but he knocked me out cold in the second. Total humiliation and the end of my short boxing career.

I found the academic work at Sherborne easy, boring and unchallenging. I passed ten 'O' levels without much effort, as OMH had taught me most of it. At Sherborne the quickest way to the sixth form was via the medical fifth and once you were in the sixth you could put your hands in your pockets! This, combined with my interest in medical matters, was the main factor in my decision to become a doctor.

My best mate at Sherborne was Charlie Pink, who was in Westcott House and my partner in crime. We used to smoke together in the woods, meet with girls from Sherborne Girls School – an expellable offence then – and plan night escapades. In the local Boots library worked an extremely glamorous and fun-loving local girl – we called her Di Boots – and Charlie and I competed for her favours. Charlie got the first date but chose a meeting-place which allowed little opportunity for serious hanky panky. I know, because I was the lookout.

When it came to my date, learning from Charlie's poor strategy I chose to meet Di Boots at a derelict mill house, a mile away from Westcott, with Charlie as lookout. I could then exaggerate the progress I made with the young lady without argument. Di was a very sporting lass and far more experienced than either of us, so we both claimed to have gone 'all the way'.

The truth only came out years later.

All Sherborne, boys had to join the CCF (Combined Cadet Force), and the majority were in the army section. It was an activity that I really disliked and the discipline was ferocious. There was also an air force section and a naval section – Charlie joined the latter and won a naval scholarship to Dartmouth. Naturally, I followed him into the naval section, which was less onerous than the army, though we did have to spend a week – during the holidays – on one of Her Majesty's ships in Portsmouth. My lasting memories of that week were the lower deck language of the ratings and the constant smell of diesel.

At the annual CCF show for parents, I dropped Charlie in the middle of the swimming pool in a breeches buoy demo and ended up back in the Army section. Everyone knew we were buddies so my protestations that it had been a genuine mistake were ignored. I wondered afterwards if the punishment was worth that short period of notoriety.

On the sports front I eventually made the house Rugby XV and Rodney Maynard was my fly half. We became good friends and during the holidays I fell for his sister, Gabrielle. She had been going out with Bruce David – a captain in Westcott House, in the school Rugby XV and two years my senior: not my favourite person. Gabrielle was a beautiful girl with a perfect figure and, most importantly, she was shorter than me.

During the holidays I used to stay with Rodney at the prep school in Woking where his father was headmaster. This gave me the opportunity to get to know Gabrielle better. Finally, I plucked up courage and declared my love for her. She did not fully reciprocate but said she liked me a lot. The inevitable 'but' was that I was four years younger than her, so 'I should not commit myself.' She also said she did not love Bruce, which made me feel much better and kept my hopes alive.

We spent as much time as we could together, discreetly and out of sight of her parents, who were very strict. I used my asthma attacks as an excuse to creep though to her bedroom when everyone had gone to bed. I was still a virgin and remained so throughout my romance with Gabrielle – her choice, not mine! We wrote to each other when she went back to University, but it wasn't the same so I had to find someone else.

At Sherborne, as with many Public schools then, the authorities turned a blind eye to homosexuality. This was in stark contrast to the attitude of boys socialising with girls, which was absolutely verboten. It was accepted that older boys could have 'crushes' on younger boys, and although this was not physical, I saw it as being far from normal. I questioned the housemaster, but he never gave a logical reason and just reit-

The Old Malthouse First XV rugger team, 1950. Dee is in the back row (extreme left), with Peter Matt next to him; GS is front right.

erated the dire consequences of socialising with girls. I felt this was morally indefensible, and became genuinely angry that a perfectly normal teenager's interest was being demonised. Charlie and I therefore ignored the rules and spent hours plotting our next meeting with Sue and Jackie, our new girlfriends, just up the road at Sherborne Girls School.

In 1953 my sister Noo left Newton Manor school in Swanage and was sent to Montesano, a finishing school for young ladies in Switzerland. In the winter her school moved to Gstaad, so Dad arranged for the whole family – by now there were five kids – to join her for a skiing holiday. The family, accompanied by Nanny, travelled overnight by train and were met in Gstaad by Kimber, the chauffeur, who had driven the Bentley down with the luggage.

We had our own instructor and learning to ski was then a slow and laborious business. Once one had mastered the kick turn, the next thing was sidestepping uphill. Walking uphill in herringbone fashion followed. Finally, we got to schussing down gentle slopes, with skis tightly parallel and legs bent. Learning to turn was the next step and this was quite tricky on the long wooden skis of the day. There were no safety bindings and the skis were attached

1955: Dee's Austin Special, with Grandma Spice.

to leather ski boots by long leather straps, which eliminated all movement between boot and ski. If one fell over at speed, breaking a leg was a distinct possibility. So, to reduce the risk, the instruction was rigorous and there was no question of progressing to the next stage until the previous one had been fully mastered.

Having learnt stemming techniques, you learned the stem christie, then the parallel christie, and the final technique was wedelling – but this took many weeks. Mum and Dad both gave it a go but decided it was not for them and they took up curling. Nanny's role was to stand at the bottom of the slope acting as clothes horse for discarded ski gear as the day grew warmer.

Two years later, at the end of our ski holiday in Wengen I decided to go for my British Ski Club gold badge. I had passed the bronze and silver tests in the previous two seasons. The 'crash and dash' part of the gold was a descent on the infamous Hahnenkahn racing course, against the clock. For once, technique did not matter. With schoolboy logic, I figured that if I took the course dead straight I would most likely fall and break my leg, resulting in time at home rather than returning to school. In the unlikely event of not falling, I would be a star – so there was really no downside.

I completed the formidable course, miraculously stayed upright and recorded the fastest time of the season! I was immediately approached by a group of middle-aged, weather-beaten and very plummy English ladies who seemed very excited about the record time. They suggested to my parents that I should be trained by the DHO (Downhill Only Club), with the idea of racing for the British under-16 ski team next season. Since there were very few English boys of my age lucky enough to ski, their choice of trainees was limited and the idea was given parental blessing.

In the winter of 1955–6 I underwent training with the DHO and entered my first downhill race. Alas, it was also to be my last, as I flew off at the second corner and tumbled down a sheer ravine, breaking both skis and damaging both cruciate ligaments in my left knee.

The only bonus was that when I should have been at Sherborne I was in St Mary's, Paddington. What was then major knee surgery meant I was excused CCF for two whole terms.

My 16th birthday fell in the Easter holidays and Dad hatched a celebratory plan. In the '50s Dad was a regular big spender in London nightclubs. After the austerity of the '40s, clubs like Rico Dajou's Casanova, Harry Meadows and Churchills were popular with businessmen, particularly those with company expense accounts. At the time the top rate of income tax was 85 per cent plus a 15 per cent surcharge on investment income, and the clubs relied on foreigners and businessmen for their income. Dad always reminded us that when he gave us 2s 6d (13p) to go to the cinema with a friend, it had cost him £5.

One of the attractions of these expensive clubs was the choice of young, attractive hostesses. On request, they would sit with clients and encourage them to buy more champagne, whilst they consumed soft drinks, charged out as champers at £10 a bottle! At a time when the average weekly wage in the UK was under £10, I remember being horrified when Dad signed bills to his company for well over £100.

After a few whiskies, sometimes Dad would buy everyone in the club a round of drinks, so he was a highly popular customer. Once a hostess had hit her sales target for the evening, she would be allowed to leave with the client, and after that any further arrangement was strictly between hostess and client.

After supper on my 16th birthday, the chauffeur was summoned and Dad announced he was taking me to town. It was my first visit to a nightclub, Harry Meadows in Conduit Street, and I was gobsmacked by the luxurious surroundings. In drab post-war Britain you did not often see red and gold flock wallpaper, never mind a titillating floor show. Through my teenage eyes, the hostesses were to die for.

The one Dad chose for me could not have been more than 19 and I was quite taken aback by her forwardness. After a few drinks, my inhibitions were forgotten. So when, at the end of the evening, 'Susie' asked me back to her place, I told her I'd love to but I had no money. She explained that this was not a problem, and took me off in a taxi to Athenaeum Court – a luxury block of flats just off Piccadilly. She was a very sweet girl, fully understanding of my over-enthusiasm, and assured me it would last longer next time...

Dad's 16th birthday present to me was not without an ulterior motive. He now had me over a barrel, and from then on if I questioned his authority at home he'd remind me: 'You wouldn't want your mother to know about Susie?'

At 16 that would have been the worst thing imaginable.

I went back to school absolutely full of it, elaborating my sexual adventure to a degree where Don Juan would have come a poor

Hooligans in the Wintney Court farm Land Rover in 1956.

second. Although some boys claimed to have gone 'all the way', few actually had, so my miserable performance remained secret. I did have to toe the line at home, but now I was a man of the world, and became even more derisive of the constraints of public school life.

Another friend who I looked up to at Westcott House was Robin Barkshire. He was a year or so older than me, was even more of a reprobate and spent most of his time under detention or loss of privileges. He had been caned twice by the Headmaster, Robert Powell, and this was a big thing in the macho ratings as the next stage was expulsion. At 17 Robin kept a car in a lockup garage and after lights out we'd creep out and go touring the countryside. The height of adventure!

Medical V1 class proved a cushy number. I persuaded my house master Frank King that I should give up all subjects not relevant to a medical career and use the extra study periods to concentrate on Biology, Physics and Chemistry. Mr Davis, our Biology teacher, was undemanding and my friend, Peter Bush, was clever and conscientious, as well as happy to share his work with me. Peter went on to become a highly respected doctor.

'Kippy' Andrews, who taught chemistry, was my favourite master. He voice was very quiet and raspy – the result of lung damage caused by mustard gas in World War 1 – but we all respected him, and not just because he turned a blind eye to our pranks. During his lessons I learnt to make sweets with sugar nicked from breakfast, and sold them for 3d a bag to fund my cigarettes, which I remember cost 1s 3d for ten.

On the academic front, I passed my Chemistry and Physics 'A' levels and Biology First MB, which qualified me for University Medical school. Both parents were keen that I should go, but Dad made it clear that, whilst my allowance would be adequate, there would be no question of any 'high living'. Perfectly fair, but the thought of another five years under Dad's control was unappealing so I dumped the idea of becoming a doctor.

The week before the end of my last term at Sherborne, Charlie and I, feeling demob happy, planned our last escapade. We acquired a jar of Potassium Permanganate crystals from the science laboratory, and late on Saturday night we crept up to the girls' school and poured it in their swimming pool. As anticipated, the whole pool turned purple. Stupidly, we then hoisted a jockstrap to the top of their flagpole.

A bad idea.

By this gesture, the authorities connected the boys' school with the pool's change of colour.

At assembly next Monday the Headmaster read the riot act amidst stony silence. He threatened to punish the whole school if the perpetrators were not found. Being among the main suspects, Charlie and I were grilled at length, but the authorities had no proof (no name on the jockstrap!) and we stuck to our well-rehearsed denial.

Meanwhile on the home front, in 1950 the family had moved from Hook to Hartley Wintney, and Dad had become a gentleman farmer. Post-war austerity (sweet rationing only ended in 1953!) and high taxes for big earners had led many successful businessmen down this route, as farm losses could be offset against top-end income tax, in addition to the perks of having your own farm.

Wintney Court was a large Victorian mansion set in 200 acres of fields and woodland, and the gilt sign at the bottom of the drive read: 'Home of the Wintney Court Herd of Pedigree Guernseys'. Dad was very proud of that. It was a model farm and a wonderful place for kids to grow up.

My love of driving was sparked by throwing the family Land Rover sideways through the fields, chasing and shooting rabbits on the run at night and behaving like a hooligan when the coast was clear. Mum had a silver AC Aceca and, egged on by her siblings, drove it flat out. In those days traffic was never a problem but Dad put speed bumps in the drive – very unsporting. In stark contrast, Dad drove slowly, often in a gear too high and on the verge of stalling. I think he did it just to annoy us.

When Dee was 17 he bought an Austin 7 Special which was a real old banger – I think it cost a tenner. He was studying at Chelsea's College of Automobile Engineering, where a fellow student was future Land Speed Record holder Richard Noble.

Dee was always far better than me at mechanical things, but when help was needed to keep his car on the road there was always Alan Southern at Phoenix Engineering, just down the road. Alan, being ex-RAF, boasted an impressive handlebar moustache. The Home Counties Weber agent, he was also a classic car enthusiast, specialising in Alvis, Lagonda and Bugatti. It was Alan who sparked Dee's interest in motor racing, and if it wasn't for him I'd have never become involved.

Chapter 2

Australian adventure

Around 1957 Dad and the farm manager decided they were paying too much for cattle food, mainly because the suppliers held a cartel. Typically, Dad decided to do something about it. He bought G&D's cocoa processing plant in Hook, which had been closed following a major fire, and the factory was rebuilt around the latest machinery to make cattle food. The idea was to give local farmers, of which he was one, a better choice of affordable supplies. Court Mills Ltd was created, and feed production started.

In the summer of 1958 I left school – one of the happiest days of my life – and my first job was selling Court Mills cattle food to local farmers. At 18 years of age, with no training, this was a tall order – particularly as my potential customers were tough, sceptical farmers, resistant to change. I could rarely answer their questions if they were about more than price or delivery. The few orders placed were out of sympathy for my plight, or because they were friends of the family. However, my job allowed me the use of a Morris Minor Traveller, a luxury I could not otherwise afford and which more than compensated for my lack of sales success.

I had read about the Australian Government encouraging immigrants from Europe with a token £10 one-way fare, and had made known my plan to go there. Fate rescued me via Doctor Jimmy Phelan, Dad's close friend and drinking partner: Jimmy was the only doctor who didn't tell Dad to stop drinking. Married to Molly, an Australian, Jimmy was a charismatic Irishman, and it was through the Phelans that I met Ian Jacoby, founder of Custom Credit Corporation, a successful Australian finance company.

An offer was made for me to work for Custom Credit as a trainee manager, and I accepted with enthusiasm. The parents were as happy to see the back of me as I was to be independent of them, and a ticket was booked on the SS *Orion*, an older ship of the P&O fleet.

In November 1958 I set sail from Southampton with my luggage and my two favourite records: The Platters and Oklahoma. I also had £200 in cash, which made me feel like a millionaire as it was more money than I had ever seen.

As a '£10 Pom', I shared a cabin, deep in the bowels of the hull, with a tall 21-year-old Canadian, Peter Martin. We became good pals and agreed to share a flat when we got to Sydney. Peter was a drummer who told me he had been kicked out of Canada for GBH (Grievous Bodily Harm) inflicted on his father, who was still recovering in hospital. I didn't believe him, but I should have.

Ship life was hectic. Even £10 Poms could enjoy all the free entertainment, and a whole new world unfurled before me. Couples, generally older than myself and paying full fares, seemed happy to take me under their wing – buying drinks and being entertained by my amateur card tricks.

The port excursions were eye opening and in Djibouti I had my first experience of an Arab market which specialised in X-rated postcards and shows for tourists. No details were spared and the shows featured some amazing antics involving donkeys – and I'd thought I was a man of the world!

Life on board was extremely sociable, and I soon fell for a lovely dark-haired 20-year-old, Nicky Dunlop. She was returning to Oz, after completing a secretarial course in London. The problem was she was travelling with her Indian boyfriend. I really couldn't see what she saw in him, besides his luxury cabin and the size of his wallet. Fortunately the boyfriend was leaving the ship in Ceylon, which was good news. So I spent time with them, playing gooseberry and usually out-fumbling him when the bar bill arrived.

When we got to Colombo the boyfriend's parents entertained us royally at the gorgeous five-star Mount Lavinia Hotel. My sharpest memory of that day is swimming to a small island off the hotel beach. When I grabbed a rock to pull myself out, the rock scuttled away – it was a giant crab!

Leaving Colombo, boyfriend mercifully gone, I wasted no time in making my move. I was pleased to find Nicky had her own cabin, far superior to mine with proper windows.

A minor setback occurred when she explained she would not sleep with anyone, unless she was going to marry them.

Unperturbed, I said I quite understood her reservations, and would she marry me? I was really quite taken aback when she accepted!

I promised her the engagement ring would be first priority when we hit Sydney, hang the expense. The Colombo to Sydney leg of the journey was shipboard romance at its best and time flew by.

When we reached dry land three weeks later, reality hit us both.

On arrival in Sydney, Nicky was met by her mother and I was introduced. We had agreed not to mention our forthcoming betrothal immediately. I was greeted by Geoff Jacoby, son of Custom Credit boss Ian, a thoroughly Ozzie Oz with an accent to match. Geoff had been delegated by his Dad to integrate me into Australian life. I can't think of a better mentor, and we became great friends.

Geoff was the complete party animal, extrovert, raconteur and comedian. At 28 years old he was one of Sydney's most eligible bachelors, but it wasn't his money or his looks that attracted an endless succession of stunning girls, but his ability to amuse and entertain – with or without booze.

Geoff rented a bedsit for me at The Ritz in Cremorne, in the shadow of Sydney harbour bridge. The Ritz was not ritzy, but it was cheap and only 20 minutes from my new career at the head office of Custom Credit. It was a ten-minute boat ride from Circular Quay, where construction work had just started on what would become a global landmark: the clamshell outline of Sydney Opera House.

Custom Credit Corporation was one of the first companies in Australia to recognise the potential of hire purchase. Excepting Mercantile Credit, it was the largest Australian HP concern, with branches in all major cities. So I was in the right place at the right time, and my face apparently fitted.

Jacoby junior recalled almost 50 years after out first encounter: 'I first met Gordon Spice when he arrived in Sydney in 1958. He was fresh-faced, blond, good looking with plenty of charm and natural wit. He was also self-effacing and could easily mix with people two or three times his age. He was very positive and you felt he would succeed in whatever endeavour he chose in life. He embraced Australia, but with his natural enthusiasm he would have embraced Timbuk One. Gordon was an intellectual – he loved our beer.' No, I did not pay Jacoby for that testimonial!

Custom Credit offered finance on domestic electrical goods, motor cars and bikes. Transaction records were kept on a card system processed by ladies with accounting machines – no computers then. At Head Office I spent a week in each department learning the business. After a month I was dispatched to work at the Edgcliffe branch. I used this as an excuse to move to the centre of town and took a flat with shipmate Pete Martin in the Kings Cross Road, known as 'the dirty half mile'. Kings Cross was the equivalent of London's Piccadilly Circus and the centre of clubland.

My salary was now A£110 per month. The Australian Pound was worth 15 UK shillings then, but would buy twice as much. At 18 I had a responsible job and a salary of £1,300 per annum, an absolute fortune compared with the £7 a week I earned in the UK.

Because of my age Geoff did not support my engagement to Nicky, who lived with her Mum in Gordon, on Sydney's North Shore. Geoff had a house complete with large swimming pool at Darling Point, an upmarket Sydney suburb, so I wasn't seeing much of Nicky. My introduction to Sydney was an endless round of parties at Geoff's and his friends' places. Weekends were spent cruising on his English Harrison Butler sailing sloop, *Talisman*.

Nicky thought I should be spending more time with her, and unless I changed my ways she would call off our engagement. There were no regrets on either side when that came to pass.

The Aussie blokes thought I was a complete dork. They had never seen a chap stand up when a lady entered the room, open a car door for a female, or talk to girls at a party. They regarded this as totally unmanly behaviour and they frequently took the piss out of my accent. I let them have their fun. I exaggerated the cut glass Brit bit and the girls loved being treated with respect.

At work I was frequently 'mothered' by ladies in the accounts departments, which I enjoyed. One day I was quite taken aback when one of them asked to borrow my Durex. I did not know that this was the Oz generic name for a rubber of the erasing variety.

Although I was earning good money, I wasn't saving enough for a deposit on a car, so I took an evening job as a junior barman at the cosmopolitan Rex Hotel in Macleay Street – a five-minute walk from the flat. I was a mere dogsbody, washing up glasses, clearing tables and rarely serving behind the bar. As a hotel, the six o'clock closing rule did not apply, so the popular bar was open all hours. Drinks at the Rex was on visiting celebrities' must-do list.

You can imagine the excitement when Frank Sinatra, Sammy Davis Jr and Dean Martin walked into the bar, accompanied by teenage idol Frankie Avalon. The stars, who were at the height of their 'Rat Pack' days, were doing a show at the Sydney Stadium, which was just down the road at Rushcutters Bay. They were big drinkers and big tippers: my car-saving fund increased dramatically. Incidentally, Peter Farquhar, an old friend who was an apprentice jockey in Sydney at the time, attended this concert; he remembers it was in May 1959.

One evening on my way to the Rex, I saw a young Aborigine snatch an old lady's bag from her shoulder and run off. He was a scrawny lad and when I caught up with him I tapped him on the shoulder.

He turned to face me and I started to explain the error of his ways, then BAM...

I came to flat on my back on the pavement. I'd never even seen his fist coming. Another lesson learnt.

I did not see much of Pete Martin, as he played drums in a club and never got back before 3:00am. After working at the Rex for a couple

Perth in 1986 (40 years later!), with Geoff Jacoby and Nelleck Jol.

of months the novelty faded, and I saw little chance of being promoted. I mentioned this to Pete, who told me there was a vacancy for a drummer at a nightclub named El Bongo (very original) and why didn't I apply?

I pointed out that I didn't play the drums, to which he replied 'No problem, I'll teach you.'

So I went for the interview, elaborated on past experience in 'the Old Country', and asked about the pay and hours? At the end they asked me to demonstrate my drumming skills – on their drums.

I explained that in England drummers used their own drums and as I was not familiar with theirs, I'd prefer to bring my own along. I offered to play a piece on 'their' cello, which I could have managed, and having swallowed the bullshit a return date was set for the following Monday.

The following weekend saw six hours of instruction from Pete, plus ten hours of practice. By Sunday night I had learnt the basic techniques for the different tempos. On the Monday I turned up without drums. I explained that my car had broken down, and I couldn't bring them on public transport, so I'd just have to use theirs – which, happily, were similar to Pete's.

I had played for two minutes, accompanied by a record, when they stopped me. I thought I'd been rumbled, but 'When could I start?' was the only query. Success!

The hours were 9:00pm to 2:00am Wednesday to Saturday, and it turned out to be lucrative and fun. El Bongo was expensive, intimate and exclusive – one of the watering holes for Sydney's society set in which Elsa Jacoby, Ian's wife, was a leading player.

Being a bit of a tart, I soon discovered that smiling at older ladies, and laying on the British accent during breaks, led to handsome tips. After three weeks, added to my Rex Hotel savings, I had enough money for a deposit on a car.

My relationship with Pete Martin came to an unfortunate end when he turned up around 4:00am one morning, well ratted. He accused me of using his drums without asking. When I denied it, he went absolutely berserk and grabbed from the wall a decorative African tribal knife – a gift from Dad – and attacked me.

Luckily the knife was blunt, he was too spaced-out to be a serious threat, and he passed out after being hit with a chair. I found the whole experience quite shattering and didn't go back to bed that night.

First thing in the morning I went flat-hunting, and by lunch had rented a bedsit just up the road. Later that day when I collected my gear Pete was nursing a mammoth hangover. He was highly remorseful and promised that it wouldn't happen again, but I wasn't going to take the risk. Suddenly I believed his original story about why he'd left Canada.

The new bedsit was tiny, with only enough room for the bed and stereo system, but it came with a parking space: all I needed was the car to fill it.

Within Custom Credit, a list of repossessed cars was produced monthly and they would normally be auctioned to recover HP arrears. When a red 1954 MG TF appeared on the list I snapped it up. It was my pride and joy, and especially savoured as I'd bought it with my own earnings. Having my own wheels, and sexy ones at that, gave me a new freedom, and the girl-pulling power was an extra bonus.

After just three months work experience I was promoted to assistant branch manager at the Gordon office. It was one of the smaller branches with a staff of eight, in a fashionable residential area that was an easy commute from Kings Cross.

My rapid promotion was not a reflection of my business skills, which by UK standards were average, at best. In the late '50s in Australia career opportunities came quickly, if you could read, write, add up and communicate. The country was desperately short of basic skills and this was the reason behind the Government's £10 immigration scheme.

World War 2 had strengthened Australia's paranoiac fear of being overrun by millions of Asians, and a White Australia policy was at that time a strict Government priority. Immigration from European countries was encouraged, but banned to residents of countries with a different skin colour. Hard to believe today, but in the '50s it was normal.

Promotion had boosted my salary so I relinquished my evening job at El Bongo and my social life expanded to seven nights a week. Some weekends I'd spend on Geoff's boat with his friends. If Geoff was away I'd use the sloop as a base, and do my own entertaining, pretending to be the co-owner if it would impress my guest.

Other weekends I'd go to Bilgola Beach where Alan Waring, a friend from Custom Credit, had the use of his parents' house, which was right on the beach. Winifred

Atwell, the famous American pianist, was a regular visitor to Sydney and she owned a house next door to the Warings. Apparently the White Australia policy was relaxed for celebrities and she was a very popular figure in Sydney. On Saturday nights she had open house and entertained the locals playing her honky-tonk piano in her own inimitable way. She was a wonderfully warm person, never played the superstar and made everyone feel welcome. I became a lifelong fan.

Bilgola was a well-known surfing beach and, being young and fit, I soon mastered the art, spending hours in the water looking for the 'Big One'. The surf boards were bigger and heavier than today, and it was hard work paddling through the breakers to pick up a wave, typically a hundred yards offshore.

One day, having failed to spot the 'dumper', I fell off the board and got swept under the white water towards the shore. I surfaced somewhat disorientated and my board, which had caught the next wave, hit me slap in the face.

That was the last thing I remembered.

Luckily the lifeguards, constantly on the lookout for sharks and swimmers in trouble, came to the rescue. I came to on the beach with a broken nose, blood everywhere and two front teeth missing. 'Painless' Frank Starr, one of Geoff's sailing mates, was also an excellent dentist. Painless sorted out the teeth well before the black eyes had disappeared – not good for the image and a source of much piss-taking by my Ozzie 'friends'.

Sadly, I hadn't bothered keeping in touch with the family, so it was a pleasant surprise when I received a gift voucher from Mum for my 19th birthday in April 1959. The voucher was for John Hardy's department store, Sydney's equivalent of Harrods. They had a booze

Geoff Jacoby in 1958.

department and I spent the lot on Fosters beer. My letter home thanked Mum for the new shirts!

Shortly afterwards, Dad visited Sydney claiming to be on a buying trip to the East Indies. I knew this was just an excuse to check up on me but, happily, we got on extremely well. Our relationship had changed out of all recognition, and for the first time ever we spoke man to man.

It came as no surprise that Dad had a girlfriend in Sydney, someone he'd known for years. Dawn was an elegant and attractive divorcee in her 40s. Dad was an inveterate traveller and wherever he landed – New York, Rio, Paris or Lagos – he'd simply pick up the phone, and within the hour female company arrived. These women were not tarts, but party-minded ladies who obviously enjoyed Dad's company.

During Dad's week in Sydney, I enjoyed impressing my girlfriends with lavish hospitality at his expense. When Dad left to go to Indonesia I continued seeing Dawn and became her toy boy, although I didn't think of it in such terms at the time.

At work, after three months as assistant manager I understood most aspects of the business, from the paperwork and selling side through to repossessing goods when customers defaulted. I was delighted to find that my manager was due to be transferred to a larger branch, and the prospect of promotion loomed large.

After interviews at head office I was offered promotion to branch manager, conditional on a month's extra training at the larger Paramatta branch, 40 miles from Sydney. I realised that this would have a negative impact on my social life – a month is a long time at that age – but the thought of having my own branch overcame the down side.

The Paramatta branch boss was Alan Brinton, an inspiring character. I learned from Alan how little I really knew about management, and he was an exceptional mentor and motivator. That month in Paramatta shot by, and I realised afterwards how important it had been to my business career.

I couldn't believe my luck! Here I was at the age of 19, earning £170 a month, with my own car, my own pad, girls galore and enough money to really enjoy life. On top of that, as branch manager I was personally responsible for HP outstandings of £1.2 million. I still had much to learn about man-management, but

Alan was only a telephone call away and I relied heavily on his help.

I became involved with every department and spent time planning with the staff how to elevate our branch in the Custom Credit league table. One vital measurement was the amount of bad debt attributable to each branch, so I spent time visiting customers who were in arrears, often in the evenings. If promises of payment were broken, goods would be physically repossessed. It was a tough training ground in credit control and invaluable experience for the future.

The National Bank of Australasia (NBA) had a 40 per cent shareholding in Custom Credit, a natural partnership for a fast-growing finance company. With NBA's backing it was decided to enter the life insurance business, and CustomLife was founded. The Managing Director would be Peter Hutton-Potts, a Brit who had been a senior officer in HM's Hong Kong Police force and was currently a director of Custom Credit. Peter was one of Geoff's closest buddies and I knew his family well. In a country full of Aussies, two Brits were natural allies.

One evening Peter told me about the start-up of CustomLife, where he would be MD, and asked me if I would be interested in becoming his personal assistant? He outlined the job requirements, which would involve travelling with him and establishing a network of offices around Australia.

It was a wonderful opportunity to be in on the ground floor of a new business, not to mention a company car! Having cleared it with Geoff, I accepted the job which was due to start in November. In mid-October, however, I received a telegram from my mother which was to change my life, although I didn't know it at the time.

The telegram said my father was extremely ill and was unlikely to live very long. I should come home as soon as possible to see him, implying this would be the last time. I knew that for many years he had suffered from bouts of bad health. On several occasions he had been on the critical list, so I had no reason to suspect a set-up.

I spoke to Peter and Geoff who agreed I should go back, and they would hold the PA job open until I returned. Knowing I would be coming back to a company car I sold the TF and bought an air ticket. By the end of October 1959 I was back in the UK.

I left behind a lifestyle I would never see again, a career with unlimited prospects, and some of the best friends I ever had.

Chapter 3

America, Birdie and Britain

I was met by the family chauffeur, Kimber, at Heathrow and driven back to Wintney Court. I questioned him about Dad's health and he was very vague. Dad had apparently made a miraculous recovery, and I subsequently discovered that he had not been that ill. The telegram was a plot they hatched to get me home and I never really forgave them for that.

In their defence, the only news they had had of me came via the Jacobys and the Phelans, so perhaps the rough justice was warranted by my thoughtless behaviour.

I told the parents that I intended to return to Australia and take up my job with CustomLife. Dad made it equally clear that, after my expensive education, it was my duty to go into the family cocoa business, WG Spice & Co, formed after he had left G&D.

Knowing I had no money, they asked me how I intended to get back to Oz? They made it clear that they would not lend me the airfare.

After its brief honeymoon in Sydney, our father-son relationship was back to square one. The only difference was that I now knew my market value and, although it was never discussed, so did Dad. Tempted by seeing the USA for the first time, and feeling flattered at being needed, I surrendered to Dad's demands. Looking back, I'm sure that Geoff would have financed the return trip, but I was too immature to think of asking.

Whilst I had been away in Oz Dad had started a new company, Personalised Products Ltd (PPL), which produced high quality chocolate bars. The distinguishing feature of the Toblerone-shaped bars was that the wrappers were personalised for specific events, such as a charity balls, or could be printed with the name of the hotel or club selling them. The concept had been successful in the States, particularly at fundraising events, and Dad had been quick to spot the potential for the UK market.

Before leaving for the States, I got stuck into selling the chocolate bars to hotels, pubs and clubs. During the charity ball season in London I attended and set up stalls to sell the bars at £1 each, 'Made specially for The Royal Lifeboat Society' or whatever. Half the money taken went to the relevant charity.

For both PPL and the charities it was a win-win situation. We were making good money and raising product awareness, and the charity enjoyed additional no-risk income. For me it was fun, mixing with the 'debs delight' set, meeting glamorous girls and being paid for the privilege.

At one of these balls I met a dark-haired beauty, Valerie Parish. I chatted her up with free chocolate in exchange for her phone number. We hit it off immediately and in the months before leaving for the States she became my number one girlfriend. I called her 'Birdie', similar to the Oz slang for a single girl, and she recently recalled our first meeting:

'The posh ball was at London's Grosvenor House, where there are two ballrooms at different levels. Gordon was selling his choccies on the split level between the two. Yes, he did get my phone number, but he also learned my address too, because there was a bunch of red roses through the door the next day... Very romantic!'

Still laughing, Birdie chortled when we met again in 2008: 'However, when you came around for our first date there was a snag. You were wearing the most disgusting shiny suit, one of many you had picked up down under. I had to train you back to British dressing habits!' Aside from attending to my dress sense, Birdie would also be my lover and wife, but that's another story.

After a family ski holiday, I left for the eastern seaboard of the States in March. I was met in Philadelphia by Dick Brown, owner of the US Cocoa Corporation in which Dad had an interest. I spent the first week at Dick and Louise's home, near Trenton, New Jersey. They spent a lot of time at the very posh Trenton Country Club, where Louise was captain of the ladies' golf team.

I was treated as a bit of a celebrity, as most of their friends had never met an English person. I was forever being asked to repeat what I'd just said because 'We simply *laaarve* your accent!' I revelled in the attention of pretty young girls with perfect teeth who hung on every word and competed to take me to drive-in movies.

Dick was ex-Princeton College and fixed me up at The Princeton Club in Philadelphia, steeped in history and tradition, and as snobbish as only Ivy League clubs can be. I took full advantage of my British status and left for work every morning in cavalry twill trousers, blue blazer and old school tie – somewhat inappropriate for factory life.

The cocoa factory was in Camden, New Jersey, a 15-minute walk over the bridge crossing the Delaware river. The basic factory operation was grinding cocoa cake, a by-product of cocoa butter, to make cocoa powder. Camden was an all black town, and the only whites in the factory were the foreman and me.

My first day at work was a complete culture shock.

The factory was indescribably dusty and all the workers were permanently covered in a layer of cocoa dust. On arrival each morning I would join the other workers in the changing room and change into a boiler suit. The highlight was listening to my black co-workers describing their previous night's exploits.

Typically, one of them would pull out his enormous plonker, grasp it in both hands and talk to it as if it was human. 'Was you busy last night, man, or was you busy? Man, you was everywhere… Aah could hardly keep up… You made the sweetest pussies cry with joy… An' yo' daddy's proud o' you, man.'

No detail was spared as they played to a new audience.

I'd say 'I don't believe you actually had three ladies in your bed with your wife at home.'

The reply? 'No big ting man… Rosie was busy with Winston… we's a-sharin' dem honey pots.'

Pretending not to believe them was all the encouragement they needed to elaborate on their prowess. These guys were hardworking but unskilled, and were paid enough to buy new cars every year, which was important to their status. In their lives sex was the number one topic – cars and baseball came a poor second. They were friendly and protective of me but could not work out what an educated honky must have done to end up shovelling cocoa cake into a hopper with them?

I could not admit I was there to learn the family business, or how pissed off I was at having walked so naively into Dad's trap. I lived a Walter Mitty life, my days spent labouring before showering off the cocoa dust and returning to the hallowed atmosphere of the Princeton Club.

Philadelphia, known then as the city of brotherly love, was the gay capital of the East Coast and famous for its many bars. My favourite was Lani's, and most clients were Irish Americans with an enormous capacity for boozing and scrapping. Rarely an evening went by without Lani breaking up a fight.

At Lani's I met Kenneth McKenzie, an ex-pat who lived with a wonderfully buxom nightclub singer named Joy. Kenneth, who was ex-RAF and played the part to perfection, was working for a specialist employment agency. His claim to fame was that he recruited Wernher von Braun, the German rocket scientist, to join the post-war American space programme.

Kenneth was a skilled raconteur, a complete Male Chauvinist Pig and excellent company. Shortly after we became drinking mates, I left the Princeton Club and rented a room in his flat. It was cheaper and more fun, though I could never understand why Joy put up with such an MCP.

At the cocoa factory, I was getting pretty fed up with the monotony of sweeping floors, filling hoppers and cleaning filters, so when I saw on the notice board that the company needed a truck driver I applied for the job.

'Can you really drive trucks?' I was asked.

'Of course,' I confidently replied. 'In England, after your driving test you automatically go on to get a heavy goods licence.' Knowing that the company truck was fixed axle, and to give credibility to the bullshit, I added that, due to my age, I had not yet passed the test for articulated lorries.

My truck-driving career came within a whisker of a premature end on the return leg of a daily run. I was delivering cocoa powder to the Hershey chocolate factory in Norristown, Pennsylvania, when I noticed I was low on fuel. Approaching a long downhill section of road, I switched the engine off, freewheeling to save fuel. What I did not know was that there was a new road works diversion at the bottom of the hill...

I applied the brakes, but sweet FA happened.

By the time I realised that the airbrakes relied on the engine running to keep up the pressure it was too late. I crashed through the wooden diversion barriers and came to a halt a hundred yards later amidst some very surprised labourers. Damage to the truck was minimal but the barrier was well stuffed.

I explained what had happened to the work gang's boss and gave him some money 'to pay for the damage'. He was as pleased as I was relieved – trucking was an advance on shovelling cocoa all day!

Discussing the recruitment business one evening, Kenneth mentioned that English secretaries were much in demand in Philadelphia. US company bosses were paying handsomely for the kudos of having an English secretary, and work permits were not a problem. So I sent a telegram to 'Birdie' Parish, suggesting she leave her job with J. Walter Thompson and come to Philadelphia to earn some big bucks. And that's exactly what she did.

In 2007 Birdie remembered that 'It was all so exciting. We had been going out for about six months when you asked me over. I had been sharing a flat in London with Sally Stokes [long-term partner of World motor racing champion Jim Clark, who later married Ed Zwart, Dutch race ace]. Sally and others were interested in my trip and some of those flatmates of mine did come to share the flat you rented later on, in New York.'

When Birdie arrived I rented a small flat in a less affluent area close to downtown Philadelphia, the commercial centre. Birdie's first weekend was spent painting our first home. Life was good. Birdie landed a secretarial job with a large advertising agency and was earning $125 per week, against my own $75. We pooled our money and after paying rent and other living costs there was plenty left over for luxuries, particularly as invitations to spend weekends with new friends were rolling in.

It was rare to find Americans who were not proud to claim English, Scottish or Irish ancestry, and looking back their generous hospitality was largely down to their fascination for all things British. We enjoyed being the centre of attention and it soon became second nature to ham up our Englishness.

After a few months at US Cocoa I was not learning much about cocoa and the novelty of driving a truck was wearing thin. So Dad sent me to New York, where I started work for Ernest Adler & Co, a cocoa broker with offices in Wall Street. I couldn't wait for the buzz of the NY Cocoa Exchange, wheeling and dealing in cocoa futures and all the other things I'd heard about.

The reality was a big downer.

My first job was working on insurance claims in a grotty office alongside monosyllabic New Yorkers. Somehow, they knew that Ernest Adler was an associate of my father and treated me like a spy. My job was to cut open hundreds of cocoa beans from damaged shipments, work out the ratio of good to mouldy beans, and make insurance claims for any losses. It was a repetitive, soul-destroying job. I had dark thoughts about being exploited by Ernest Adler, a Jew who wore fur coats, and my father, his friend.

However, I put up with it because my private life could not have been better. Birdie, who'd accompanied me from Philadelphia, landed an excellent job in Manhattan, and we rented the top floor of a large house in Brooklyn Heights, with three bedrooms. She then phoned three girlfriends in the UK and persuaded them to come over to enjoy the rich pickings of secretarial life in New York. Within days of arriving they all landed jobs, earning between $125 and £175 a week – considerably more than they could earn in London, and with less tax.

The rent for the Brooklyn apartment, which had two doubles and a single bedroom, was $300 a month. I charged the four girls $100 per month each, but this included free commuting to Manhattan in the old Chevy I'd bought in Philadelphia. My own pay was still only $75 a week and the arrangement worked well.

When the snow came, on Friday nights we'd all pile into the Chevy and head for the ski resorts in upstate New York or Vermont. Parking the car out of sight, one of us would check into the motel as a single: the other four would cram in afterwards – fantastic value for money. The skiing was never much good compared to Europe, but the après-ski was brilliant. Accompanied by four of England's finest females, I rarely had to buy a meal or a drink.

Birdie's recent recollections of life in New York are that 'It was just as exciting and colourful as I'd hoped. The clothes were strangely exotic, with big changes between the seasons in hats and coats – and there was just so much

going on, all the time… and the sheer size of the cheap meals! Remember, Britain was only a few years out of post-war rationing and some pretty drab times, so the sheer vibrancy and colour of life in the States was exhilarating at such a young age. My memories are of places like the Stork Club, and ice skating at the Rockefeller Centre.

'I rather bravely went to see the Alfred Hitchcock thriller *Psycho* on my own in New York – but we had been regulars at drive-in movies in Philadelphia. Of our trips outside the city, the most vivid in my mind, some 47 years later, were those to Niagara Falls, the hick town that was Toronto back then, and skiing in Vermont.

'It was all a great adventure as a young adult – the Christmas atmosphere was absolutely wonderful – I would not have missed any of it… But that life would not continue indefinitely,' Birdie concluded.

In November 1960 Ernest Adler told me that Dad was visiting New York and asked me to pick him up at the airport. Birdie and I met him at Idlewild airport (now JFK) and on the journey to Manhattan Dad sat beside me with Birdie in the back.

Dad was very chatty – I assumed he'd had a few on the aeroplane. A bizarre conversation followed, which according to my and Birdie's joint recollections went like this:

Dad: 'You're living with Valerie, aren't you boy?'

Me (surprised he knew): 'Yes Dad, I am.'

Dad: 'Do you love each other then?'

Me (although we'd never discussed it): 'Yes Dad, we do – isn't that right, Birdie?'

Birdie: 'Yes, of course we do.'

Dad: 'Well, boy, I think you should get married. What do you think about that?'

Me (playing along): 'Good idea, Dad. Birdie, how do you feel about it?'

Birdie (joining in the fun): 'Sounds OK with me.'

Dad: 'That's agreed then, boy. I'll fly you back for an engagement party at Christmas and you can get married in June – you'll be 21 by then.'

Me: 'Fine, Dad.'

The subject was then dropped, and driving to the Waldorf Hotel small talk included anything but marriage.

Spending Christmas in England was now our priority, but eventually we got round to the subject of getting engaged. Neither of us can remember the details, but we agreed we loved each other, got on well together, had much in common, and could see ourselves happily married. So… why not?

I've never known to this day what was in Dad's mind when he suggested we get engaged. I knew that the very last thing he wanted was for me to get married, and certainly not to Birdie, who had Jewish blood. I always believed that the Spices also had Jewish blood, and often expressed that belief, much to the annoyance of the family. That did not stop Dad holding highly anti-Semitic views, frequently voiced, which today would get him locked up.

I once asked him why, if he disliked the Jews so much, was he always in business with them? He never gave me a satisfactory answer, but agreed that commodity markets were predominantly Jewish. I concluded he was in denial of his ancestry – something that probably went back to his early days with non-Jewish Gill and Duffus, and his commitment to elevating his family to the middle class.

A week before Christmas 1960 we flew back to London and had our engagement party at Wintney Court. I met Fred and Marie Parish, Birdie's parents, who lived in Hadley Wood, Hertfordshire. I got on well with Fred, who was a down-to-earth character and one of the most generous men I have known. Birdie was the apple of Fred's eye and he was genuinely pleased that she had found her man. Fred owned two of the best carpet shops in North London: his sons, Tony and Malcolm, also worked in the business, which was highly profitable and funded a lavish lifestyle.

Returning to New York after Christmas we fell into the routine of working in Manhattan Monday to Friday and taking off for the mountains at the weekends. In March I was sitting in a traffic jam on the Triborough Bridge when a Ford pickup ploughed into the back of the old Chevy, writing it off and giving me a very stiff neck.

I mentioned the incident to a chap I met in a local bar who happened to be an attorney. He asked if he could take up the case on a no-win-no-fee basis. Naturally I agreed, but pointed out that my injuries were minor and that I would be leaving the US shortly. I thought the chances of compensation were minimal.

'Whiplash is never minor,' he said, 'just leave it with me.' Two weeks later he phoned to ask if I'd settle for $500, to which I hastily agreed. I never had the balls to ask him how much he was making from the deal!

When the cheque arrived, I took the girls out for a slap-up meal and still had $400 to spend.

Opposite: Brother Dee and GS at his wedding to Birdie in 1961.

In mid-April 1961 Birdie returned to the UK to plan for a June wedding and to find a flat. At the BOAC baggage desk at Idlewild a pretty American girl, Ruth, checked-in Birdie's bags and we had a good chat. After Birdie and I had made our fond farewells, I noticed on the way out that Ruth was still there, so I resumed our conversation. I mentioned how lonely I was going to be, alone in New York without my fiancée, and it would cheer me up if she would have supper with me.

She had recently broken up with her boyfriend and agreed we should drown our sorrows together. It was an added bonus that Ruth had a flat on the Upper East Side of Manhattan, for it was a much easier commute to Wall Street than from my pad in Brooklyn, particularly as I was now carless.

We enjoyed my last few weeks in New York together, knowing we were just living for the moment. This was the start of the Swinging '60s, which had begun in America during the '50s. Looking back, it shows how immature I was, and what unsuitable marriage material.

I flew back to London in mid-May and on 2 June 1961 Birdie and I married at Hadley Wood Church. We honeymooned in Ischia and settled down to married life in a flat Birdie had found in Bayswater.

For my 21st Birthday, I had been given an Austin A40 – the choice was either that or a Morris Minor, but it had to be black, as Dad thought coloured cars were vulgar. Dee, two years older than me, had been given a similar car for his 21st and he modified it extensively with a Downton-tuned Formula Junior engine, uprated suspension and gutted interior. Dee was on National Service in Holland, and raced his A40 at the Zandvoort and Zolder race-tracks. He also became a regular club competitor at Goodwood, racing against names such as Mick Cave (A40), Doc Merfield (V8 Anglia), Mike Young and Chris Craft (Anglias).

Had it not been for Dee's A40, I would never have got involved in motor racing – but more of that later.

During our first year of married life we moved from Bayswater to a basement flat in Lennox Gardens, just behind Harrods. I commuted to the Personalised Products Ltd (PPL) factory in North London on a 50cc Honda Monkey bike: even in those days it was quicker than by car.

When not at the factory I was out selling to pubs, hotels, clubs and anyone else who wanted their names on our upmarket chocolate bars. It was a hard sell at 5s (25p) a bar when the Cadbury's equivalent price was 1s (5p), but repeat business was good and customers paid for the exclusivity value.

Around the corner from our flat was a well-known watering hole, The Australian. When we were turfed out at closing time, half a dozen friends – mostly Old Shirburnians – would come back to our flat and drink into the small hours. I had installed an extremely naff bamboo bar, which at the time was the dog's bollocks, and since most of my friends were on the breadline it didn't take many months before my 21st inheritance was spent.

It was the irresponsibility of youth and we soon found that we could not afford life in London.

In 1962, Personalised was moved to Court Mills in Hook, home of the cattle-feed business, which had been closed. The factory now ran as a cocoa processing plant for WG Spice and Co, and Dee worked there after finishing his National Service. PPL's move to Hook coincided with Birdie and I leaving London.

We sold the short lease on the Lennox Gardens flat for a tidy sum and moved in to a cottage, close to Hartley Wintney, owned by Mum and Dad. It was convenient for the factory and my salary was reduced in lieu of paying rent!

One day at Goodwood when Dee was testing his A40 I persuaded him to let me have a go. I had never imagined what fun it would be or how easy it was, and respectable lap times came with the minimum of effort. I was completely hooked and decided to get my own racing car and become a racing driver.

Conveniently, around this time I was sitting in a traffic jam on the Chiswick flyover – well before the M4 was built – when I was hit very hard from the rear, right into the car ahead. Extensive damage meant the A40 was a write-off. Since I was the innocent party, the insurance company paid up without question.

Suddenly I had the cash to buy whatever I wanted. Heaven!

Imagine my father's wrath when I bought an MG TF1500 with the insurance money. It almost led to our permanent estrangement, but the argument that I needed a company car, and should not have to use my 21st birthday present for business use, was reluctantly accepted. Once more it was back to the Morris Traveller.

The choice of an MG TF had been influenced by having owned one in Australia and remembering it was pretty fast. It showed how little I knew about cars and turned out to be a complete disaster.

Chapter 4

Virgin racer door to door

At the beginning of the 1962 season I applied to the RAC for my provisional racing licence. My objective was to get the six signatures needed for a full competition licence. After a practice day at Goodwood early in the season, it became obvious that the TF was not competitive in standard trim. So I went to Derrington Motors of Kingston-on-Thames in Surrey, then a world-famous preparation and performance parts company.

At enormous expense they fitted an aluminium cylinder head, upgraded carburettors and a new exhaust system. Harder brake linings, stiffer shocks, lowered suspension and the famous Derrington aeroscreens completed the job.

I entered my first race – a five-lap sports car handicap at Goodwood. Driving down from Hartley Wintney, accompanied by Dee in his A40, the spark plugs kept fouling up and we only just made scrutineering in time. In the practice session, with fresh plugs, the car went well for two laps but then started to overheat, and a blown cylinder head gasket was diagnosed.

No race, no signature.

And that's how the season went. If it wasn't plugs oiling up it was blowing head gaskets. Despite, or perhaps because of, numerous cylinder head skims, enlarged radiator cores, the addition of an oil cooler and many other modifications, we could not solve the problem. Not only that, but frequent visits to Derringtons to try to sort out the problems meant I was fast running out of cash. From five races entered in 1962, I failed to start in three of them and failed to finish in the other two!

Not only had I failed miserably to meet my objective but I had gone stony broke trying. I still had the bug, though, and with the opti-mism of youth I determined to try again – but next year with the right equipment.

Chocolate sales were going well, but relations with my father hit an all time low when I was caught red-handed fiddling my expenses.

I had an agreed business petrol allowance of 6d per mile, and my weekly wage of £10 equated to 400 miles at 6d per mile, so I soon realised that it was more profitable to be driving than sitting in the office. To boost my income I'd sometimes jack up the rear wheels and let the Morris 'motor' at a standstill at low engine speeds in fourth gear, busily recording profitable miles in the drive whilst I went back to bed.

My father unexpectedly called at our cottage early one morning whilst this was happening. The shit really hit the fan and, quite rightly, I was fired on the spot.

Although I didn't see it at the time, it was the kick up the backside that I needed. Now I really had to get out and earn proper money, particularly if I was to continue motor racing.

In late 1962, scanning the classifieds for a job, I spotted an advertisement promising instant fortunes for self-employed salesmen, with cars, to sell the *Encyclopaedia Britannica*. I duly reported to their offices in Kilburn, and was hired, along with a motley selection of other wannabe salesmen.

The following day I reported for an in-house one-day training course. All earnings would be entirely commission-based. As an American company, the sales techniques were uncompromising and effective: probably the best door-to-door sales training available in 1962 UK.

I was fascinated with the psychology behind the sales approach, which was unique in my experience. The sales pitch was based on making potential customers keen to own a set of Britannicas, and making them feel they qualified by answering some simple 'market research' questions. However, if certain key questions were not answered correctly, you knew you were wasting your time and should not to proceed with a full presentation. How did it work?

EB assumed its salesmen would not be of high intellect, which was generally true. To succeed they must not deviate from a well-rehearsed script. Training concentrated on brainwashing the new recruits to follow the format in every detail, even to the way you knocked on the door, entered the house and where you sat your customers.

In return, along with the hype that goes with American sales culture, they promised extremely high earnings. Commission rates were set between £30 and £120 per sale. The cheapest set of Britannica volumes was £150, for a basic set, and the most expensive a hefty £600. The latter comprised a leather-bound set, a set of *Children's Britannica*, a world atlas, a choice of Anglican, Roman Catholic or Jewish bibles, and a bookcase to house them all.

The rules of selling were simple:

Make more appointments than you can possibly keep.

Only present to husband and wife – never individually.

Stick verbatim to the script: do not add your own sales patter.

If you get the wrong answer to any of five critical questions in the ten-minute questionnaire, leave immediately.

If the customer has not signed the order within five minutes of the end of the presentation, be courteous but leave immediately.

It was that simple and it really worked. We were all given a large leather briefcase with a sample volume of *EB*, literature on all the add-ons and benefits, and a presentation book which you had to read to your customer, ensuring that they were reading it too.

One of the cleverest aspects was the appointments system, which was designed to build high customer expectation. The telephone approach was disguised as market research and the critical question was 'If we made it possible for you to own *Encyclopaedia Britannica*, is it something you would use?' If the answer was 'Yes' you would make an appointment for that evening, certainly no later than next day.

The target was to make six evening appointments daily, and many more at the weekends.

Typically you'd keep three of the six appointments, depending on how many full presentations you squeezed in.

Your priority calls next morning were to apologise for the appointments you missed. You then explained how busy you were trying to fit in all those who were desperate to hear about the super deal on offer. After a few missed appointments, complete strangers pleaded to be part of your busy timetable and when you finally appeared the job was half done.

An overloaded appointment book was the key to success. Following up on the six names and addresses which customers had to provide when they ordered a set, (one of the conditions for participating in the promotion), meant that after a few weeks no cold calling was necessary.

My sales manager gave me two names and addresses for my first calls, ostensibly leads from adverts in *Reader's Digest*. I followed the script religiously and remember the excitement of making my first sale – worth £30 in commission. I thought it must be beginner's luck but this notion was dispelled when my second customer ordered an even more expensive set. What a confidence booster – I was on the start to a fortune!

However, when I was handed my commission cheque for the first week I noticed that my first two sales were not listed. My manager told me both orders had been cancelled – something customers had the right to do within 48 hours of signing. Subsequently I discovered that your first presentations were set up by the company with the sole purpose of giving confidence to new salesmen. Clever stuff, and it worked a treat.

My sales career with *EB* rapidly took off: I had never earned so much in my life. The motivation to work long hours, seven days a week, came easily.

After my first month I had earned almost £2,000 in gross commission (without tax) and was nominated *EB*'s Salesman of the Month. The trophy, a gilt model of a salesman striding along with a volume of *EB* under his arm – as naff as you can imagine – was presented with fanfares at a company lunch. It was an embarrassingly over-the-top affair, geared to motivate new recruits as much a to reward the winner.

In common with many direct sales organisations, *EB* had a high turnover of salesmen with an average employment time of only two weeks. By the end my second month I began to understand why – it was demanding and emotionally draining work.

The high earnings had the effect of making me overconfident of my own sales ability and I conveniently forgot that it was *EB* who had taught me in the first place. Without reference to the company, I tried to upgrade my unit sale values by concentrating on big spenders. I made arrangements with doormen at The Hilton (the newest five-star Hotel in London) to provide names and room numbers of visiting Arabs, in exchange for £5 per name.

I thought I was on to a winner, particularly after my first sale which was for five expensive sets, paid for in cash (one for each wife). The company script went out the window and that was the beginning of my downfall.

Instead of concentrating on the basics, where I had a conversion ratio of one sale per two presentations, I started looking for the 'Big Ones'. These more glamorous sales took longer to complete and I had no training in selling to wealthy people.

After three months I was burning out and in my last month earnt less than £1,000. That would have been great when I started but now I was no longer enjoying it. I decided it was time to move on.

The good news was that in little over three months I had saved £5,000, the equivalent of several years' salary from Personalised Products. More than enough to buy a racing car, and run it for the season.

It never occurred to me to buy a single-seater, they were for the professionals and I still only had a provisional licence. In the Marque Sports Car races at Goodwood, I'd noticed that Morgans were fast and reliable, and at Graham Warner's Chequered Flag garage on the Great West Road in Chiswick I found a smart dark blue Lawrencetune Morgan +4 for sale. With my newfound wealth burning a hole in my pocket it was irresistible.

In February 1963 I bought it for £2,000.

Chapter 5

Lawrencetune Morgan

The year 1963 was significant for the midsummer death of my father, some sharp lessons in business, and my first full season of Club racing.

Birdie and I continued to live in Hartley Wintney and, following my success as an *Encyclopaedia Britannica* salesman, I had been reinstated at Personalised Products, but now on more sensible pay. I kept my Morgan in a lockup garage at Phoenix Green, which all the family knew about with the exception, I thought, of Dad. Later I overheard Dad at a cocktail party telling one of his pals that 'Gordon has a racing car in the village and does quite well with it, but he thinks I don't know!' I took this as tacit approval but it was never mentioned.

The Morgan was as good a choice of car as the TF had been bad. I competed in 11 races that season at Brands Hatch, Snetterton, Mallory Park, Goodwood and Aintree. The Morgan covered more road than track mileage, as only pure racing cars used trailers or transporters in that era.

The scratch – as opposed to handicap – races were for Marque (production) Sports Cars, the organisers being the BARC (British Automobile Racing Drivers' Club) and BRSCC (British Racing & Sports Car Club). I was regularly beaten by more experienced drivers like Neil Dangerfield, Adrian Dence and Hugh Braithwaite, but I normally finished near the front and achieved two class wins and several second and third places.

My most satisfying result came at Brands in the Boxing Day meeting, where, after a wet qualifying session, I started from my first pole position ever. Unfortunately the track dried out during the race and I had to settle for fourth place behind two E-types and Dickie Stoop's Porsche. At the same meeting Dee overturned his A40 in spectacular fashion at Paddock Hill Bend, as recorded by a photo which appeared on the back page of *The Times* next day.

My first 1963 race was at Brands in April: en route I collected my friend, Tim Milligan, from Guildford. We carried a spare set of wheels with racing tyres and our first task was to change wheels for scrutineering and practice. Tim hit the wheel nut spinners with a copper hammer with little result. Out came the owner's manual. We were discreetly reading it under the tonneau cover when a nine-year-old pointed out that the spinners must be hit against the direction of rotation. Naturally, we pretended we knew this all along – quite embarrassing really!

Birdie was the timekeeper and pit signaller and Tim, a newly qualified solicitor, was my regular helper. Historic racers will know his brother, Michael 'Spike' Milligan, an eminent gynaecologist and Gentleman Driver, who enters his historic race cars under the name FM (Fanny Mechanic) Racing.

Perhaps the racing itself was tempered by the knowledge that we all had to drive our racers home afterwards. It was an era when any club driver who wore fireproof racing overalls was regarded as a poser. It was Peter Proctor's horrific accident in a Ford Anglia at Goodwood that led to a complete change of attitude.

During 1963 I began spending time at Lawrencetune Engines in West London. Chris Lawrence, the boss, was a first-class engineer who inspired strong loyalty from his staff. Even when he broke his promises you wanted to believe his explanations, such was his charisma.

My own faith in Chris – call it gullibility if you like – was to cost me dearly.

At Lawrencetune's modest premises in Avenue Road, Acton, I learned the basics of race car preparation, including how to change stub axles – a recurring Morgan weakness. I was helped by Len Bridge, the works manager and fount of all knowledge, and Rod Cooper, an aspiring rally driver and a talented mechanic.

I decided to leave Personalised Products as my heart was no longer in the job and it was not helping my racing aspirations. Towards the end of 1963 I started working at Lawrencetune full time, without pay, in exchange for free race preparation of the Morgan.

It soon became apparent that the business was extremely short of cash, mainly because of the amount being spent on in-house racing projects. In 1963 there were two of these, the Morgan SLR and the prototype Deep Sanderson sports racing car.

The SLR was an aluminium-bodied coupé built around a Morgan chassis and running gear. Four cars were built and two are regularly competing today – and looking much better than when they were new. Commercially, though, it was a dead duck and a serious drain on resources.

The Deep Sanderson was a glass fibre rear Mini-engined GT car, designed from scratch by Lawrence. It was named after Chris's uncle Tony Sanderson, a wealthy motor enthusiast who had done a bit of racing. Lawrence told me that Tony, who had retired to the South of France, was financing the whole project.

I should mention here that all five Spice children were fortunate enough to be beneficiaries of a Trust fund set up by Dad. From the age of 21 we received a small income from the Trust and at the age of 25 we were entitled to a share of the capital. Since by early 1964 Lawrencetune was in urgent need of cash to

The Lawrencetune Morgan +4 at Brands Hatch, 1963.

Dad

In July 1963 my mother received a phone call from Dad, who was in Guernsey. He had suffered an oesophageal haemorrhage – not his first. Normally he'd have been rushed to St Mary's in Paddington, or the British Military hospital in Paris, as they knew his history, but this time Dad made it clear he did not want to go to hospital – he'd had enough. He died shortly afterwards.

He was only 52 years old but had packed more into his life than most of us could in 100 years.

survive I persuaded my mother to advance me £3,000 against my inheritance, as the money was needed immediately and could not wait until my 25th birthday. In anticipation of my investment in the company an agreement was made with Chris Lawrence.

I saw the investment in Lawrencetune Engines Ltd as an expedient way to learn the racing business, at the same time as enjoying the perks. I could not borrow the full amount but the £3,000 loan would be enough to finish building the Deep Sanderson in time to run it at Le Mans in June 1964. Lawrence agreed to repay this money as soon as funds were received from sponsor Tony Sanderson.

Just to be safe, the loan went in as a debenture secured on the assets of Lawrencetune Engines Ltd, with an option to convert to shares subsequently. I assured my mother that the money would be repaid after Le Mans.

At Lawrencetune I was the dogsbody. My duties included booking and invoicing customers, sourcing supplies and... fighting off creditors.

Despite many broken promises, such was Chris Lawrence's natural charisma that creditors continued supplies to his company with ever-extending credit. Paydays were a nightmare but somehow the company survived.

After the 1964 race at Le Mans, covered elsewhere, Lawrence announced that he and his wife, Jenny, would drive to the South of France to collect the promised money. We returned to Acton and it was left to me to explain the situation to our long-suffering creditors.

About a week later I got a telephone call at home from Jenny saying they had been involved in a major car accident near Paris and Chris was in a critical condition. He was taken to a hospital in Paris where his spleen was removed.

Back at Acton, the company was hopelessly insolvent. So I called a creditors' meeting, where I explained the situation. I promised that all in-house racing would cease immediately and we would concentrate solely on commercial work. If they were prepared to go along with this, it was likely that all creditors would be paid in full within six months. If they did not agree, I would call in my debenture and put the company into liquidation. It was a great relief when the creditors agreed to the plan.

From then on race preparation was only for paying customers and work that did not produce instant cashflow was dropped. All non-essential overheads were axed and it was amazing how quickly we got on top of the creditor situation. Within two months, staff were back on full pay and creditors were down to 90 days.

No one had heard from Chris since Le Mans but the recovery plan was going well, everyone had their heads down, and we could see light at the end of the tunnel. Then the unexpected happened.

On a Monday morning in September we arrived at work to find all the tools and equipment had been stripped from the workshops! Over the weekend Lawrence had removed anything that could be moved and taken it to his home workshop at Bradfield in Berkshire. Lathes, welding gear, head grinding equipment and spares had all disappeared.

Despite the sacrifices of the past three months, without the tools of the trade the business was not viable. On legal advice liquidation was the only option and a Receiver was appointed. I explained to the creditors what had happened, but by far the hardest part was telling the loyal staff that they no longer had jobs.

Predictably, Lawrence claimed that his uncle had not come up with the cash, but by then whether he had or hadn't was academic. Besides the misery caused to staff and suppliers, I had worked for nothing for over a year. My few practice laps at Le Mans had cost well over £3,000.

Another hard lesson learnt.

Chapter 6

Downton: an education

If you look hard enough, every cloud has a silver lining. One of Lawrencetune's creditors had been Downton Engineering, one of the leading BMC Mini tuning companies. Located south of Salisbury, it took its name from the local village.

Downton, which had supplied the engines and spares for the Deep Sanderson, was co-owned by husband and wife Daniel and 'Bunty' Richmond. I'd had many conversations with Bunty, whose credit control was the fiercest I ever encountered, and ensured that Lawrencetune stuck rigidly to an agreed repayment schedule. At the time of receivership the Downton debt had been substantially reduced, and I think that was a major factor in Downton offering me a job as sales manager.

At the interview I explained my racing ambitions. I asked if, in exchange for a reduction in salary, it would be possible to borrow development engines for my racing Mini? At the time I owned no such vehicle.

Daniel Richmond – 'Sir' to me – said he thought the firm could help. My weekly salary was consequently reduced by £5 a week but I was confident that commission on new car sales would cover this.

By now, Birdie and I had moved to Berkshire Cottage in Sunninghill. It was too far to commute to my new employers, so we rented a small flat in a converted barn close to Downton and only went home at weekends.

My job as sales manager was fascinating, mainly thanks to daily contact with Bunty and Daniel, who were truly oddball characters even by motor racing standards. On my first day I parked my red Ford Cortina GT in the car park in front of the showroom and Daniel went berserk. No one had told me of his passionate hatred of Ford cars, or his contempt for Ford drivers.

Daniel made it clear he didn't want to see it on his premises ever again so I arranged the temporary loan of an Austin 1100 from my mother. With the proceeds of the Cortina sale I bought a racing Mini. These were rapid deals, as Daniel Richmond refused to speak to me until the Ford was sold… and a major part of my job was answering sales enquiries from customers, which needed his input.

Being a BMC car, the 1100 met with Daniel's approval and he started talking to me again as if nothing had ever happened.

Bunty Richmond was one of the plainest and worst-dressed women I had ever met. She was also one of the most charismatic and had the gift of making you feel very special. She was a fearsome lady but a compliment from her more than compensated for her sharp tongue.

Following the Lawrencetune fiasco Bunty had ordered that credit should never be given to any customer, for any reason. An amusing example occurred when a chauffeur arrived to collect Tony Armstrong-Jones' new Downton Mini: at the time he was married to Princess Margaret. It was late on a Friday afternoon but he had no cheque to pay for what was a substantial sale. The Royal family had assumed their credit was good and the invoice would be sent to Kensington Palace.

'Not so,' said Bunty, and I had to arrange overnight accommodation for the driver, and the money would be wired to the local post office next morning. Instead of going back to Sunninghill that night I had to stay over to collect the cash, before releasing the Mini to a bemused palace chauffeur!

One of my duties was to serve Bunty a large Martini at 11:30 pronto every morning: a large measure of gin with a sniff of the cork of a Martini bottle. After several of these she'd accompany Daniel to The Bull pub for lunch, preceded by bottles of vintage Krug champagne – Daniel drank nothing else. Anyone who didn't like Krug champagne was a peasant in his book.

As with many gifted men, Daniel Richmond was a complete eccentric. He knew that anyone wearing a flat cap was a Communist, and anyone who drove a Ford was a yob. Test-driving with him was quite unnerving as he drove very fast and faced his passenger whilst explaining his latest engine tweak, and appeared to pay minimal attention to the road ahead.

Daniel was the brains behind the development of the Mini Cooper engines. He was also

GS with first wife Birdie and whippet Charlie Min, circa 1965.

a friend of Alec Issigonis, designer of the Mini, and Alex Moulton, designer of Hydrolastic suspension as fitted to later Minis and 1100s. Both Issigonis and Moulton were regular visitors to Downton but on Wednesdays they all met to play model trains in the loft of the Issigonis home in Abingdon. I just wish I could have been a fly on the wall at their brainstorming sessions. Daniel always returned from these meetings in happy form: driving with a few drinks under the belt was not unusual in the '60s, and certainly not regarded as antisocial.

Downton had been recently appointed as a BMC dealer and one of my tasks as sales manager was to sell new cars. This proved to be difficult due to two rules laid down by Bunty. Firstly, no discounts were to be given on new cars, and secondly, no trade-ins were allowed. With other BMC dealers discounting new cars and taking trade-ins I saw little prospect of boosting my salary with commission. On the rare occasions I sold a new car it always turned out to be to 'a friend of the company', which it probably was, and it was made clear that there was no commission payable on those sales. It didn't really matter though – I was thoroughly enjoying the work and learning invaluable business lessons from Bunty.

I'm dwelling on my spell at Downton as it had a significant impact on my future career, as it had for others who fell under the Richmonds's influence. For example, Jan Odor and Richard Longman both served their apprenticeships at Downton and went on to build successful businesses. Janspeed Engineering became a highly respected tuning company, and after Daniel died Richard Longman Ltd became the new Downton Engineering. Richard went on to win two RAC Touring Car Championship titles in Longman Minis in 1978 and '79.

Downton had customers all over Europe and one of these was Philippe de Saint André, who had a BMC dealership in Perpignan. The Richmonds were extremely protective of Downton's reputation as the Rolls Royce of BMC tuners so when Philippe asked Bunty if he could have the Downton agency for France, I thought he stood no chance. It says something of his Gallic charm, in the form of outrageous flattery of Bunty and all things British, that she agreed.

I was sent to Perpignan to check out his premises and workshops and was given a memorable gastronomic tour of the region. A few weeks later I drove Daniel and Bunty to Perpignan for the press party announcing the Downton agency. Bunty was given the red carpet treatment and after cutting the ribbon gave a welcoming speech in fluent French – a lady of many talents.

More recently I attended a Downton staff reunion, organised by Barry Hawkins, a long-term Downton employee who was very close to the Richmonds. Barry reminded me of the following story: 'I was following Gordon home, both of us in Morris 1300s. He was trying a bit too hard on snowy roads. I saw him slide into the banking and his car flipped over. I stopped and there was Gordon and what turned out to be the power unit, 30 feet into the field without a trace on the unmarked snow.

'Gordon was not too bad but did need a little attention. So I called at his flat to tell his wife what had happened. Totally unmoved she said "Well, he'll just have to eat his dinner cold".'

I should add that when Birdie and I were discussing this book in late 2007 she told a drawing room full of visitors, 'Oh, Gordon was always crashing in those days. It was just something I got used to…'

Shortly after I eventually left Downton, I was unexpectedly summoned to a meeting with Daniel and Bunty. Over lunch at The Bull, Daniel explained that they were thinking of retiring and would like me to buy the business.

I told him that I did not have that kind of money and even if I did I lacked the experience and technical know-how for its continued success.

Daniel explained that money was not a problem – they'd lend me the money interest free and I could pay it back as and when.

Looking back, I think I made the right decision in declining the offer. Downton was synonymous with the Richmonds, and without their inspiration, eccentricity and the huge support they enjoyed from influential customers, it would not be the same.

In late 1965 I received the balance of my inheritance and was mindful that it had to be invested wisely and not frittered away on motor racing. Whilst I was earning a fair salary at Downton it was certainly not enough to fund the lifestyle I wanted. I knew that both Dee and Noo were financially secure and the idea of becoming the poor relation was unthinkable. This was a major factor in my decision to leave Downton and start my own business.

The big question was: what should I do?

Chapter 7

From speed shops to candles

I can't remember what sparked the idea of opening a car accessory shop. A friend, Dick Card, thought it was a good idea, and being Competitions Manager of Lucas he had good knowledge of the automotive aftermarket. More importantly, Dick knew Stirling Moss and he suggested we approach Stirling to use his name to promote the business.

To ensure this was a sound idea, I did some market research. I stopped hundreds of shoppers in local High Streets and asked them to name two racing drivers. Invariably the first name was Stirling Moss and often that was the only name they knew. We were on the right track!

We duly met at Stirling's London house in Shepherd's Market. I proposed that, in exchange for naming the first shop 'Stirling Moss Accessories', he would receive five per cent of the gross takings, plus a similar percentage for any further owned or franchised outlets. No investment was required from him,

Skoda bolts

In 2008 Former Spice employee Paul Parker recalled his brief experience of City Speed Shop employment in these (slightly edited) words on the Atlas website: 'I worked at City Speed Shop from March to late December 1971. The shop was on two levels, downstairs it was accessories, steering wheels, anti-theft steering locks, wheel spacers for Minis and Anglias, driving gloves, Jackie Stewart corduroy hats and myriad other ephemera. Upstairs were Nomex race suits and underwear, Bell helmets and a wide range of racing equipment.

'The shop attracted the usual quota of nutters and persons seeking car spares. One day a rather Monty Python character crossed the threshold and asked me for a set of bumper bolts for a Skoda.

'When I explained that this was an accessory shop and not a motor factors – thus we did not sell spares, he became quite belligerent. The potential customer started saying things like "Call yourselves a motor spares shop?" and so on.

'Gordy was upstairs checking out the helmet stock. He overheard the customer complaining as we were standing at the bottom of the staircase. Gordy did not suffer fools gladly, and came down to see what was going on, demanding an explanation from me.

'I told him about the request for Skoda bumper bolts. Gordon paused for a few seconds, looked at the customer then turned to me and said "What the fuck's a Skoda?" Said punter exited rapidly very red in the face whilst I subsided into minor hysterics... and Gordy went back to checking the stock.

'Working there was a hoot and I enjoyed it immensely in those carefree and different days.'

the books would be open to audit by his accountants, and he would be in a no-risk situation, irrespective of the success of the business.

Stirling, who had not raced since his dreadful accident at Goodwood in 1962, agreed in principle and we agreed to meet with our respective lawyers, to thrash out an agreement.

Stirling's lawyers had very different ideas as to how best to protect his name. Their legal demands included approval of all products sold, setting of profit margins, co-signing of cheques and guarantees of minimum royalties – to mention but a few.

The meeting didn't last very long.

At the end, ever the gentleman, Stirling said 'Sorry, old boy, but I have to take the advice of my advisors.'

Doubtless, if I had pulled off that coup the business would have taken off faster than it did under the Gordon Spice Ltd (GSL) banner.

The first shop was in a new shopping block in Ashford, Middlesex, about half a mile from the main shopping centre. A 21-year lease was agreed with one year rent-free, and seven-year reviews. Being a secondary site the rent was relatively low and parking was easy.

Birdie helped fit out the shop and the opening stock was purchased. The majority of it was sourced from specialist manufacturers of sporty car accessories – items like leather-rim steering wheels, straight-through exhaust pipes, triple air horns, spoilers, alloy wheels, driving gloves and more.

The more mundane stock was delivered on a daily basis by local motor factors. It must be remembered that in the '60s new cars were pretty basic. Items like radios and aerials, wing mirrors, fog and spot lights, head-rests and car mats – all taken for granted today – were not fitted to cars then. Consequently many car owners wanted to personalise their second-biggest investment with the stuff we were selling.

Initially, business was slow – in the first week we took £75 – and I set about increasing sales by selling to the motor trade. I recruited Dick Card from Lucas to help Birdie, who worked part-time in the shop. Dick and I would call on trade outlets, getting orders to increase sales. Our best trade customer was a local BP service station where I had persuaded the manager to put in a merchandising unit, close to the cash till in the forecourt shop.

Every evening I would check their stock and next morning deliver replacements for what had been sold, less trade discount. There was no financial commitment by the manager, as I owned the stock and he only paid for what had been sold. This business built up quickly, but the BP Area Manager thought company policy was being compromised, which led to a meeting with the Marketing Director of BP's retail operations.

At that time there were virtually no forecourt add-on sales but I persuaded the BP bosses that their captive audience provided a unique opportunity to increase petrol station profitability. During an afternoon session at Miranda's – an infamous Piccadilly strip club and popular watering hole of the then BP bosses – they agreed to back the concept of what later became BP AutoShops.

I was given carte blanche to select product ranges, merchandise their stands, all supplied from the Ashford shop. BP even paid me handsomely to train their managers in the art of selling car accessories – with all of six months' experience!

These training sessions took place in the Reading headquarters of Church and Co, which manufactured merchandising units. They became the approved supplier to BP and I was paid commission on every sale.

By the end of our first year sales totalled £20,000, our stock value was £7,000, and we made a loss of £2,500. I replaced Dick Card, who was on £30 a week, with Roger Henwood, recruited from Montagu Burton, on £12 a week. In the second year sales increased to £60,000, stock to £25,000, and we achieved financial break-even. However, the shop was so full that you could hardly move, partly because I could never say 'no' to a good sales rep.

During the second year, in partnership with my brother Dee, we opened City Speed Shop in Bishopsgate, in the City of London. John Hansford – a most likeable and talented chap – was an excellent manager and the shop was an instant success. I am grateful to former employee Paul Parker for his memories (on the Atlas website) of working at Bishopsgate – see the accompanying panel entitled 'Skoda bolts'.

To alleviate the lack of Ashford storage space, I took a long lease on two lockup units at the rear of the Ashford shop. They cost £275 each and the ground rent was fixed at four guineas a year for the whole period. The lease expires in 2092 and currently those garages yield an annual rent of £2,400!

Spicy opening

I quote from *Autosport* (Pit and Paddock) in 1969:

'To mark the opening of his sixth motor accessory shop, SloughSpeed Accessories in Slough, Gordon Spice assembled perhaps the most spicy contingent of females yet seen under one roof. The shop, which is similar to the other five in Gordon's group, is in an ultra modern shopping centre and should serve the Lola home town well.

'Amidst the smog and the crowd, guests spotted included Paul Hawkins, Mick and Karen Cave, Nick Gold, John Rhodes, Ginger Devlin, Valerie Pirie and SloughSpeed partner, Richard Pakeman.'

In 1968 the decision was taken to find suitable premises from which to service the Ashford shop, City Speed Shop and our growing number of trade outlets. I was lucky enough to find the ideal warehouse at Thames Side, Windsor – an old bakery with bags of space, a rent of 10s (50p) per square foot and wonderful river views from my office window.

After two years' trading the business was building a reputation for stocking a far wider range of car accessories than its competitors. The new market for motor racing equipment was growing fast as RAC-approved racing overalls and crash helmets became compulsory. We were plain lucky to be in at the start of it all.

The new warehouse enabled us to expand our range. Without the time constraints of retailing, I had time to find more trade customers whilst Birdie and Roger took care of the admin side. Racing Minis was giving the company good PR and the extra income helped fund the business.

I began to get approaches from car enthusiasts wanting to get into the accessory business and, as a result, developed an unusual form of partnership. Basically, I selected partners with sufficient money to pay for the fitting out of a shop and some working capital. My financial contribution came in the form of stock: very useful in cashflow terms, as extended credit was negotiated with suppliers for every new shop opening.

It was important that my partners were hungry enough that they could not afford to lose their investment, and would work hard to be successful. In return, they would own 50 per cent of the new company and share in half the profits, after drawing a modest salary. They were obliged to buy stock from the wholesale side of GSL, which supplied them at cost plus ten per cent. This might sound onerous, but we now bought all our stock direct from manufacturers at an average 50 per cent discount.

Typically, wholesalers supplied retail outlets at 33.3 per cent off retail prices. Buying from GSL, my partner shops were enjoying a 45 per cent discount, without the larger investment demanded by bulk buying. Partners were also allowed to buy locally from motor factors, but only such products as were not stocked by GSL.

It was also in our second trading year that we opened our third shop – The Rallyman in Egham, Surrey. The original South African partner in this business turned out to be less than honest and when he unexpectedly fled from the UK I found myself fully owning the shop.

The following year, in partnership with an old friend, Hugo Tippet, we opened our fourth shop, The Aylesbury Tappet in Aylesbury (Tippet-Tappet, get it?). Hugo was a delightfully eccentric chap, an enthusiastic Lotus 7 club racer and a man of total integrity. Hugo's brother, Charles, was also a keen racer: in the late '70s he became the Financial Director of GSL – the best we ever had.

Our shop openings were launched with unabashed publicity, and were generally well supported by the press, who were lavishly entertained (see the panel headed 'Spicy opening').

The SloughSpeed shop was unusual in that Halfords had a well established store just three doors away. They were well known for cutting prices in those days and it was our policy not to compete on price but to concentrate instead on good availability and a wider choice. Ably run by Richard Pakemen, who was married to the sister of an old school pal, the shop prospered, and a seventh shop in Reading was soon added.

Between 1968 and 1970, in addition to supplying partner shops we developed the wholesale business, providing a similar service to other independent accessory shops.

Attracting new customers was helped by my involvement in Mini racing, initially as a privateer and later with Equipe Arden and Cooper Cars. Many of the drivers worked in the motor trade and they seemed to enjoy doing business with someone involved in racing.

Our product range expanded and we started importing and distributing racing gear on an exclusive basis. American Trackstar full-face crash helmets were the first of such ventures, when full-face helmets were more a fashion statement than a safer option.

One of the attractions of sole agencies was that the importer decided the pricing structure and profit margin. Prices were set to allow decent discounts to our official stockists, and

Glamour girls at SloughSpeed shop opening party in 1969, including sister Zani (back row third from left) and Birdie (right-hand side on floor). Partner Richard Pakeman is in the centre.

it was the most profitable side of the business. We also started to break new ground, learning about manufacturers' promotional budgets… and how to tap into them.

However, the business was being constrained by lack of working capital and the reason for this was simple: the more business we did, the more we were owed. As our debtors increased we had difficulty paying suppliers on time, and there was a limit to their patience.

I was moaning about this vicious circle one evening in the pub when the answer came in a flash of alcoholic inspiration: we should convert the wholesale business to 'cash & carry'. The change would require a cash injection, as we were always up against our bank overdraft limit, but approaches to the bank for additional facilities were turned down flat – and not even referred to Head Office.

I set about finding an equity partner.

I had two options. The first was my brother, Dee, one of the early casualties of the new – and often ignored – drink-drive legislation. Having lost his driving licence for a year, he was in Australia. I wrote to him explaining my plan and the need for a £10,000 investment.

As a backup, the second option was a friend, Charles Sawyer-Hoare, who had expressed interest in investing. I knew Charles socially, as he was one of The Belvedere drinking crowd in Ascot. After closing time we would meet at the Peanut roundabout in Windsor Great Park for some night racing. Races were over five laps – or less if one of the lookouts on the four approach roads sounded the alarm. Crazy days!

Charles owned a successful Renault dealership and was married to Ginny, who later married Frank Williams. Ginny was well heeled and I suspected it was her money that Charles was planning to invest.

I thought that a good way to get to know him better would be to travel abroad with him. As I was due to go to New York to negotiate opening a new accessory shop, I invited Charles to join me. We agreed that all expenses would be shared 50/50 and it turned out to be a most interesting trip, from which I learnt two things.

The first was that, however much money Charles had to invest, I could never be in business with him. The second was, stick to the territory you know… I'll explain the two lessons as they happened.

On a previous visit to New York to negotiate UK distribution of Trackstar helmets, I had visited the General Motors building on Fifth Avenue in mid-town Manhattan. In the basement was an enormous and popular theme restaurant called AutoPub. Here you sat in a replica vintage cars to eat your meal, and the decor was given over to racing car memorabilia: they even had racing cars hanging from the ceilings – very American.

Adjoining the restaurant was a shopping mall with boutique designer shops selling upmarket products ranging from jewellery to golfing gear. Strangely, there was no car accessory boutique. The shops were franchised by Longchamps Inc, the restaurant group that owned AutoPub, and I approached them with the idea of taking a boutique to sell exclusive British car accessories. The idea appealed to Alan Lewis, the CEO, but I needed to test the water before signing a lease. We finally agreed to a rent-free period of one year, and in lieu of rent Longchamps would take a small percentage of all sales – a very satisfactory outcome from my viewpoint as it reduced our initial risk in an unknown market.

Charles and I were staying at The Gladstone, a modest two-star hotel. The day before I was due to meet Alan to sign our agreement, I received a phone call from a man claiming to be colleague of Alan. He was keen to welcome us to New York and invited us to dinner that evening. Naturally we accepted and arranged to meet at an Italian restaurant in uptown Manhattan.

We were greeted by our host at the door and taken to a large table at the back of the long narrow restaurant. I noticed that the doors were shut behind us by one of the two gorilla-like doormen with bulging jackets – obviously armed, just like in the movies.

The next thing we noticed was that we were the only customers and the closed sign had been put up on the door. Bloody hell…

We had an excellent meal – the full tootie – and our swarthy Italian hosts were charming. They explained that they were in the insurance business, knew about our agreement with Longchamps, and that they 'looked after' many New York retailers, including those in the GM building. They were concerned that our new business would be successful and for a small percentage of our takings they would make sure that we had 'no trouble'.

The penny dropped that we were being offered 'protection', and would be in deep shit if we didn't accept. With the two bouncers still sitting by the locked door, we accepted their offer of 'insurance' – there was no option.

Our newfound partners said they'd meet us at the hotel next day after we signed with Longchamps. As we left, our host mentioned 'By the way, gentlemen, we don't like our partners staying in second-rate hotels, and we've had your bags taken to The Plaza. Don't worry about the check, in New York, you're our guests.' Again… bloody hell!

They weren't bullshitting either: all our stuff had been packed, moved to the Plaza, unpacked and put away – nothing was missing. Not surprisingly, we felt extremely frightened.

Events were out of control and we had neither the balls nor the experience to deal with the Mafia. The move to the Plaza was the final straw. Charles and I sat up most of the night planning our next move. It became clear we would not be opening in New York. At first light we left the Plaza via the fire escape and hot tailed it to the airport, all the while expecting to be stopped.

That is how I learned the 'stick to your own territory' lesson. When I phoned Alan at Longchamps, he claimed not to know our Italian friends. But someone in his office did…

We were due to visit an export customer in Bermuda the following weekend, so we took the first flight out and arrived a few days early. Our customer in Bermuda was a charming local Bermudan named Robin Trott. We had been supplying Robin with shipments of Weber carburettor conversion kits for road cars, and, since Bermuda has a strictly enforced 20mph speed limit, I wanted to find out where he was selling them.

It transpired Robin was secretary of the local car club, which organised sand racing, which had become a popular sport. Weber kits were the cheapest way to get more power and he had cornered the market. One interesting thing I discovered in Bermuda was that the Government had put a limit on the width of all cars. Morris Oxfords, one of BMC's most successful contemporary exports, were one inch over the permitted width. They got around this by putting the cars through a hydraulic press as they were landed. This squeezed in each side by half an inch – problem solved!

On the flight home from Bermuda I presented Charles with his bill for half the expenses of the trip, as agreed. They were less than anticipated as our hotel bill in New York City had been paid by the Mafia, but Charles was not at all happy. He argued, for example, that I would have had to hire cars with, or without him, so that should be down to me. Whilst Charles was amusing company, his tightness warned me that a business partnership would end in tears. Lesson two learnt… just in time.

Dee had travelled overland to Oz in a VW campervan and trailer, complete with mobile discotheque and dolly girls. After speaking on the phone he returned to the UK in more conventional style and in March 1971 we shook hands on a business deal. In exchange for his investment he became a 40 per cent shareholder in Gordon Spice Ltd. We agreed that the 60/40 ratio of our shareholdings should be maintained for the foreseeable future.

It turned out to be the best partnership anyone could wish for. Throughout the next 15 years in business together we enjoyed total trust. Not once did we argue about money – it was rarely discussed.

Dee's investment, support from our suppliers and a little help from our bank (with personal guarantees), enabled the first Gordon Spice cash & carry to be opened in June 1971. We made it easy for our customers to convert to being cash & carry shoppers, and their businesses thrived on the considerably reduced prices. Such was our relationship that we did not lose one single trade customer.

GKN Spa was the first car accessory cash and carry to open in the UK and we were the second. Our stock range was wider and more appealing and included racing and tuning equipment hitherto simply unavailable anywhere else at trade prices.

Our opening mail shots were as unsubtle as they were hard-hitting. Pictures of scantily clad dolly birds with captions like 'UP YOURS' (profit-wise, we mean) and 'GET 'EM OFF' (the shelf, of course). Several editors complained about lack of taste, but the trade loved it and new business flooded in. The new 4,500ft² premises at 12b, Central Trading Estate, Staines, was soon bursting at the seams. We increased selling space by adding mezzanine floors within the building and by 1974 we had 11,500ft² of selling space on five floor levels.

We tried to make shopping at the cash and carry a fun experience. Dee was in charge of recruiting the checkout girls, chosen for their outgoing personalities rather than their mathematical skills. Their repartee with customers built enormous goodwill and when mistakes or delays happened at checkout, their pretty faces

Subtle trade mail-shots promoting the first Gordon Spice cash & carry at Staines in 1971.

usually won the day. It was the one area of the operation that was a bottleneck and often the entire staff would be involved on checkout. It was not unknown for customers to write their own invoices.

Between August 1971 and August 1974 sales increased from £130,000 to £660,000. Given that the average trade price of each item was under 60p, the volume of product going through checkout really was staggering.

Shortly after moving in to 12b, an opportunity arose to buy two state-of-the-art exhibition vehicles with roofs that raised electrically to provide two storeys of exhibition space. The vehicles had originally cost £30,000 to build, but the company which commissioned them had gone bust and we picked them up for £6,000. We really had no idea what we were going to do with them, but, for reasons never envisaged, they turned out to be the buy of the year.

Gordon Spice (Exhibition Vehicles) Ltd was formed and, with considerable help from John Hine, the original owner, the first major job was landed. It involved a three-month tour of Eastern Bloc companies for The Ames Pharmaceutical Group. Ivor Jauncey, a friend who happened to have the right HGV licence, drove the vehicle and it was down to his resourcefulness that the tour was such a success.

At a time of major political instability (1972) it was a high-risk undertaking, but the Ames company were great people to deal with and happy to pay a price which reflected the hazards of the region. By the end of the 6,000-mile export drive, the cost of buying the two vehicles had been well and truly covered.

Subsequently, during the miner's strike of 1974, the vehicles more than covered their costs yet again. When the power cuts came, both vehicles with their 15kW generators were backed up to the warehouse, so that during the period of the 'three-day week' we were able to trade twelve hours a day six days a week – the only business in Staines with proper lighting. Business boomed and the checkout tills were red hot.

It's an ill wind that blows nobody any good… and the coal miners strike proved the cliché. Candles were in huge demand and very soon UK supplies had been exhausted. So we hired a six-ton truck, and the redoubtable Ivor Jauncey was despatched to the Continent with loads of cash, and instructions to fill the lorry with candles. In Holland Ivor found a wholesaler supplying churches

and caterers, so he bought up as many candles as the truck would take. I telephoned buyers at Harrods, Fortnum & Masons and other posh retailers, agreed prices and promised delivery within two days.

Next thing was a call from Ivor, now at Dover docks, explaining that HM Customs & Excise deemed that tapered candles were decorative and therefore must be treated as luxury goods, attracting purchase tax of 33.3 per cent. Clearing cheques would take too long, so Dee headed off for Dover with the cash. Meanwhile I was back on the blower renegotiating prices with the buyers, some of whom cancelled. We sold enough to cover costs but the profit of the exercise sat in many pallets of unsold stock. Certainly Spice households would never be short of candles!

There was a happy ending: the following year, when VAT was introduced to the UK, and Purchase Tax abolished, Customs & Excise refunded all purchase tax paid on any goods in stock at the time.

It was also around this time that Birdie was doing promotional work for BMW Concessionaires GB Ltd, who expressed an interest in buying one of the exhibition vehicles. She pulled off the sale of the smaller of the two vehicles for a worthwhile £5,000 and earned a healthy commission for her efforts.

So celebrations all round!

1973: One of our exhibition vehicles – with generator!

SELLING IN THE SEVENTIES

Chapter 8

Mini racing years

As has been mentioned, part of my pay package at Downton was the use of in-house 1,300cc BMC development engines in my newly acquired racing Mini. Even with help in the evenings and at weekends from my work colleagues, it was not until July 1965 that the car was race-prepared, and deemed worthy of a Downton engine.

My first ever Mini race was at Silverstone on 10 July – a round of the RAC Saloon Car Championship. It also happened to be a support race for the British Grand Prix, truly a baptism by fire!

I knew I had to learn an entirely new driving technique in a front-wheel-drive car but saw no problem with that. My main concern was not to make a fool of myself in front of so many top saloon car drivers.

Details of the race itself elude me – it was too much of a blur to recall – but I see the race was won by Sir Gawaine Baillie in a Ford 4.7-litre Mustang, and I came 14th overall. It was a respectable first-time effort: I had not fallen off and had beaten several cars in my (up to 1,300cc) class.

Tyres for the weekend had left me pretty skint, so my second and final 1965 outing was at Brands Hatch on 30 August – another round of the same championship.

As a driver I must have improved, as I was the fastest Mini and came seventh overall and second in the class, beaten only by John Fitzpatrick in a Ford Anglia. Overall winner was Jack Brabham in another Ford Mustang: it was great to be in the same race as a real hero.

I left Downton at the end of 1965 to open my first car accessory shop but stayed on good terms with my former bosses. Daniel very kindly agreed to support my racing with the free use of development engines, and it was this generous gesture that was to earn me professional status by the late '60s.

1966: sponsored success

In February 1966 I opened the shop in Ashford, so racing was not the first priority. I found that Saturday trading accounted for half the shop's weekly takings so I needed to be there, but it was also the day of qualifying for Sunday's races. Perhaps retailing was not such a good idea after all.

That 1966 season I competed in six National status saloon car races at Silverstone, Brands Hatch, Oulton Park and Crystal Palace. The best result was at Crystal Palace, where the bigger classes had their own race and we were going for overall victory. I came second, splitting the works cars of Rhodes and Handley and surprising a few people into the bargain – myself included.

At the British GP support race at Brands in July, I came third in class behind John Young's Superspeed Anglia and Rhodes's Mini. I began to think I was getting the hang of it but I still had much to learn, as was demonstrated a month later at the same circuit.

Driving Minis was a very physical business due to heavy steering caused by understeer, then having to induce oversteer before the corners. I was learning the technique, but not without a few offs on the way, and the next race was a case in point.

It was the Guards International Trophy meeting and my absolute hero, Jim Clark, was also driving in the saloon car race – in a works Lotus Cortina. I knew he would lap me in the race and was determined not to get in his way.

Sure enough, he appeared in my mirrors as I entered Clearways before the pit straight. My plan was to give him space on the inside of the next corner, which happened to be Paddock Bend. That part of the plan worked but I was so spellbound watching the maestro go through – with his nearside wheel a full twelve inches clear of the kerb – that I turned in too late. I skidded over the marbles and hit the barriers a mighty clout, ending my race in ignominy.

By the end of the season I'd worked out that despite Downton's help I simply couldn't afford to go racing without some serious trade support. Over the winter I set about finding some backing.

First I secured a contract with Castrol for free fuel and oil. It helped that my business was wholesaling their racing oils and greases. I also had a good relationship with Dunlop's Dick Jefferies (competitions manager) and he agreed to supply tyres – the biggest expense by far – at retail price, less 40 per cent discount. Better than that, I could buy as many as I needed. This turned out to be a significant agreement as Dunlop R5 Green spots for Minis were in very short supply at the time: even second-hand they sold for silly prices.

Daniel Richmond agreed to continue loaning their engines, but as Downton were supplying Cooper Cars – now the official works team – the stipulation was made that I must not beat them. That was academic at the time and I didn't give it a second thought.

The works number one driver was the spectacular John Rhodes, undisputed Mini king at the time, and the late John Handley provided strong backup in their second car. BMC were used to winning internationally in the '60s, and their Minis and Cooper S variants were the cars to beat in the smaller capacity classes. However, they did face some stiff competition from Ford, initially in the form of Superspeed Anglias and later from Broadspeed Escorts.

1967: Trade salvation

With my newfound trade support, my aim for 1967 was to compete in all rounds of the RAC Saloon Car Championship, the first being at Brands Hatch in March.

In practice, I qualified behind the works cars but not far out of touch. In the race, both works cars, which were using all kinds of new

1968: Equipe Arden with BMC Works team in background: (left to right) Norman Seeney (mechanic), GS, Jim Whitehouse and Alan Edis. (Maureen Magee)

engine bits, hit problems and I found myself in the lead. Aware of my pre-season commitment, on the last lap I slowed down and waited for John Rhodes to pass, which he duly did. I still could not see Handley so I crossed the line second in class.

Question was, how best to capitalise on this unexpected turn of events?

This did not take long to work out. Prize money was small then, but the bonus money from trade suppliers was significant. The trade assumed that works cars would do all the winning, so bonuses paid to factory teams were justified by OE (Original Equipment) contracts. I approached my contracted trade suppliers, Dunlop, Castrol, Champion and Ferodo. I put it to them that I could beat the works cars, and explained the reason for not having done so at Brands. As I was on a very tight budget, I asked if they would pay me winning bonus money if I was only beaten by the works cars? Surprisingly they agreed and the extra income generated over the season made a very useful contribution.

As anticipated, Coopers soon sorted out their reliability problems: for the rest of the season they beat me fair and square.

But it was the Dunlop contract that was the real saviour. If you needed racing tyres, used or new, John Pearce of J.A. Pearce Engineering

Arden Mini at Croft in 1968. (Maureen Magee)

in West London was the man who monopolised the market.

John only dealt in cash, and paid for used racing tyres by the depth of the tread. A new Mini tyre had 7mm of tread and he would pay £21 per tyre. Similarly a half used tyre was worth £10.50 to him and he would sell it for £20. As I was paying £6 per tyre (£10 less 40 per cent) this was more profitable than the accessory business!

So the financial success of every meeting was largely measured by the number of tyres I could buy from Dunlop: the less tread used the better. Most of qualifying was spent doing a few laps, coming in, fitting a new set and repeating the process. Mixed weather conditions were a Godsend as it justified buying both wets and slicks and the investment in ten sets of alloy wheels soon paid off.

On the Monday morning after a race meeting I'd drive the fully laden shop delivery van to John's warehouse in Southall and negotiate a price for the weekend's spoils. John, who looked like a tramp and always wore the same grease-impregnated flat cap, was a canny negotiator.

Before arriving I'd measure the depth of all the tyres on offer and work out the value. If his offer was less, we'd be in for a long session. I was in a strong position as Mini tyres were in

1968: a touch of understeer, with Bernard Unett in an Imp giving chase. (Brian Kreisky)

great demand – even at the scandalous prices he was charging.

It was the wheeling-dealing with tyres that enabled me to enjoy my first full season of Mini racing. By the end of the year the racing had shown a profit!

Results-wise, the season was one of mixed fortunes. The highlights were the second place at Brands, followed by third in class at Silverstone and third overall at Mallory Park and Oulton Park: on all occasions finishing behind Rhodes and Handley.

Other competition came from Harry Ratcliffe in the British Vita Mini, the Broadspeed Anglias of John Fitzpatrick and Chris Craft, and Don Moore's Mini – driven by Timo Makinen.

I was pushing the limit, as witnessed by many off-circuit excursions and several DNFs, but I was gaining much-needed experience every race. I was also earning recognition as the quickest non-works driver, and this would lead to my first works drive – albeit for one 1968 race only.

Given the works

At the Silverstone round of the 1968 RAC championship in May, Ginger Devlin, Team Manager of the Cooper Car Company,

approached me. He asked if I knew the Nürburgring circuit in Germany? Without thinking I replied 'Of course, sir, like the back of my hand.'

Devlin then explained that Johns Rhodes and Handley were scheduled to do the Nürburgring 6 hours race in June, but Handley had to go into hospital for a minor operation. They were looking for a co-driver for Rhodes. I couldn't believe my luck and the conversation went rather like this…

'How much?' I asked.

'£200' said Ginger

'How much?' I asked again, thinking it was a hell of a lot of money to ask me to pay.

'OK then,' Ginger replied, 'we're on a limited budget, but we can run to £200 plus travel and hotel expenses.' The penny dropped that they were actually offering to pay me to drive!

We shook hands on the deal. I was told to report to the team's hotel at the circuit on the Thursday before the Sunday race.

One minor problem was that I'd never even seen the Nürburgring, I just knew it was very long (over 14 miles a lap) and quite dangerous. This was years before Armco barriers were the norm, and the 'Ring was full of sheer drops, blind brows and large trees…

I flew out on the Monday, hired a BMW 1600 from Hertz at Cologne airport and drove up to the Eifel mountains. At that time the circuit was open for practice to anyone prepared to pay two Deutschmarks per lap.

First thing Tuesday, having disconnected the speedometer (sorry, Mr Hertz) I set out to learn the circuit, accompanied by a tape recorder, stopwatch and not a little apprehension. I just had to memorise the circuit's 175 corners spread over that daunting 14.2 miles. More importantly, I had to remember the order they came in.

I gabbled into my recorder snippets such as: 'Flat right-hander – hedge on the left – brake hard by haystack on right – slow left-hander then flat out over blind brow, staying left for late apex right-hander…' – and so on, just like the rally co-drivers. As I got faster, I had to slow on the straights to let the tape recorder catch up. At the beginning of the second day, having listened to the tape for half

Arden Mini at Brands Hatch in 1968.

the night, I could confidently talk my way round the circuit.

Halfway through the Wednesday, the tyres were bald and the brake pedal was soggy. So I had the brake pads and tyres replaced by the local garage. Now my lap time was down to a competitive 11 minutes 30 seconds. To offset costs, I started charging what turned out to be a plentiful supply of local enthusiasts three DM per lap to accompany me.

That Wednesday evening in the bar, I was befriended by two local Fräuleins, who hunted as a pair and unselfishly enjoyed the spoils together. Their enthusiasm for bed sports was only matched by my embarrassment a few days later when I had to try to convince Birdie that you really can catch crabs from foreign lavatory seats.

On Thursday John Fitzpatrick arrived. He would drive the Broadspeed Anglia with Chris

The unofficial official works Mini

Another of John Blackburn's responsibilities at the Cooper Car Company was dealing with foreign race organisers' enquiries for the Cooper team cars to appear overseas. Often these were impossible requests for logistical reasons, so we prepared a spare 'works' car, identical in every respect to the real thing. It was kept at my Ashford lockup.

John would explain to such overseas inquiries that he couldn't produce two cars, as one was 'undergoing a major rebuild' (often true!). However, Gordon Spice could be available that particular weekend, if they were interested? Once start and prize money had been agreed, we set off with a trailer behind a rather tatty Mercedes, borrowed from Mike

Sandford, a friend who worked at Elmbridge Motors in Surbiton. Our cover story was that the Cooper transporter had broken down, hence the Mercedes and trailer rig.

On one such trip to Jyllandsringen in Denmark, a Mickey Mouse circuit where the main straight was all of 500 yards long, our replica Mini needed gearbox repairs after Saturday practice. I left John, who was a competent mechanic from his Calypso Racing days, to fix the problem. It turned out to be an all-nighter for him but his efforts did not go unrewarded: we won our race and shared a record windfall.

A vital part of Blackburn's job was to make sure that John Cooper never saw the *Autosport* race reports...

Craft, and with his kind and expert tuition I got my lap time down to just under 11 minutes. By now I knew every bump, damp patch and landmark from the little tree that you had to line up before the blind Karussell, to the haystack approaching Flugplatz. Though far from being a Ringmeister, I still felt confident that I could put on a reasonable show.

Nürburgring expenses had been high and the hire car had served its purpose so on Thursday afternoon I reconnected the speedo, drove back to the airport and returned the car to Hertz, parking it so that damage to one side was out of sight. The letter they sent me a few days later, telling me I had lost my deposit and asking for more, was a classic. 'We observe that the tyres are without profile... The brake pads are worn out... 300km, is this right...? The passenger armrest has been pulled out...' etc.

Thank God it happened long before credit cards.

I joined up with the Cooper team at the airport, pretending I had caught an earlier flight. The big day dawned – official practice – and John (Rhodes) was put in to bat first. When my turn came, after an exploratory lap savouring the pleasure of my first works drive, I went for it on the second lap, keeping a small safety margin as an off would be disastrous.

I was as surprised as anyone that my time was 20 seconds faster than John's. To alleviate

my embarrassment, after swearing Rhodes to secrecy I told him the full story. Being the sportsman he is, John thought it was a helluva laugh. Ginger Devlin, who worshipped Rhodes, was not impressed – but his revenge was to come later...

The pressure was off so I spent the few laps that Ginger reluctantly allowed me driving at the same pace, knowing that John would match me, which he did.

Come race day, naturally John started and for the first hour was keeping Fitzpatrick's Escort in sight. After pitting for tyres and fuel, I exited just behind the Escort, now being driven by Chris Craft. To my increasing consternation, every passing lap had my pit board showing 'minus 5 secs, minus 10 secs, minus 15 secs'. Bad News. What Ginger Devlin did not tell me was that I was lapping 10 seconds quicker than in practice... the bastard!

My mind in turmoil, I drove on the ragged edge, thinking I was letting the team down. The inevitable happened. Going down the sweeping downhill bends of the Hatzenbach, with forest on each side, I overcooked it and ended up ten yards off the circuit, down a bank with the passenger side against a large pine tree.

Amazingly, only the wheel spats were missing and there was no other visible damage. I noticed the scene of my off was out of sight of any marshal's post – not uncommon at the

1969: Spares for Movi

One of John Blackburn's tasks as Cooper's Marketing Manager was to market the Cooper name in Europe. Hunky Juncadella, the wealthy Spanish aristocrat and GT 40 racer, bought the Cooper franchise for Spain, and under the name Movi-Cooper ran two Mini Cooper cars in the Spanish Saloon Car Championship. Movi also sold all the Mini go-faster parts of the time, but the Spanish government levied a massive 200 per cent import duty on foreign cars and spares.

Hunky raced the ex-Paul Hawkins GT40 in the Spanish Sports Car Championship, and the car was prepared in Hawkeye's workshop in Slough. Bernie, a young Australian mechanic, looked after the car, drove the transporter to each race and was responsible for getting the Carnet de Passage stamped at every border. The RAC Carnet was designed to prevent the sale of cars or spares abroad without duty being paid.

One of the scams at the time, exploited by at least one well-known current F1 entrant, was taking new racing cars into Europe on a Carnet and selling them for cash. On the return trip the new car was replaced with a wrecked racing car of the same make which mysteriously bore the same chassis and engine numbers!

When I saw the prices being charged by Movi for Mini parts, I suggested to Juncadella that my company could supply them at much better prices, namely UK retail plus 50 per cent. This depended on Bernie hiding the parts in the transporter and omitting them from the Carnet. This enabled Movi to buy everything half-price.

Since it was Bernie who was taking the risk, I paid him commission on the value of each shipment, and guaranteed to pay bail money or fines if he got caught.

Bernie never got caught: a nice little earner!

'Ring. Luckily, within seconds the car was surrounded by strapping young campers. They lifted Mini and me back on to the track and, after removing debris from the grille, sent me on my way.

I finished the stint, trying to ignore a slight pull to the right, and handed over to John, mentioning that I thought I'd bent a steering arm. Luckily, later in the race electrical problems led to a lengthy pit stop which put us out of contention and distracted attention from my earlier indiscretion. We finished a lowly fifth in class and 14th overall. When questioned after the race, I put the missing spats down to contact when lapping a slower car: more acceptable than admitting to an off.

The excuse was accepted but I knew Ginger Devlin was secretly smiling – his John Rhodes would never have done that!

1968: A British title

Having campaigned my own privately financed Mini in the up to 1,300cc class for three years – albeit in only 20 races – I was very excited to be offered a semi-works drive with Equipe Arden for 1968.

On the business front things were going well, but I was working long hours and it was increasingly difficult to find time to prepare the car. So this 'arrive and drive' deal, with none of the financial worries, was a welcome change.

Negotiations for my contract were with Alan Edis, then a rising star in the British Leyland hierarchy. Some 35 years later Alan was heavily involved with Steve Neal's very successful assault on the British saloon car championship, culminating in Steve's son, Matt, winning the 2006 BTCC title.

Birdie and I got on well with Alan and his glammy wife, Chris. Despite Alan's serious approach, this extremely clever man had a dry wit that was easy to miss if you weren't on your toes. Records reveal that I was paid travel and hotel expenses and, in lieu of a retainer, was allowed decals on the car to advertise my business.

The Arden team, owned by the late Jim Whitehouse, ran out of a converted piggery in the rural depths of Tamworth-in-Arden in the

Midlands. If you had to guess what Jolly Jim did, the last thing you'd think of was engine tuning. Yet Jim was an absolute genius. Slow-speaking with a broad country accent, he was a deep thinker and had that rare gift of being a good listener. His reputation as one of the best engine builders in the country was totally justified.

The Arden Mini, running in liberal Group 5 form in the up to 1,000cc class of the 1968 British Saloon Car Championship, was competitive from day one. We did not have it all our own way: when the works Fiat Abarths appeared, driven by Toine Hezemans and Rob Slotemaker, they would normally beat us. These Abarths were out and out racing cars and we considered them to be well outside the spirit of the regulations – typical foreigners!

The popular driver Tony Lanfranchi, driving the rear-engine Nathan Hillman Imp, was also a fierce contender for class honours. Our off-track friendship survived our many on-track skirmishes. Enjoying a pint together was more important than falling out!

Of the 11 rounds that year we had four DNFs. Unlike previous years, only one was due to crashing out, so I must have been maturing.

Of the other seven rounds, we finished in the top three, taking wins at Oulton Park and Croft. It was enough to win the one-litre class of the 1968 British Championship by a healthy margin, but I remember the frustration of never being in contention for overall honours. For that I'd have to wait another seven years.

Around October 1968, when I was talking to Cooper Car Co and Downton about the next season, Alan Edis asked for a recommendation as to my replacement. I had no hesitation in suggesting Alec Poole, who I knew was a very quick driver, and with his Irish charm would fit in well.

Alec went on to be the outright 1969 British Saloon Car Champion.

Thruxton in 1969 – leading team-mate Steve Neal!

Silverstone GP meeting, 1969. (Peter Darley)

Posing with team-mate Steve Neal in 1969. (Peter Darley)

1969: Simply the best...

In October 1968, over lunch at The Bull Hotel in Downton, I found nothing had changed with my former employers in Wiltshire. Krug champagne for Daniel and dry Martinis for Bunty. The Richmonds told me of their plans to enter a 1,293cc Mini Cooper in next year's British Championship. They even offered to pay a retainer, but that was not the reason it took me all of five seconds to accept.

I knew Downton's Ray Sheppard would produce a competitive car and it meant promotion from the 1,000cc to the 1,300cc class. There would also be the chance of overall wins when the races were divided and the two smaller classes had a separate race.

Looking at the bigger picture, and some hidden agendas that 40 years of hindsight

reveal, our new team had every chance of beating the official factory cars based at Abingdon. Lord Stokes had taken over BMC to form the doomed British Leyland and the Abingdon boys were demoralised at the savage cuts they had to make in favour of their preferred sport of rallying. Indeed, they had to prepare racing Mini Coopers S-types at short notice for Rhodes and Handley, whom they knew would be facing increasingly stiff opposition from the Broadspeed Escorts of John Fitzpatrick and Chris Craft.

The Cooper Car Company's contract to prepare and enter the works Minis had been terminated on the orders of British Leyland's new management. That fired up Cooper's will to beat their old employers no end, and Downton felt the same. After all, it was Cooper which had originally created the Mini Cooper and S concept and Downton who had done all the engine development work. Another element was that Cooper Car Co had just been bought by the Sieff family, owners of Marks & Spencer, the deal being motivated by Jonathan Sieff's enthusiasm for motor racing.

Along with the Sieff connection came David Blackburn, who held the sole BMW franchise for the UK, and was now a director of Cooper Cars. Enter one John Blackburn, nephew of David, entrepreneur, bon viveur, handsome, smooth-talking and married to Liz. John was appointed Marketing Manager of Cooper Cars.

Without factory support the Cooper/Downton team needed serious sponsorship to be viable, and this was provided by Britax Ltd – leading manufacturer of seat belts and a close neighbour of Cooper in Byfleet, Surrey. Thus the team was renamed Britax-Cooper-Downton.

John Blackburn and I were kindred spirits and we hit it off from our very first meeting. During contract negotiations John became my 'man on the inside' and insisted I hold out for a £1,000 retainer and 40 per cent of prize and start money, as he knew it was in the budget. To put this in perspective, at the time you could stock a car accessory shop for £2,000.

All that money for something I'd happily have done for the pure fun of it!

Steve Neal and I viewed each other with the deep suspicion that only team 'mates' appreciate. Sod the competition, beating your teammate was paramount. Friendly and supportive for the world to see but plotting and scheming behind each other's backs.

Regarding driver status, John Cooper agreed that whichever of us had scored more points after four races would become the number one driver. After races at Brands, Silverstone, Snetterton and Thruxton, I was well ahead of Steve on points. The two cars were absolutely identical apart from the seat and race number: our rivalry came to a head at the second Silverstone meeting in May.

I was ahead of Steve after practice but on the warm-up lap for the race I noticed my car was handling strangely. It immediately dawned on me that Team Manager Ginger Devlin, who I regarded as thick as thieves with Steve, had swapped our cars. Quite early in the race, Steve and I got into a motorised punch-up which resulted in the need for two new bodyshells. Steve ended up against a bank at Club corner, whilst my car finished on its roof in the middle of the track!

It wasn't the first time we had clashed, and neither was it to be the last, but this was an expensive shunt. At the inquest, both of us naturally blamed the other. I argued that if John Cooper's ruling had been heeded, the contretemps would have been avoided. John Cooper was such a gentleman and hated confrontation: it transpired John had put off telling Ginger or Steve, neither of whom would have taken kindly to the decision.

At Crystal Palace two weeks later, the four saloon car classes had been divided into two races, and this represented a realistic chance of my first overall win. The BBC televised the race, Murray Walker gave his usual seat-of-the-pants commentary, and I ended up winning my first outright race victory.

The delight at my first win was disproportionately heightened by Steve coming fourth behind Craft and Rhodes!

The first seven races had produced three wins at Brands, Mallory and Crystal Palace, two second places at Silverstone and Thruxton (behind Broadspeed Escorts) and two DNFs at Snetterton and Silverstone. By mid-season, though, Ralph Broad's development of the Escorts resulted in Craft and Fitzpatrick regularly beating us for the rest of the season.

1969 had brought success beyond my wildest dreams and established me as the fastest Mini driver in the UK. More than that, my racing income for the season – including unofficial earnings – was enough to stock five new accessory shops. To avoid high income tax, all the money went into funding the expanding car accessory business.

1969: BOAC 500 Brands Hatch. Retired! Juncadella is on right-hand side.

On the podium at the 1969 Jarama 1,000km: (left to right) F. Godia-Sales, Juan Fernandez, Alex Soler-Roig, Jochen Rindt, GS and Jose Juncadella.

Spanish perks

One of the reasons the 1969 season was so memorable for me was that it led to the opportunity of driving a proper sports racing car for the first time in my career: a Ford GT40.

Movi Cooper were the concessionaires for Cooper Cars in Spain, and I was involved in testing their Group 5 Mini Racer which they entered in the Spanish Touring Car Championship under the Escuderia Montjuich (EM) banner. The owner of both Movi and EM was Jose Maria Juncadella de Salisachs (nicknamed Hunky), a wealthy member of the Spanish aristocracy as well as a gentleman racer.

Hunky went racing in style and I got to know him well – an incredible stroke of luck. Escuderia Montjuich owned the ex-Paul Hawkins Ford GT40, which they raced in the Spanish Sports Car Championship and other European endurance races. Hunky didn't have to ask twice when he approached me to drive with him at the BOAC 6-hour race at Brands in April.

The overwhelming sensation of driving a GT40 for the first time was one of pure joy. It helped that it was a well sorted car: it actually went in the direction you pointed, the steering was light and it was extremely comfortable. All the things a Mini wasn't! I'd expected to find it a challenge to handle the 450bhp, but it was the easiest car I had ever driven and within very few laps I was on the pace.

In the race, which was won by Jo Siffert and Brian Redman in a Porsche 908, we retired after 95 laps with clutch problems. But Hunky did not seem bothered and promised me further drives.

The call came sooner than expected, this time to drive at Jarama in a round of the Spanish Championship. The GT40 was entered in Group 4 – the category for sports cars with a 5-litre engine limit for which a

minimum of 50 cars had been homologated. The faster Group 6 category was for sports prototypes with a 3-litre limit, much reduced weight and no minimum production.

As Janos Wimpffen says in his *Time and Two Seats: Five Decades of Long Distance Racing*: 'The balance of the mixed Group 4 and 6 tenure up to 1971 would witness some of the most exciting cars seen in the history of motor racing. Not the FIA nor any of the manufacturers expected this.'

Juncadella always liked to do the opening and closing stints and was happy to leave the middle stints to his co-driver. This meant plenty of seat time for me and I remember this race well. With just over an hour to go I handed over to Hunky for the final stint. We had a two-minute lead in Group 4 and were lying third overall behind two Group 6 Porsches.

With half an hour to go, Hunky made an unscheduled pit stop – he was thirsty and wanted a Coke! Owner or not this was simply not on and he was unceremoniously sent back out – without a drink – to finish the race.

What should have been an easy cruise now became a drama. The happy ending was that we won the class by 20 seconds and came third overall – my best sports car result to date. The

Driving the boss in his Ford GT40 after Jarama victory!

race was won by Alex Soler-Roig, a wealthy Spanish surgeon who had hired Grand Prix star Jochen Rindt as his co-driver!

This was also Hunky's best ever result – from the post-race celebrations you'd have thought he'd won the championship. Later in the evening, between hugging and kissing, he thrust a pile of pesetas in my pocket that I thought it would be rude to refuse. When I got home I changed them for proper money and found it was over £400.

A few weeks later Hunky asked to meet me at the Hilton Hotel in Paris the following Friday – the GT40 was entered in the Montlhéry 1,000km race, a round of the Spanish Championship. A first-class air ticket duly arrived – Hunky didn't do Economy. I can't recall what happened in the race but I do remember trying to find the limit on the famous banking in qualifying, always feeling I could have gone faster.

That evening, back at the hotel, Hunky told me he had ordered a Ferrari 512 to enter at Le Mans next year and to keep that week free. That was reward enough for the weekend and I was flying high for days!

John Cooper with cigar, 1969. (Peter Darley)

Later in 1969 John Cooper was invited to open the Barcelona Motor Show. I suspect Juncadella had fixed it, for Movi Cooper was Barcelona-based.

Before the show opened there was a formal dinner at which John was the Guest of Honour, and Hunky had thoughtfully provided some very attractive young ladies to accompany our entourage. When the dinner was over, Hunky suggested we accompany our escorts to a private party. He would not be going as he was with Cuka, his gorgeous girl-friend, but with a wink and a nod he recommended we attend.

We were driven to a most beautiful hacienda, with a courtyard behind high walls, where the men were all in DJs, the ladies in long dresses and the atmosphere highly sophisticated. As we chatted at the bar the penny dropped that this was no normal house party, the ladies were there for the men to enjoy. The establishment was patronised by gentlemen known to the management and, as Hunky's guests, the night was on him. Just one of the perks of the Spanish aristocracy, tacitly accepted by their wives, and practised with complete discretion.

Viva España!

My last GT40 race of the season was the Barcelona 12 hours, held on the roads around

At Jim Whitehouse's memorial 40 years later (2008): (left to right) Steve Neal, GS, John Rhodes, Barry Williams and Alec Poole. (Norman Seeney)

Montjuich Park, after which Hunky's team was named. We were out after 400-odd laps with transmission failure, but the race was won by another of Escuderia Montjuich's eight entries, a Porsche 908 driven by Juan Fernandez, who would be co-driving the Ferrari with me next year.

Incidentally, Chris Craft and David Piper came second in a similar 908, and the last classified finishers were Chris Marshall and John Britten in a Triumph Spitfire!

1970: Arden Mini finale

For 1970 my heart was set on racing in the European Formula 5000 series and, as will be seen in the next chapter, I drove the Kitchiner K3A until the money ran out. However, with the demise of the Britax-Cooper-Downton team, and British Leyland's withdrawal from saloon car racing, I was invited to drive for Equipe Arden again.

The team was fresh from Alec Poole's overall victory in the previous year's championship, and Alan Edis and Jim Whitehouse decided to enter a 1,293cc Mini Cooper S in the 1,300cc class. I made it clear that F5000 races would take precedence, which, looking back, was a mistake.

I do not actually remember much about the 1970 RAC British Saloon Car Championship, but time spent in the BRDC library, reading through old copies of *Autosport*, has refreshed my memory.

The season was remarkably similar to that of 1969, except the cars were run to Group 2 specification, and there were less Minis competing but more Ford Escorts.

I missed the early rounds – mid-fielding and having accidents in the Kitchiner K3A – but came fifth overall and won the class at Silverstone in late April. According to *Autosport* 'Gardner again, but Spice steals the show.' This was followed in June by two more class wins – including the Tourist Trophy race at Silverstone – but from then on history repeated itself.

In my last three appearances in the Arden Mini in July and August, I came second in class, each time beaten by Fitzpatrick's Broadspeed Escort.

I don't remember being fired but my name doesn't appear in the reports for the rest of the season!

Chapter 9

Single seat = parties and pain

I met Tony Kitchiner in summer 1969. He was the most enthusiastic man I had ever met in the racing world and had high ambitions as a race-car constructor. His confidence was catching and I let him know I was keen to progress from saloon and sports cars to the Real Thing: single-seaters. Tony invited me to his workshop at Stamford Brook Arches in Chiswick, West London – premises that were extremely modest, very cluttered and absolutely filthy.

The egg trick: setting it up.

Here, between servicing cars to pay the bills, he was converting a compact Formula 2 monocoque chassis to a full-blown Formula 5000 car that would be a sure-fire winner. This was the K3A.

Tony explained that the budget for the 1970 season, including building the car, was £1,500, of which £400 had already been spent buying a 4.7-litre Ford V8. Chevrolet 5.0-litre engines were the norm in F5000 but Tony had 101 reasons why a Ford would be better, not to mention the cost.

The radical racer was smaller and lighter than the opposition, had a short wheelbase, and featured a unique slatted nose cone and a rear wing that extended well behind the rear wheels – this to satisfy Tony's theory that the leverage would increase downforce and reduce drag for a higher top speed. The saving grace was that it was easy to drive: when things got hairy it could be put sideways, Mini-style, without losing control.

Our season started well with two sixth places at Oulton Park and Zandvoort. When mechanical gremlins did not interfere, we enjoyed some fair results. The team's income was entirely reliant on start and prize money, plus whatever cash could be drummed up from the odd sponsor. Our best result was a fourth place at Monza which caught the imagination of the motoring press, who saw it as a David and Goliath performance. The prize money from that Italian result was enough to transport the car from Monza to Anderstorp in Sweden by the next weekend.

Financially, we were skating on thin ice and a miracle would be needed to complete the season.

Tony's commitment was incredible throughout, but sometimes he'd go down a

58

route that seemed crazy. One example was his obsession with producing his own fibreglass wheels, which would be lighter and far cheaper to produce than the alloy wheels used by everyone else. He duly produced beautifully crafted wooded bucks for laying up the wheels: after a few days of curing we were off to Thruxton to test the revolutionary wheels.

One gentle lap, into the pits – no problem.

Five faster laps, into the pits – no problem.

Unfortunately, taking off for the third stint there was an expensive grinding noise and the car came to a halt. While the car was stationary, the discs had acted as a heat sink and started to melt the fibreglass! Tony understood the problem, but it was back to the drawing board.

Before Monza, Ulf Norinder – one of Birdie's favourite racers – had invited all F5000 team personnel to his retirement party. It was held at his Swedish estate, 200 miles north of his home circuit, Anderstorp, south of Gothenburg. The word was that girlfriends and wives would be redundant on this occasion, and to allow more than 24 hours for the celebrations.

So Anderstorp was a must.

The Anderstorp weekend was marred by the death of Derrick Williams when his Lola collided with Fred Saunders's Crosslé and landed upside down. It was pure luck that I avoided the accident: Derrick was six feet in the air as I went under him. A nasty one, I thought, but it was not till next time round that I realised just how bad.

On that sombre Sunday evening a meeting was held to decide whether Ulf's party should go ahead, the decision complicated by the conservative Swedish press latching on to the dilemma and making it clear what they thought. The teams thought differently: cancelling the party would be the last thing Derrick would have wanted and it wouldn't bring him back – so the party proceeded as planned.

Next day we were coached to Ulf's party home which was a slice of Sweden measuring six miles by sixty, with every facility imaginable from Go-Kart racing on forest tracks to water skiing on the lake adjoining the main house.

Party hostesses showed us to our rooms in the surrounding chalets and at 6:00pm all assembled for cocktails on the magnificent

Left: Lining it up.

Right: Tray gone – egg in glass.

The egg trick

Over the years I've learnt a few party tricks that have not only been fun to do but have been an effective icebreaker with everyone from Japanese racing sponsors to City big shots. On occasions they have been a source of revenue – by betting against their success.

One of my favourites is the Egg Trick. This was first shown to me by successful club driver Mick Cave, who had raced his Austin A40 against brother Dee's similar car at Goodwood in the '60s.

At their lovely farm house near Thruxton, Mick took us all down to the cellar, where he produced a long axe, a tray, a Bryant & May book of matches, a glass of water and a fresh egg. Cave then placed the tray centrally on the floor, over the half-filled glass of water, and balanced the egg centrally on the sleeve of the matchbox.

The challenge was to get the egg into the glass, without it breaking, using only the axe. To everyone's amazement he simply swung the axe in an arc, struck the side of the tray, and the egg plopped straight into the glass without breaking.

As long-handled axes are not always available, I modified the trick using a heavy shoe instead of the axe, placing the glass of water on the table, instead of the floor. As long as the egg is perfectly aligned over the glass it works, provided the tray is hit absolutely horizontally. If it is hit at an angle the egg will fly off, as the trick depends on the rim of the tray knocking out the match box: gravity takes care of the rest.

One of the best things about the trick is the audience participation. In a restaurant, selection of the heaviest shoe gets all the surrounding tables involved. Clearing space for the tray to land gets the punters running for cover. A few practice swings with the shoe, just missing, raises the tension. If the atmosphere is right, *ie* the punters are feeling no pain, it can be 'a nice little earner'. All made easier with the help of an attractive personal Debbie McGee – in my case Creech (of whom much more as this book progresses).

Start by making the trick fail, by hitting the tray at an angle. While preparing for the second attempt, your assistant takes bets that next time it will work. After two or three 'double or quits' the bets pile up and when there's enough at stake you make it work.

Occasionally, if the egg hits the side of the glass, it will crack but not break. If this happens, rescue the egg from the glass, hold it up to show it is perfect. Gently throw it to one of the audience. If cracked, it will almost certainly break in their hands – their problem not yours!

Sometimes the maître d' would get upset, particularly when other customers try the trick and fail. On occasions we have been asked to leave, but more often the waiters were desperate to learn how to do it: a good negotiating point when the bill arrived.

Practice before your first public performance!

lawn, with a trad jazz band playing in the background – utter luxury. Next thing, helicopters swept in dropping clothes and toiletries for the guests. The T-shirts were printed 'Oy Oy! This is Ulf's Party' and I treasure mine to this day. To top this, more helicopters arrived with scantily clad young ladies swinging from underneath, the idea being to drop them off on the lawn. As it happened, a breeze had blown up and the only safe way they could be landed was in the lake: there was no shortage of rescuers.

Maryanne Flack – known as Flacky – was Ulf's PA, and one of her responsibilities had been to recruit enough 'good-time girls' to look after Ulf's 100-odd guests. Flacky told me there had been no shortage of applicants and she'd simply selected them by their looks, personalities and free spirit.

What a thoughtful host!

The first party night went into the small hours and it became clear that this was to be a marathon. Three bands played round the clock, those with sporting aspirations drove

Go-Karts and motorbikes, or went shooting or water skiing, whilst others had massages, entertained the ladies or just watched them enjoying each other – another first for me.

On the second day, the few who had brought their partners were dragged home and the party became a Bacchanalian feast. Limitless supplies of food and booze were on hand as one day drifted to the next. Politically incorrect and unimaginable today, it might sound degenerate, but it was organised with such style and good humour that everyone entered into the spirit.

At one stage our host, Ulf, a tall striking Viking with shoulder-length flaxen hair and enough gold chain to pay the national debt, made an emotional pot-fuelled speech which had everyone blinking. We had presented him with a retirement gift and in his own inimitable way he made it clear how touched he was. Sadly, they don't come like Ulf any more.

I had to fly back early – on the Friday to be precise – to sober up for a saloon race at Silverstone. I understand the party continued to the Sunday. Endurance racing had nothing on that.

Without doubt the event of the year, and eminently worthy of Para 9 Clause (j) as presented in Birdie's divorce petition a couple of years later.

The next round of the championship was at the Salzburgring – a spectacular circuit dwarfed by the surrounding Austrian Alps.

Argentine GP at Buenos Aires, 1971: leading Silvio Moser in first my outing with ex-Howden Ganley F5000 McLaren-Chevrolet M10B. (LAT)

Tony Kitchiner with GS at the 1971 Argentine GP. (LAT)

The race coincided with the week of the Salzburg Car Show, which I was visiting, and knowing the dire financial position of the team I was half expecting Kitchiner not to turn up.

When he did he was penniless and we had to borrow money to pay for the fuel for the two-heat 50-lap race. In practice Trevor Taylor wrote off the new works Surtees TS5A in a high-speed accident that ended Team Surtees European F5000 season.

The priority for the race was just to finish, as without the prize money the team wouldn't get home, so it was with great relief that we came fifth on aggregate, just behind Ulf Norinder's Lola T190.

The race was won by Mike Hailwood in another T190 and second place went to Howden Ganley in Sid Taylor's McLaren M10B. I didn't know it at the time, but I would be racing Howden's car the following year.

With six races to go, Tony and I decided to call it a day. The constant hassle of being under-funded was getting to Tony and with growing business commitments I was in no position to help. We parted as friends.

My First [and last] Grand Prix – January 1971

After Salzburgring, having completed half a 'character-building' F5000 season with Kitchiner, I decided the equipment I had been using was responsible for the poor results. Typical racing driver – nothing to do with a lack of skill!

In September I sold Berkshire Cottage in Sunninghill. After paying off the mortgage, there was still a tidy sum left over and I conveniently decided it was not a good time to reinvest in property. I persuaded Birdie that we should rent whilst looking around, so we took a two-year lease on Kingsbury Cottage in Old Windsor.

In November I heard that the non-championship Argentine Grand Prix – scheduled for 24 January 1971 – was open to F5000 cars to make up the grid. Since the start/finishing money was set at rewarding Formula 1 levels, I was seriously interested. After protracted negotiations with Howden Ganley, I bought his McLaren M10B, funded partly by a bank loan and partly by the Berkshire Cottage sale. With the help of Barry Bland and Peter Gaydon at MRC, I secured an entry to the Argentine Grand Prix.

Tony Kitchiner prepared the car with the brief that it had to be reliable, just a plain old-fashioned M10B with no experimental bits. The McLaren was shipped to Buenos Aires, with Tony as team manager, race engineer and mechanic. I was truly at the threshold of international stardom!

There had been yet another revolution in the Argentine and each team was allocated security guards and drivers who were with you 24/7 – even sleeping outside your hotel room. Heady stuff, but not as exciting as being on the grid with names I had only read about in awe. The prize money was critical to the plan and paid right down to last place. I completed practice at a safe pace, ending up near the back of the grid, learning both the circuit and the car, mesmerised by the superstars hurtling by and trying to keep out of their way.

The penny still hadn't dropped that F1 was not for me.

The GP was in a two parts and I finished the first heat towards the back of the field. Mission half-achieved! The second leg was a race of attrition, with numerous accidents and blow-ups, but I stuck to the strategy to finish at all costs, made easier because halfway through I was totally knackered. I remember the race was won by Chris Amon in a Matra MS120, and I finished eighth overall between Reine Wisell's Gold Leaf Team Lotus 72C and Wilson Fittipaldi's older Lotus 49C.

Despite a few days celebrating in Rio with Birdie on the way home, I arrived back in the UK flush with cash – enough to pay off the loan with plenty to spare.

On the car accessory front, by 1971 business was thriving. We appointed a chap named Karl Wieland and his wife Dot as Public Relations gurus for the company. They were an unconventional couple, artistic in a hippie way, but, most importantly, Karl was a car nut. They gave us a pot plant – of the smoking variety – as a Kingsbury Cottage housewarming gift and it grew like a Triffid, despite regular trimming.

One of Karl's clients was a West Country industrial heating manufacturer, Powrmatic, and he persuaded them to sponsor my F5000 efforts.

Tony Kitchiner prepared the M10B, but his priority was constructing groundbreaking racers, so he never fully committed to the McLaren. After an early season crash at Snetterton, necessitating a major rebuild, the car reappeared mid-season dubbed a Kitchmac – get it?

Tony persuaded me that his nosecone was better than the original, with horizontal slats that looked like a washboard, and cheaper than a McLaren genuine part. The rear wing was modified and moved backwards to increase downforce, and the M10B became a real hybrid.

I still didn't know enough to argue.

Apart from a few accidents – all part of the learning curve, I told myself – the 1971 season was dogged with reliability problems, from running out of petrol to full-scale blowups. My best result was a fourth place at the last meeting at Brands in October. It was a combined F1/F5000 grid and, before we had time to

Kitchiner explained

Mike Kettlewell's review of Gordon's 1971 season in *Motor Racing 1972* revealed some of the difficulties encountered. 'Gordon Spice started off with three engines, but disasters reduced this total to one, an amalgam of all three concocted by Tony Kitchiner. Spice crashed his ex-Ganley car testing at Snetterton, prior to the second round of the championship, requiring a new monocoque. This and a road accident shortened Spice's year somewhat, but on several occasions, especially in the wet, he was able to show he has what it takes to drive a powerful single-seater.'

Nicked!

I nearly missed Ireland's Mondello Park meeting in May 1971 after a brush with the Metropolitan Police in London. On the Thursday evening before we were due to fly out I was enjoying a few pints in a pub on the Kings Road. At closing time the landlady upset me by pouring my unfinished pint down the drain.

Refused a refund, I insisted on the police being called – first mistake.

'Giving trouble are we, sonny?' was their response before bundling me into the back of their Panda – then straight to the nick.

After a sobering night in a cell I appeared next morning before a magistrate: he was totally disinterested in my version of why the police had been called, or that I should have been on my way to Dublin. A £5 fine followed.

Apart from launching the Kitchmac over a bank in practice, my memory of that Irish weekend was a party given by motor racing entrant Sid Taylor. One of the sport's great characters, Sid had the amiable and extremely talented Brian Redman driving his McLaren M18, which won the first heat and retired after leading the second.

Left: 1971 Argentine GP – a moment of contemplation, or 'What the hell am I doing here?!' (LAT)

Brands Hatch, 1971, the last race of the season: leading Trevor Taylor's Leda prior to red flags after Jo Siffert's fatal crash. (LAT)

The cigarette trick

This trick is performed to demonstrate the power of the mind over pain. Take a lit cigarette – if you can find one nowadays – knock off the ash and blow on the lit end to make it glow. Take the cigarette and hold it by each end between thumb and forefinger. Sounds extremely painful, and it is until you know how…

What you do is take an ice cube, conceal it in your pocket and hold the end of your index finger against it until it is frozen. Then remove your hand from your pocket, making sure your finger is dry – very important. Place the burning end of the cigarette on the frozen part of your finger and hold it there until you feel it start to get hot. This will take several seconds, whilst the frozen finger is brought up to normal temperature. The silence will be stunning!

When you remove the cigarette, blow on it to show it is still alight – that is why it is essential to dry your finger – then pass it on to the next challenger. If accused of having a dead finger, just repeat the trick using another finger. Without ice, it is very painful!

Good luck with these, but if you fancy something a little more edgy turn to Chapter 10 for the knife trick.

Mallory Park, 1972: at Pole position in the Powrmatic-sponsored KitchMac, alongside Alan Rollinson's Lola T300. (LAT)

break down, on the 15th lap the race was stopped when Jo Siffert had his fatal accident in the BRM. This was the first time for me that the reality of the danger really struck home.

No post-race celebrations, just the thought: 'There but for the grace of God...'

Overall 1971 qualified as an even worse season than 1970. However, I did catch the eye of at least one reporter, regarding which see the sidebar labelled 'Kitchiner explained'). I see from the record books that Frank Gardner won the Formula 5000 championship by a country mile in a Lola T300 with Mike Hailwood second in a Surtees TS8. In the overall standings I came 16th equal, and it was little consolation that also on four points were Jean Pierre Jaussaud and Howden Ganley (both in Barry Newman McLaren M18s) together with Keith Holland and Tony Trimmer.

I still had hope, though, and took encouragement from the fact that Peter Gethin, an established superstar who won the Italian Grand Prix that year, finished in only 12th place with seven points. I ignored the small detail that Peter drove just two races to my 15...

Roll on 1972!

With the opening of the cash & carry in 1971, my first priority was the business, and allowing Tony Kitchiner's continued involvement for 1972 must have been the easy option.

The season started well enough and at my first F5000 race, at Mallory Park, I stuck the Kitchmac on pole, with Allan Rollinson alongside on the same time. A damaged front spoiler dropped me to fourth place in the race, but it was an encouraging start.

A week later at Snetterton I shared the front row with Gijs van Lennep in the works Surtees TS11 – ahead of Graham McRae and Brian Redman. On lap two I took the lead from van Lennep and held it for the next 12 laps. Then a front spring broke, van Lennep took the lead, and for five laps I kept Teddy Pilette behind me in third place. On the 18th lap of 25 my Kitchmac's suspension collapsed completely – another DNF. Van Lennep won, Pilette was second and Redman third. My first F5000 win had eluded me. Again.

Business pressures only allowed me to compete in a further another four races that season, but each one was dogged with mechanical problems, mostly due to poor preparation. The year was a high point in business but the lowest point so far in my chequered racing career.

The KitchMac at the Silverstone GKN Trophy meeting, 1972. (LAT)

The Kitchiner-Ford K3A F5000 car at Oulton Park, 1970. (LAT)

Chapter 10

Back to tin-top roots

Following an inauspicious start in F5000 in 1970, followed by unmemorable seasons in 1971–2, the chance to return to my roots in saloon car racing came in 1973. It was business colleague Ernie Unger who introduced me to Stan Robinson. Stan was a larger than life character, great company and a patron of Bacchus – so we had much in common. Stan also owned a Ford dealership and that introduction prompted the start of my ten-year affair with Ford Capris.

I was in the middle of a traumatic divorce from Birdie – my fault entirely, I hasten to add – and stony broke. So the idea of driving someone else's car, without personal financial hassles, was very appealing. Stan had opened a Ford dealership in County Durham called Wisharts of Crook. He had no personal aspirations to be a driver, but was a serious enthusiast and dead keen to go motor racing.

The Wisharts mechanics were Dave Cook and Terry, both excellent men, and Dave proved to be a highly skilled engineer. Peter Clark was a manager at Wisharts and doubled up as mechanic when needed. He was also a useful driver and we drove together on several occasions. Cook and Clark later went into business preparing racing Capris – hence CC Racing.

The car was a yellow 3-litre Group 1 Ford Capri GT, Essex road-registered RPU 931K. It ran within the unusual 'racing by price'

Touring liberties

I was joined on the 1973 Avon Tour by my then current girlfriend, Vivian. She happened to share a London flat with one of James Hunt's female friends and we had both moved in. In the evening, drinking beer and smoking spliffs, James would expound on his Formula 1 ambitions, and then disappear early next morning – to the gym or off running.

I'd tell him what a wanker he was: that he was not called 'Hunt the Shunt' for nothing. I told him that if he had to live in cloud cuckoo land, he should go and do it elsewhere.

Three years later he became F1 World Champion.

I digress. Vivian had brought along her 'best friend' to the overnight Avon Tour stop in Bath. This friend was an RAC timekeeper and, like many best friends, was considerably less attractive than herself.

After an evening at the bar with Stan and the boys, Vivian announced that her friend needed a bed for the night and, with the hotel fully booked, she'd have to sleep with us. I was in no state to argue and when we got to the room it was made clear that I would not be allowed my usual rights without sharing them with her friend.

Even in the '70s this was extremely liberal thinking, but it did my kudos with the Wisharts crew no harm at all… it would never happen in County Durham!

formula. The Capri was in the over £1,500 class, eligible for both the 1973 Britax and Castrol Production Saloon Car Championships. These were normally 10-lap races and our first class win was at Brands Hatch, where I had the advantage of having just competed in the Shellsport Celebrity Race in a Ford Escort Mexico, where I finished third.

A second win in the Capri came at Silverstone, and a third victory at Oulton Park in April. I often came second – eight times during the busy season in two championships – although I also won at Thruxton in June. Overall race wins usually went to the big car class – Chevrolet Camaros with V8 engines and twice the power. Former motorcycle champion Stuart Graham was particularly successful in the Yank tanks, as was the late Richard Lloyd. A well-financed BMW-Rothmans team of 3-litre saloons led by Tony Lanfranchi and rapid journalist Roger Bell also featured.

In addition we took the Capri to the Nürburgring 24-hour race, where we had enormous problems at scrutineering – our first taste of German officialdom. After an all-nighter to make the car comply with their interpretation of the rule book, it was particularly satisfying to finish the race. Our lap chart showed we'd won the class but the organisers didn't agree and we had to settle for second place.

My first taste of Belgium's Spa Francorchamps road circuit came in their 24-hour race of 1973. My co-driver for Spa was John Hine, an ex-Formula 3 racer, from whom I'd recently bought the two exhibition vehicles. The old 14km Spa circuit was fast and challenging – even in a Group 1 Capri we were approaching 150mph into the blind Masta

The 1973 Avon Tour of Britain: Wisharts Capri with Stan Robinson. (LAT)

Tricky burn-up at the Nürburgring

The evening before a 24-hour touring car race at the Nürburgring in 1973, the bar at the Wildenschwein in Adenau was crowded with drivers and mechanics – most of them German. We would be racing on the old 21km Nordschleife circuit, constructed during Hitler's time to demonstrate the superiority of German cars (in my view it is the best circuit in the world). After qualifying, Stan Robinson and I had been given a hard time by over-zealous scrutineers, and the mechos were still at work.

That evening seemed a natural time for some teasing at the Germans' expense, and this started with the knife trick. I was delighted to find none of

them could do it, and I wasn't going to tell them how to.

This led to my mentioning, in a friendly way, that one could naturally not expect German drivers to have the swift reactions or self-control of the Brits. '*Mein leiblings*,' I started, 'mind over matter is vital in a racing driver...' and I launched into the cigarette trick as described in the previous chapter. At their insistence, I repeated the stunt several times.

The challenge was irresistible, but, despite their dogged efforts – surprise, surprise – not one of the fit young drivers could hold the glowing ciggy longer than two seconds. The number of plastered fingers at breakfast next morning was testament to their courage!

kink. We failed to finish that year, but I fell in love with the circuit and returned home determined to try again.

The 1973 event that stands out in my mind was the inaugural Avon Tour of Britain. Stan, who had somehow massaged sponsorship from Woolworths, was navigator in our racing Capri. The event was a mix of circuit races and

special stages, run over three days to a strict schedule, using public roads to link the competitive stages. As a rally driver I was pretty useless, probably because I'd never done it before.

On a foggy night special stage I decided to take it easy and wait for Ari Vatanen, who I knew was starting in his rally Escort 30 seconds behind us, and then just follow his tail lights to

The knife trick

The knife trick demonstrates the exceptional reactions of the professional racing driver! Take a table knife – or spoon or fork – and hold it between both index fingers, horizontally at eye level, facing your adversary. Challenge them to catch it when you drop it any time within five seconds. The challenger must hold their catching hand above the knife. When you drop it, they grab for the knife, invariably missing it – but only just. The knife must be dropped absolutely horizontally for this to work.

Try it before reading on and you will see how difficult it is.

Actually it's very simple if you know how, and has little to do with fast reactions. The technique is to ignore the

line of patter that the knife dropper will invariably use to put you off, and concentrate on the knife. When the knife is dropped, resist the natural reaction of grabbing for it. Just follow it down and catch it from above, at somewhere around knee level. This way, with a little practice, you will catch it every time and the more proficient you become the less you will have to bend down.

An even more impressive version of the trick is to put both hands behind your back and catch it from that position. Don't try this until you can catch the knife conventionally at least ten consecutive times.

You should now be confident enough to take a bet on succeeding!

the end of the stage. Sure enough, he caught up and flew past before I even had a chance to give him space. Within seconds he had disappeared into the fog; there was zero chance of staying with him. I remember thinking 'What a madman, and what a way to earn a living!'

During most of the tour we didn't have much clue as to how we were doing, but we'd won most of the races, survived the stages, and persuaded the organisers to cancel the public road stage where many of us had made a complete Horlicks.

Nevertheless, we were surprised to find that, with one rally stage remaining, we were lying second overall, a few seconds behind James Hunt's Camaro. The stage was a short hill climb through a forest and the superfit James ran the course on foot, giving him a clear advantage. I regarded this as highly unsporting, knowing that I could never follow suit!

James maintained his lead and Stan and I had to settle for second place, albeit just 26 seconds behind the future World Champ. Very good for the ego!

The encouraging result on the Avon Tour inspired Stan to greater things, and this took the form of a massive American Plymouth Hemicuda for 1974. But first I had my private life to sort out…

I had just moved in to a tiny cottage at Thorpe Green, thanks to a £10,000 bank loan agreed with a new Bank Manager in exchange for moving the company's business to NatWest. After Vivian (for whom see the sidebar entitled 'Assorted liberties'), Leslie had become my live-in girlfriend: she was a top speech therapist, who specialised in teaching autistic children. We were together for six happy months, but our romance came to an abrupt end when I fell madly in love during the 1973 Caribbean tour, described in a later chapter.

The object of my affection was Stephanie, who lived in Guyana with her two kids. She had separated from her partner, a wealthy jeweller who owned gold mines, and she and her family all lived in Georgetown. Stephanie's Dad and brother were both pilots for Bookers International, which owned plantations in many parts of the world.

When I returned from the Caribbean before Christmas, I had the difficult job of explaining to Leslie that Stephanie would be coming to live at Rambler Cottage – in three days' time… Leslie and I both knew our relationship would never be permanent, which made things easier,

and my guilt was short-lived after Stephanie arrived. She was quite gorgeous, with stunning Irish eyes, and was an instant hit with my family, which made a nice change.

I would have married her at the drop of a hat.

Any such plans were thwarted when, on returning from work one Friday evening, I read her 'Dear John' letter. She missed her children desperately, and had flown back to Guyana to be with them. Her decision was completely out of the blue and I was poleaxed.

History had repeated itself and this time the boot was on the other foot.

My first selfish thought was about next day's dinner party hosted by my racing pal, Billy Gubelman. Who could I take with me? To appear alone would be unthinkable. So I called up Annie P, an old friend who recently separated from Stephen Proctor, owner of Britax. I explained the situation but she was not free that Saturday: she had arranged to take their family Nanny out to dinner – an original

excuse! But she had a friend, whom apparently I'd met before and who had just split up with her boyfriend of six years. If I promised faithfully to behave like a gentleman, she would ask her to accompany me to the party.

I had misgivings about a blind date – what if she was ugly? But time was short and I was desperate, so I arranged to collect my mystery date on Saturday afternoon from Annie's house in Chelsea.

Next day I drove to London, accompanied by Wisharts mechanic Terry, and my old whippet Charlie Min (see the sidebar 'Charlie goes missing') sitting in the back. Charlie was 12 years old and very special. He had travelled everywhere with me since my divorce from Birdie and was trained to keep a low profile – especially at race circuits, where he would hide under a rally jacket and go for hours without a pee. When I was living in a 'no dogs allowed' bedsit in Staines – demonstrating extreme poverty to my ex – Charlie learned to lie quietly in a carrier bag so that I could carry him

1973 Avon Tour of Britain: trying to be a rally driver. (LAT)

Charlie goes missing

Former Spice employee Alan Morgan remembered my wonderful whippet, Charlie Min: 'A small anecdote. After late night opening on Thursday evenings at the Staines warehouse, we would all repair to the pub. At this time Gordon had an aged whippet called Charlie. Charlie had the run of the warehouse, but dutifully followed Gordon into the car when it was time to go.

'One particularly wet and cold Thursday, we were in the pub as usual but Charlie had found his way outside. When we left, he was nowhere to be found. Gordon was very concerned, but after a fruitless search we all had to go home.

'The next day, somebody rang the warehouse from East London to say that he'd got Charlie. Apparently, what had happened was that the poor soaked dog was standing, shivering, next to a car. A passer-by, thinking that it was his owner's car, let Charlie in. He immediately curled up on the back seat and went to sleep. The driver did not discover that he had an unexpected passenger until he got home!

'Gordon was extremely relieved when he got the call the next day.'

in and out of my room. His one downside was that being very old he had bad breath.

On arrival at Annie's house, I was relieved and delighted to find my blind date was a real knock-out, a slim 22-year-old beauty with long dark hair, model looks and a wonderfully engaging personality. Her name was Mandy Watson.

We drove Terry to Paddington to catch a train to the North, and then down to Hampshire for dinner at the Gubelmans: I couldn't wait to show off my newfound trophy. As was his habit, Charlie stood in the middle of the back seat, his breath drifting forwards. I hastily explained to Mandy it was the dog that was the culprit, and she'd soon get used to it.

Over dinner no mention was made of Stephanie and any questions as to how I knew Mandy were tactfully avoided. I knew they were dying to know but was not going to admit to a blind date. She was very much the centre of attention and I was very proud to be with her.

Thank you Annie P!

At the end of the evening I persuaded Mandy to come and see the extension I had started to build at home. Rambler Cottage was a small, one-room character cottage with open fires at each end, and a double bed in the middle. Chatting away, with Andy Williams records playing in the background, time flew by and it was soon too late to drive back to London.

We woke at 6:00am and hurried to Mandy's home in Putney, where I was sent off to sit by the river for an hour. Meanwhile, Mandy took early morning tea to her Mum, pretending she'd been there all night. After breakfast at the Carlton Towers we spent the morning admiring the street paintings around Hyde Park and doing the things that two smitten people do.

I should mention here that from the start I always called Mandy 'Creech' – short for creature. From here on that is how I'll refer to her.

When I dropped her home after lunch, I knew I would be seeing her again whether she liked it or not.

For insurance I had pocketed her gold Dunhill lighter.

1974 was a bleak season. The only thing vaguely funny about the huge Hemicuda was some journalist wag's headline: 'Gordon's got a whopper'. We never managed to get the car sorted, and whilst the engine was powerful, we couldn't get it to run reliably. After much testing and one DNF appearance at Silverstone the car was sold.

The faithful Capri was brought out for the second Avon Tour of Britain. Unlike the first Tour, which had favoured the racing drivers, 1974 was monopolised by rally drivers, who filled the top ten places. After crashing with Peter Hanson's BMW during the Snetterton night race, which cost maximum points, Stan and I finished towards the back of the field.

The 1974 season also failed to impress the new love of my life, Creech, who was now living at Rambler Cottage. Yet my racing fortunes were about to change in a most unexpected way.

Chapter 11

New lives

Oulton Park Gold Cup meeting in the snow, 1975. My first and last F5000 win!

My return to Formula 5000 coincided with my changing social life, so bear with me whilst we travel to Portugal. In August 1974 Creech joined me for a holiday in the Algarve, where I had been staying with John and Liz Blackburn at their home in Carvoeiro. John had opened a bar, The Steering Wheel, which was very popular, and the village was home to many ex-pat Brits.

Having collecting Creech from Faro airport, I was later mystified as to why she was so coy when it came to undressing. It turned out that the night before, when sorting out her bikini line, she'd left the Immac on too long – and the result was a Hitler look-alike moustache!

John and I always threw an evening drinks party, and with gin costing just £1 a gallon drinks were generous and the ambience super-relaxed. Before guests arrived, the ceremonial stirring of the punch with trousers down was a source of schoolboy amusement. Especially

After the Mallory shunt in August 1975, a somewhat shortened monocoque.

when the Polaroid snaps appeared later in the evening.

One of our guests was Chris Reed, with his wife Sylvia. Chris had retired from the City to the Algarve before he was 40, having made a small fortune in currency speculation. Earlier that day Chris had mentioned that he was off to the post office in Portimao to wire some money to London. The Canadian GP at Mosport was imminent and Chris supported John Watson, then driving for the Highgate-based Hexagon Formula 1 Team.

The party seemed an ideal chance to question Chris further, so I opened by asking how much he spent on sponsorship, and why?

'Only ten thousand' came the reply – Chris just enjoyed helping the small British team in F1 and spent money when they were running short.

Chris asked: 'You do a bit of racing, don't you, Gordy? Have you tried F1?' It was too good an opportunity to miss, so I explained I was a failed Formula 5000 driver looking to make a comeback. The only thing stopping me was lack of cash. I mentioned that, for the cost of a few Hexagon payments, he could become an entrant in F5000 for a whole season.

Chris responded: 'Got to go now, but come up to the house tomorrow and I'll give you a cheque.' Talk about sobering up – I hardly slept that night. Next morning it was Creech who convinced me Chris was serious and there was nothing to lose by going to see him.

'Glad you came up – just got to find my chequebook' were his opening words, and then he disappeared. When he came back, cheque-

book in hand, I told him I'd rather he had time to think about it. I promised that as soon as I got home I'd work out the figures and telex him some choices. A week later I did just that, recommending he take the middle-priced option, which was to buy a 1974 Lola and do 12 races, with a total budget of £30,000.

Next day he telexed details of how to draw the money and Reed Racing was in business!

Once Chris had given the green light, it became a priority to set up Reed Racing and prepare for the first round of the 1975 Shellsport European F5000 Championship. Assessing the previous year's form, with emphasis on reliability, I bought Brian McGuire's 1974 Lola T332 and retained Bob Salisbury to run the car. I was really delighted to get Bob on board: I met him when he was working for Bob Gerard and running Billy Gubelman's Formula 2 car – and doing an excellent job. We had similar outlooks on life, and his wife Maggie – another ex-Gerard employee – came as a team bonus. Bob had premises near Loughborough, where the couple lived. Assisted by 'gofer' and apprentice mechanic Dave Branson, Bob race-prepared the Lola and chose Roy Fewkes, the 5-litre Chevy engine specialist, to build our engines.

The leading lights in F5000 that season were Teddy Pilette and Peter Gethin, driving for brewery magnate Count Van der Stratten's Team VDS, both in new Lola T400s. Other leading drivers included Alan Jones, David Purley and Dave Walker in Chevrons, plus Guy Edwards, Vern Schuppan and Ian Ashley

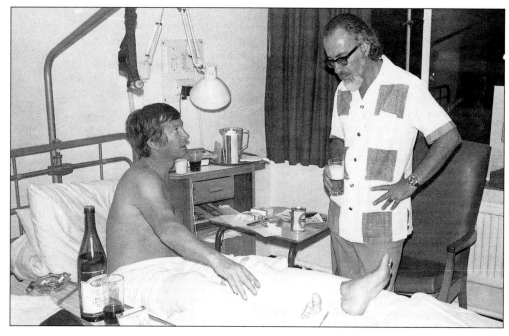

A hospital visit from
Guyanese Minister of
the Interior, Kit
Nascimento.

(Lolas) – all full-time professionals, so I knew the competition would be tough.

I shall never forget the Good Friday round at the Oulton Park Gold Cup meeting. I was stricken with flu on the Wednesday and only left my sick-bed for Thursday's practice. A heavy fall of snow cut the session short, but I surprised myself, Bob and Creech by qualifying fifth fastest: second row of a 3–2–3 grid and ahead of several far better drivers.

On race day, more overnight snow necessitated salting the track. After it dried out, apart from a few wet streams across the track from melting snow banks, it was deemed raceable. The organisers recommended wet tyres but I opted for slicks and found it was like driving on ice. After the warm-up laps we changed to wet tyres, whilst the majority on wets changed to grooved slicks.

My Lola handled superbly. By the end of the third lap I was up to second place behind David Purley, and two laps later passed him under braking into Old Hall corner. On checking the mirrors a lap later, there was not a pursuer in sight: I genuinely thought the race had been stopped!

Meanwhile Pilette, also on wets, was fast catching up. After ten laps he took the lead, which he held until pitting a few laps later with a flat battery. Several cars went off in the difficult conditions so I drove conservatively. After 50 laps – an hour's racing – I took the chequered flag first, some 20 seconds ahead of Edwards and Purley.

After countless attempts this was my first F5000 win – the most prestigious of my career to date – and it mattered not a jot that it had been entirely down to the right tyre choice! The *Daily Mail* headline referred to 'Veteran Driver, Gordon Spice', which I thought was a bit cheeky. After all, I was only 35 at the time.

The same meeting also coincided with the third round of the British Touring Car Championship. That race followed so quickly after the F5000 that I didn't even have time for a fag!

After an hour in the Lola, driving the Capri was a doddle and I came third overall, behind the Camaros of Stuart Graham and Richard Lloyd: my second class win of the season.

At the Silverstone round in April, I demolished the car against the Armco at Woodcote, and, at Chris Reed's request, the car was rebuilt and finished in British Racing Green. At the next race, at Zolder (Belgium), we came seventh on aggregate and an encouraging fourth in the second heat.

I was keen to do better at Zandvoort in Holland two weeks later, because Chris Reed was planning to be there. But good results were becoming harder to obtain as the new Lolas and Chevrons got sorted out. My maximum pace was not only slower than theirs but rather more hazardous! However, Zandvoort was a most enjoyable weekend.

The night before practice we toured the infamous canal area of Amsterdam. That was an eye-opener – every taste catered for, on display, leaving nothing to the imagination, and all legal under Dutch law.

Avoiding a bucket of water thrown from a second-floor window by one of the ladies of the night who figured we were time-wasters, Bob came across two house bricks. A lasting memory is of Bob sitting on the side of a bridge, a brick in each hand, calling out 'Cheap castrations here – only five Guilders.'

The race went well and I came fourth behind the T400s of Peter Gethin, Pilette and Scott. More importantly, Chris was delighted. I see from Wolfgang Kopfler's book, *F5000 in Europe*, which covers the whole era of that powerful formula, that in the next two races we ran competitively amongst the leaders, but a broken engine at Thruxton followed by a holed radiator at Snetterton resulted in two unfinished races.

The next race at Mallory followed the third Avon Tour of Britain, where Stan and I finished fourth in my regular BTCC Capri. We decided to do some testing on the Friday, before official qualifying on Saturday. I always found testing more demanding than racing: to be relevant, you had to find the limits and drive on the edge. Doing just that, I turned into the Esses at the end of the Stebbe straight. The Lola, however, oversteered off, hitting the railway sleepers head on. The sleepers were close to the track, and speed was reduced from 120mph to zero in about

three feet. It was driver error – I had failed to spot a deflating left-rear tyre. My last memory flash was taking my hands off the wheel before hitting.

I was out for the count and Creech takes up the story:

'I'd just come back from Birmingham, after collecting Gordy's suit which I'd left at the hotel after the Avon Tour. I had to park on the outside of the track but I noticed things had gone very quiet – practice had been stopped – and then I noticed car number 3 had crashed at the Esses.

'I thought that's OK – it's Pilette's car. Then someone said "Mandy, it's Gordy." I dropped my bag and flew over. His number was 43 but the smash had shortened the car, leaving only the 3 visible. It was a horrible sight, Gordy was unconscious with helmet off, his head resting lopsidedly on his shoulder, and his legs mangled up where the tub had been destroyed. After what seemed ages, the St John's ambulance arrived and David Purley took charge of the rescue operation.

'Whilst David's crew were cutting him out of the car he regained consciousness and was obviously in considerable pain, so I sat on the side pod feeding him nitrous oxide, which the ambulance crew provided. After half an hour of careful cutting – all being aware of the fire risk – it was 'one-two-three… lift' and the crew finally pulled him out sideways and stretchered him to the ambulance.'

2 February 1977: Creech and GS at their wedding lunch.

On impact the front tyre had knocked off my helmet – breaking the frangible chin-strap as it was designed to do. The steering wheel whacked me in the face, resulting in a severely broken jaw and several missing teeth. Simultaneously, my legs had been forced backwards, causing bad friction burns to my knee as they accelerated through the fireproof overalls. My legs were fractured in 11 places: add to that the inevitable blood and gore and – it was not a pretty sight.

As I drifted in and out of consciousness, the journey to the Royal Infirmary in Leicester seemed to take a lifetime. The ancient St John's ambulance never exceeded 35mph and pleas for more speed were ignored.

Creech takes up the story again.

'When we eventually arrived at Accident & Emergency, they assumed I was his wife, though we weren't even engaged. That meant I could stay with Gordy. He was in a lot of pain and quite angry. When he said "If they don't give me something – and fast – I'm walking out of this f.....g place," I knew his brain was OK. The staff were fantastic and the Sister in charge stayed with us until finally they knocked him out with painkillers – even though she should have gone off duty hours before. They decided it was too dangerous to anaesthetise him so soon after concussion, and the operation was scheduled for next morning.

'I returned next morning and the operation took about six hours. When I asked to see the orthopaedic surgeon to find out how it went, I was surprised at the staff reactions. All became clear when a crewcut six foot six inch giant of a man, in green overalls and a jaycloth

July 1975: my last F5000 race at Snetterton. I retired after the radiator was holed by a stone thrown up by a spinning Ian Ashley. (LAT)

on his head, came in. If he'd had a bolt though his neck he'd have passed for Frankenstein's monster. With a broad smile he gave the thumbs up and grunted two words 'He... OK.' He was a Polish exchange surgeon who spoke no English, but his simple words were strongly convincing, and he proved to be a top-class surgeon.'

After a week in intensive care I was fit enough to be moved to an orthopaedic ward, which was quite ghastly. Both legs were in plaster from crutch to ankle, with a cut-out at the knee ready for plastic surgery and skin grafts, and my jaw was literally wired shut. Food was taken by straw through the gap vacated by my front teeth. But in my uncomfortable state the worst thing was the noisy environment in the overcrowded ward, full of comparatively healthy young bikers in for a few days with broken limbs. The place was unbelievably rowdy and one of their games was to compete on how far they could pee into a bowl on the floor without leaving their beds!

No telephone, no TV, no privacy and very little sleep – I had to move on.

When I let the hospital know that I was leaving to go south to a private hospital nearer home, the Royal's staff were quite arsy. Bob collected me in a Bedford CF van and drove me to the BUPA hospital near Slough, where I stayed for another ten weeks whilst the bones healed and flesh was grown on my kneecap prior to skin grafting.

Wire-cutters were kept close to hand and before leaving hospital Mandy received instruction on how to cut the wires in the event of choking.

Mike 'The Bike' Hailwood, one of my old playmates from earlier F5000 days, dropped into hospital one day with a pile of *Mayfair* and *Playboy* magazines. His parting line was that his Mum had died in the room below, just days before... he hoped I'd have better luck! Mike and his wife, Pauline, had recently moved to Maidenhead and had become good chums. Mike was a devoted family man with two young kids but his free spirit never changed. His tragic car accident a few years later, when his daughter was also killed, devastated the car and bike racing fraternities.

In November I was allowed out to visit my sister Zani, who had just given birth to her second child, Scott, at Princess Christian Hospital in Windsor. As my legs were still plastered I sat in my wheelchair with both legs horizontal.

After leaving Zani I persuaded Creech to leave me at my office in Staines for an hour before returning to hospital. When she returned she found the boys had taken me to the local pub, where I was enjoying my first Special Brew for over three months. The first was followed by a second and, being out of training, it wasn't long before I was completely paralytic. It gave me enough Dutch courage to phone Matron at the hospital. I told her I would not be coming back that evening, did not intend to stay another night there, and would be returning tomorrow to discharge myself. She was less than pleased.

Feeling no pain, Creech took me back to Rambler Cottage and somehow got me into bed – quite a feat considering my state. I woke next morning with the worst hangover I've ever had, and it put me off Special Brew for the next 33 years. That day Creech drove me back to the hospital, and, after signing numerous disclaimers, I checked out. It was not before time – I was becoming institutionalised.

As soon as the plasters were removed I planned to go to Barbados to get my legs working. The dilemma was that business had taken a downturn and needed some intensive care, but Creech and I went ahead with our holiday anyway.

Returning from Barbados without crutches, I had to strengthen my legs, so I started cycling to work – a round trip of eight miles. One evening I'd arranged to meet my friend and business partner Keith Cundell at The Robin Hood pub in Egham on the way home. After a few jars, cycling did not seem such a good idea. I phoned Creech, who was in the middle of decorating the cottage, and asked for a lift home. When she arrived she looked gorgeous, despite tatty clothes and paint in her hair.

I bought her a drink and mentioned that it was about time we got married. Keith fell off his bar stool and exclaimed, 'Ignore him, Mandy, he's drunk – doesn't know what he's saying.'

Creech was equally confused – the subject had never been discussed – but I was dead serious. The pub had no champagne so we toasted our engagement with Babycham before driving over to Dee's house to break the news. A very late night followed.

Next morning in bed, both nursing heavy heads, Creech said she'd quite understand if I wanted to change my mind.

'Definitely not', I said, 'it just takes some getting used to.'

And that was that.

Chapter 12

Racing with a tropical flavour

Timehri Circuit in Guyana, 1971: (left to right) GS, Alec Poole, the Guyanese Minister of Sport, 'Birdseed' and Eric Vieira.

Between 1971 and 1976 I raced in the Caribbean each October and November in the grandly named International Caribbean Series. As with many good things in life, the initial opportunity had come unexpectedly, and it proved to be a most enjoyable and profitable period of my two careers.

In 1969 I had asked Keith Cundell to sell my old 1,293cc Cooper by displaying it in his Elvaston Mews showroom. Keith was then manager of Downton (London) Ltd, and he

later became an important part of my business life. Within a few days he received an enquiry from Pete Ullyett, a Mini enthusiast and Company Secretary for British American Tobacco (BAT) in Guyana. Pete bought the car, won everything he entered, and became a Gordon Spice fan.

By early 1971 Keith was my partner in GS (International Spares) Ltd, a company we had set up together to export spares and racing equipment. Keith operated autonomously

from the new cash & carry warehouse in Staines, and Pete, a Bajan (Barbadian) by birth, was a good customer of the export company.

Along with Eric Vieira, George Jardine, Philip de Freitas and Joey King, Pete was one of the founders of the Guyana Motor Racing Club (GMRC). He was also a friend of Mark Steele, BOAC's Marketing Manager in the Caribbean, based in Barbados. BOAC were relatively new carriers to the Caribbean and had a decent budget to publicise their new routes. This led to Pete asking Keith to produce a two-car team to race in Guyana and Barbados under the Team Speedbird banner. The deal agreed was that the Guyana and Barbados racing clubs would pay for one-way shipping of the cars, and BOAC would cover flight and hotel costs. An extra bonus was that Miss Speedbird would accompany the team to maximise press and TV exposure.

I asked Alec Poole to produce a second car as he had raced in the region before with Mike Crabtree and I knew he would enter into the spirit the venture. Keith bought me the ex-John Nunn 1,143cc Austin Healey Sprite, and our cars were duly shipped to Guyana.

In mid-October we all flew out to Georgetown and were royally greeted by members of the GMRCC at Timehri airport, which adjoined the South Dakota circuit where we would race. I had just alighted on the tarmac, hungover after 14 hours of flying, when Pete Ullyett insisted I drive his Mini – by headlights if you please – because he wanted to see if I thought the engine was delivering full power. I suggested we wait till daylight but no – it had to be done now – so that's exactly what we did. Talk about customer care!

That first week in Guyana was a real eye-opener. We enjoyed full celebrity treatment, parties every night, countless interviews and press calls every day. Alec and I fully exploited our celeb status with stories of our racing exploits. Nobody questioned our claims to fame, which became more outrageous at each interview. In those days communications between Guyana and the outside world were minimal, thank God.

On our first day in Georgetown I fell madly in love with Miss Speedbird, a glamorous redhead, a mean go-go dancer and one hell of a character. The fact that I was still married to Birdie, while she had a fiancée in England, just added excitement to our affair, which we both knew would be short-lived.

1,143cc Downton Sprite at Timehri.

I was ever fascinated at her cool dignity when representing the face of BOAC, which was in a stark contrast to the party animal I knew she really was.

Saturday practice for racing on Sunday was another revelation. The Clerk of the Course started by announcing that they needed more marshals: there was no shortage of volunteers. Marshals were issued with a broom and one flag each, either black, yellow, red or striped. Their brief was: 'If sometin' happen you wave de flag so de drivers know sometin' up... De broom's for sweepin' away de mess.'

Volunteer timekeepers were also recruited. Drivers were briefed: 'When you'se on hot lap you flash de headlights and de lap will be timed. If [you have] no lights, wave de arms and de timekeepers will know.'

Halfway through practice a Bedford army lorry, full of indigenous troops, appeared on the main straight and practice was stopped. Afterwards, the marshal who had let them through was berated by the Clerk of the Course until he asked: 'Would you try to turn back a fully armed platoon of soldiers with a flag and a brush?' End of bollocking!

The race meeting, sponsored by local brewery Banks Beer, attracted teams from Trinidad, Barbados, Costa Rica, Antigua and Jamaica, as well, of course, as many local teams. The range of competitive machinery was mind-boggling – everything from V8 specials through to 100cc motorbikes. The rivalry between the different countries was intense.

Alec's car and mine were competitive enough to win, but we realised that pleasing the spectators was more important than blowing off the local opposition, and providing a good spectacle should result in invitations to return. Besides, keeping racing cars running in an equatorial climate for seven or eight races was a top priority. I don't think Keith Cundell, acting as my mechanic, or Henry Freemantle, Alec's man, ever worked so hard.

So we unashamedly played to the crowd, most of which were enthusiastically support-

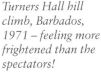

Turners Hall hill climb, Barbados, 1971 – feeling more frightened than the spectators!

ing Banks Brewery in an all-day drinking marathon.

One of the local drivers, Kit Nascimento, was running in the same races as me, driving an MG Midget with a Downton engine that Keith Cundell supplied. Kit also happened to be Minister for the Interior for Guyana, so we worked on him for introductions to buyers in Government departments such as the GDF and GPF (Defence and Police forces), Guysuco (Sugar) and Guybau (Bauxite). All were significant buyers of spare parts for predominantly British vehicles.

Racing provided a unique opportunity to boost the Minister's reputation as a driver, and keep him firmly on-side. So when I found myself leading the first race, with Kit following, it didn't take much genius to miss a gear and let him pass. I could see the crowd going mad as I drew alongside him and harried him for five laps – a local amateur mixing it with a foreign professional was their nirvana!

On the last lap I resisted the temptation to let him win and passed him. Silly really, but ego prevailed and he was already a hero…

As the day progressed, mechanical failures and accidents resulted in smaller grids, so the organisers combined the classes and we found ourselves racing with single-seaters, saloons and specials – anything still running. The Sprite had lost its clutch and Pete insisted I drive his Mini, which was great.

Now local drivers understood the need to keep the cars dicing together, rather than strung-out in a F1 type procession. Once they got the hang of it, it was more fun and less wearing on the cars, but above all the thousands of spectators just loved it. The full programme of 20 races was completed and the meeting voted the best ever, with record attendance and press coverage. Team Speedbird's future was assured.

An evening prize presentation party around the pool of the Pegasus Hotel had been organised. Alec Poole, through his Irish contacts, had

Bushy Park circuit, Barbados, 1972: 'Bizzy' Williams (Terrapin) leads Silborne Clarke (Formula V), Dave Brodie (Chevron) and GS (Austin A40).

Barbados, 1972, with export partner Keith Cundell and Gabriel Konig.

somehow persuaded Guinness to sponsor the evening... and what an evening it turned out to be.

Miss Speedbird was presenting the prizes from a dais, full of local dignitaries, on the opposite side of the pool. Winners would walk around the pool to enthusiastic applause, collect their prize and return to their tables. After the first of these marathons (and another drink) I decided to shorten the journey by swimming across the pool, emerging like a drowned rat in front of the dais. That set the mood for the evening. Everyone adopted the shorter route and soon winners, losers and most of the guests were soaked to the skin.

It could only happen in the Tropics!

Later in the evening we organised a large gilt birdcage for Miss Speedbird to showcase her go-go dancing, taking on all comers. Her whole body was sprayed in gold with skimpy matching costume. Dancing like a wanton vamp, no one could believe this was the same demure young lady who had presented prizes earlier. For the rest of the trip she was known simply as 'Birdseed'.

After a further week in Guyana, where we took more orders than we could possibly finance (another story), it was on to Barbados. There we booked into Paradise Beach, another BOAC five-star hotel. The circuit at Bushy Park was not yet completed, so the Barbados Rally and

Racing Club ran a hill climb at Turners Hall.

The Friday before the race Alec's Mini, together with overseas drivers, was paraded through the streets of Bridgetown on the back of a low-loader. The commentary over the tannoy by Ralph 'Brugger' Johnson, a larger-than-life character and club social secretary, was hysterical. 'Everyone come to Turners Hall on Sunday. See de only 150mph Mini in de world' (news to Alec!). On passing a cemetery: 'Even de dead will come to Turners Hall.' 'Bring your wives, your concubines – even you mother-in-laws.' All very Bajan.

Turners Hall hill was a mile-long hill climb, running through a sugar plantation with cane growing right to the edge of the road – perfect camouflage for hundreds of spectators who'd avoided paying and a nightmare for the organisers. It was extraordinarily dangerous, especially when they spilled on to the road to watch a car disappearing up the hill. They only moved back to the sides when they heard another one approaching. The photo says it all.

Due to non-existent crowd control I drove the Sprite, now fitted with a new clutch, extremely carefully. On Sunday an estimated 6,000 spectators materialised. After everyone had done two of three scheduled runs, a tropical downpour turned the hill into a river and the meeting was abandoned. There was great relief all round that no one had been hurt.

GS (Longman Mini) leads local gaggle at Bushy Park circuit, Barbados, 1974.

There was serious competition amongst the Bajan enthusiasts to buy the Sprite, as it would be an ideal racer for the twisty Bushy Park circuit when it opened next year. The car was finally sold to a local racer, Richard Hutchinson, at a price which more than covered expenses for the tour.

Whilst in Barbados, Keith and I were approached by Richard Rose, Geoffrey Goddard and Pete Ullyett, who wanted to open a car accessory shop using my name. We agreed, providing our export company became exclusive suppliers for all imported products.

Gordon Spice (Barbados) Ltd was duly formed and a shop was leased in McGregor Street, just off the main shopping street in Bridgetown. Initially we had no financial interest in the Barbadian shop, but within a couple of years the business was floundering. We had extended more credit than was wise, but, if the business was put into liquidation, we would have to write off much of the debt. So we agreed to take it over and run it ourselves until the debt was cleared.

We employed Ted 'Mad For It' Edgell as manager, and he did an excellent job. He was a great character, and typically would say: 'Trust me – I have a white brain in a black body.' Ted remains a friend to this day.

For the next three years, eight weeks in the Caribbean before Christmas 'on export business', with a few race weekends thrown in, became a welcome break from cash & carry life at Staines. The business generated in Guyana, Trinidad, Barbados and Jamaica accounted for a significant part of Keith's export sales. The Barbados shop under Ted's management became profitable and repaid its debts, and it was not too much of a chore to pop over from the UK to 'check the till' on a regular basis.

The word spread fast and it was no problem finding drivers to share the fun of the series. Visiting racers included Gabriel Konig, Mike Crabtree, Bob 'Mary' Howlings, Dave Brodie, Barrie 'Whizzo' Williams, Billy Gubelman, Robs Lamplough and Richard Longman.

The locals organised a frantic social life. Derek McMahon – one of Derek Daly's early sponsors and friend of Alec Poole – was a popular competitor, famous for drinking his hotel dry of Vodka. Capri entrant Stan Robinson was totally in his element and wanted to stay for life.

In Georgetown the grand old British Embassy had become a house of ill repute known as The University. (Coincidentally, Creech's grandfather, who was Head of Colonial Audit, had been based in the self-same building some 60 years ago.) With the wide range of cultures and languages in Guyana, 'The Uni' became a popular spot for budding linguists: 'Just off to Uni – to brush up my

Bushy Park, Barbados, 1974: Richard Longman is driving the other Longman Mini.

Portuguese/Spanish/Chinese...' they would say. Student satisfaction was unusually high!

In 1972 the Barbados Rally Club had asked for a female driver to be included in Team Speedbird so Gabriel Konig, complete with her Chevrolet Camaro, joined the team. She later married Philip de Freitas, the Guyanese distributor for Vauxhall and a keen racer.

Keith Cundell had bought Mick Cave's old Downton Austin A40 for me to drive. Known as The Old Grey Mare, it proved a very well sorted racer – and boosted my morale with several wins after a rotten F5000 season.

The 1972 Miss Speedbird, a dazzling blonde, announced that she was getting married at Christmas. Our disappointment was short-lived after she fell under the Caribbean spell for a last fling. The average duration of the lucky few she befriended was four days, and after she'd lined up her next target she made it clear when your time was up.

This was the first year of the Bushy Park circuit in Barbados. A packed programme of 21 races attracted over 18,000 spectators. To put this in perspective, pro rata to the quarter-million population, it was the equivalent of two million people attending a Grand Prix in the UK. BRDC, eat your heart out...

In 1973 BOAC pulled out and our new sponsor was International Caribbean Airlines (ICA), and we raced as the ICA Eagles team.

Amusingly, the new Miss ICA, a somewhat plain local lass, was closely escorted at all times, which proved a rather unnecessary precaution!

This was the year I fell madly in love with Stephanie, as recounted in an earlier chapter, and for four weeks she was my constant companion. It was also the first year that Jamaica was included in the tour. British drivers included Mike Crabtree driving a Willment Escort RS1600, Alec Poole in a Royale-FVC sports racer, and Richard Longman in a 1,300cc Mini.

At Spice we had shipped over a Ford 1600 Ginetta G12, which was uncomfortably hot to drive. After clutch problems halfway through the Timehri meeting it was a relief to be asked to drive a local Mini to complete the event. The Ginetta ran in the single-seater class, so wins were thin on the ground, but ICA team honours were upheld by Alec and Mike. It was quite a relief to pre-sell the G12 before shipping it on a banana boat to Jamaica.

The circuit in Jamaica was at Vernon Fields, a disused USAF base in the middle of nowhere. The main straight was a runway, joining two twisty bits at each end, and divided by traffic cones – quite the most dangerous configuration imaginable. With cars flat out in opposite directions, with a closing speed of over 200mph, it had all the ingredients for disaster.

On top of this the crowd control was appalling, and we seriously considered withdrawing the ICA team. However, the organisers agreed to provide a helicopter and medics for race day, so we risked it.

On the Sunday we were relieved when a military chopper arrived: what we did not see was the tannoy cables on high poles being installed after it had landed. Halfway through the meeting the pilot decided he didn't really need to be there and took off for base. He hadn't noticed the wires either, and his rotors got tangled in them, causing him to crash in the adjoining car park. Several cars were comprehensively written off but miraculously only the pilot was hurt.

After that the Ginetta developed a starting problem and was strategically retired.

I think 1974 was the vintage Caribbean year. Team Speedbird was reinstated and included Alec Poole, driving 'Big D' McMahon's 1,850cc BDA-Escort, and Bob Howlings in a Brabham BT 21/30. Keith Cundell excelled himself by providing me with a very quick Longman 1300 Mini.

The rapid Mini won all its races in Guyana. At Bushy Park, Team Speedbird notched up nine wins in the 15-race programme, Alec and I with three apiece and Howlings with two.

Crowd control at Bushy at Park was much improved. Early morning on race day, the high catch fencing was sprayed with tar. This proved an effective deterrent in stopping the many local gymnasts from climbing over.

In 1975, following the F5000 accident at Mallory in August, I returned to Barbados on crutches, accompanied by Creech. We'd rented a beach house at the Southern Palms Hotel, and swimming, Banana Daiquiris and competing with the Germans for sunbeds soon had my legs working again.

In addition to Big D's BDA Escort, Alec Poole drove the Mini intended for me, while Barrie 'Whizzo' Williams was a crowd favourite in his early Ford Capri. Other drivers from the UK included ex-Formula 2 racer and airman Robs Lamplough in a Mallock U2 and Billy Gubelman in an ex-Wisharts Capri.

I was invited to be Clerk of the Course. Totally unqualified for such a role, I declined. A good decision, as proceedings were soured by inter-island rivalry. Praising the sportsmanship of the English and Irish drivers, and referring to boycotting at the prize-giving, *The Bajan* newspaper reported: 'It was the type of childish attitude which most West Indians thought the

Trinidadians had grown out of since the hectic days of inter-colonial cricket, but it is still coming to the surface in motor sport.'

Barbados 1, Trinidad 0. Ouch!

Early in 1976 I returned to Guyana for their February meeting. After six months without driving I needed to check out whether I could still hack it. I was relieved to find that I enjoyed racing a much as ever and was still on the pace. The Formula 5000 accident was history.

I returned to the UK with confidence intact and told Stan Robinson that I would be delighted to drive his Wisharts Capri in the 1976 British Touring Car Championship. It marked my return to the premier British saloon car series and the end of my Caribbean adventures.

Hard at work in the Caribbean, circa 1973.

Chapter 13

Blooming cash and carries

We must now back-peddle a few years again, to 1971.

Up to that time Gordon Spice Ltd had done a small amount of export business, but the company was not geared up for all the paper-work palaver and it was, frankly, regarded as a bit of a pain. Enter Keith Cundell – who we've already met wearing several hats – who had now left Downton in London to set up his own export company, specialising in racing and spares for British cars.

It was fortuitous timing as GSL had just moved to Staines and any contribution towards the increased overheads was welcome. Gordon Spice (International Spares) Ltd was duly formed in a 50/50 partnership with Keith. He operated autonomously from the Staines warehouse.

Swapping from wholesaling to a cash & carry operation, plus virtually doubling our sales each year, was not without problems. These surfaced particularly on the finance and admin side. The company was sales-driven, and information that the bank needed – like forecasts and cashflow projections – tended to be hit and miss.

The situation was getting out of hand, so we recruited Ernie Unger. A seasoned professional whom I'd met in the '60s, Ernie was a middle manager with the Ford Motor Company. He proved a key player in introducing financial disciplines that we desperately needed at that stage. Unlike us, Ernie had the benefit of formal business training with Ford and was the ideal man to install systems and controls that were foreign to us. His people skills were zero, and he was equally unpopular with managers, staff and customers, but he did the jobs that were essential, as I constantly had to remind my colleagues.

It was also Ernie who introduced me to Stan Robinson in 1972, at a time when my F5000 campaign had hit the buffers: that introduction rescued my racing career.

Joanna Lumley in FPT race gear.

Computer pioneers

With annual turnover having increased to £1.2 million in 1975 and an average unit sale around 80p per item, over 5,000 items passed through the checkouts daily. Even with all hands to the pumps, such numbers produced logistical problems, with laborious handwritten invoices all being calculated manually.

It was the delays at checkout and the inconvenience to customers that finally prompted the decision to computerise the operation. This also meant bringing in computerised stock control. For entirely different reasons, however, this radical change resulted in enormously increased profit and was the forerunner of exponential growth of the company.

In the '70s computerisation was considered a risky and costly strategy. None of us knew anything about computers: we would be the first cash & carry of any kind in the UK to pioneer that route. We asked the LSE (London School of Economics) for advice. They suggested an inexpensive way forward would be to pass the project to one of their computer studies students, who could use it for his PhD thesis. An extremely bright student rose to the challenge, and worked his socks off for six months. He subsequently achieved his PhD and we used his paper as the basis for computerisation.

At the time, the USA led the computer revolution and the few UK suppliers were normally agents for American or Japanese manufacturers: desktop computers simply did not exist. Limited capacity processors were twice the size of freezer cabinets and had to be cocooned in an air-conditioned, sterile environment.

Prior to the computer, a sticky label was stuck on every item of our stock as it was checked into the warehouse. The label showed the recommended retail price: the cash & carry price was detachable by the customer, before he displayed the product. With the computer system, stock was marked only with a part number: pricing appeared on the invoice and was clearly displayed on the shelves.

In the mid-'70s inflation was running at around 18 per cent, so manufacturers typically increased their prices twice a year. Often we had to replace stock at a higher price than we had sold it, because to re-price stock on the shelves was bad PR and too time-consuming. Post computerisation, prices could be increased by simply changing one shelf label and feeding the new price into the computer.

Our first computer system cost over £50,000, which represented the total 1975 profit. Yet it paid for itself in 'stock profits' within the first three months – a far bigger bonus than anticipated.

Initially customers complained, as often we were more expensive than our competitors. These objections were soon overcome by pointing out that they now had current information on their invoices, rather than a meaningless till roll receipt. So they could now take their own stock profits. Another spin-off was that we were the first automotive cash & carry to produce a catalogue of all 20,000 stock lines.

Customers were happy to pay £20 for a catalogue to revalue their stock.

In August 1975, with roaring UK inflation, my last instruction before my F5000 accident was to increase our stocks across the board. Buy as

Doctor Who with Griffin helmet.

much as could be physically stored was the intention, and it was duly done.

Leaving hospital in November that year, I found the situation out of control. Sales had slowed down, the warehouse was chock-full and, for the first time, we could not pay our bills promptly. Analysing what we owed, the old 80/20 syndrome applied (80 per cent of sales come from 20 per cent of the stock), and the same percentages applied to our creditors.

I was due to go to Barbados to recuperate, but I could not leave the company in such a dire situation… it would spoil the holiday! So I phoned our ten major suppliers, who accounted for 80 per cent of our overdue debt.

I explained our predicament and offered them two options. Either they could extend an extra three months credit, or they could take back our surplus stock to reduce the debt. I said I would understand if they opted for the latter course, and hoped it wouldn't affect our future relationship. Either way, I guaranteed that their accounts would be within normal trading terms by the end of February.

Without exception our suppliers agreed to the extra credit. Thanks to excellent trading over Christmas, we were able to pay off all arrears a month earlier than promised. This created an unexpectedly high degree of good-will and brought home the importance of

Supplier party frolics (the supplier's the one in the middle!).

Invitation to a Spice supplier party

By way of saying 'thanks' to you,
Spice have a stag night, bold and blue,
We truly hope that you can come
To see a lot of tit and bum.
Why not turn up and be a brick,
You may get a chance to use your...
   knife and fork.

Our cabaret: 'tis very mucky,
Keep on smiling you could get lucky,
Suppliers awards we will be making,
Don't take offence at our piss taking.
We hope you'll all join in the hunt,

Your prize could be a tasty... bottle of
   scotch.

If there's not enough crumpet, you'll just
   have to share one,
Dress is optional, you don't have to wear
   one.
The night's as long as we can stand,
Unless your thing gets out of hand.
No women allowed, it may spoil your
   luck,
We hope you end up with plenty to...
   remember us by.

supplier support – particularly in the boom and bust years that lay ahead.

To foster these ties, we threw regular parties for our suppliers: we were their only customer that did this. A typical invitation, lacking in 21st-century political correctness, gives the flavour (see the sidebar). Brother Dee organised these shindigs, which were held in the warehouses with no expense spared. Top hostesses were hired and entertainment varied from ferret racing to mud wrestling.

1976 was a particularly busy year for the company. In February the computer system went live and the transition went smoothly. Each checkout had a one-line VDU (visual display unit) – computer screens as we know them were not available – and customers ended up with a fully descriptive invoice. Delays at checkout became a thing of the past.

Our main competitor was the GKN-Spa Group which had several branches and had pioneered the automotive cash & carry concept. Their MD, Peter Unwin, had been behind their success but had resigned after falling out with GKN management. Peter was a humourless accountant, an incredibly hard worker and a ruthless buyer.

Peter approached us after buying control of RSA Motor Factors, a Leicester-based wholesaler. He pointed out that that operating as a group would improve our buying power and, from GKN experience, he knew what the best terms were. He would look after RSA and the proposal made sense. A joint holding company was formed and RSA became a cash & carry.

Peter was a human dynamo and worked 24/7. Within months he had bought Windway Motor Factors in Cardiff, so GSL became a half-owner of that business too. Both companies had been picked up for a song and our investment, mainly in stock, was minimal.

Around this time we recruited Brian Merry, an ex-Regional Director of GKN-Spa and known as 'Mr Motor Trade'. Brian had a complete understanding of the motor aftermarket and opened our eyes to the fast-moving products that would sell to the same customers alongside our more sporty range. Sure, the products were boring, but they enabled us to become a one-stop cash & carry: our customers didn't need to shop elsewhere.

To tempt him away, we had to pay Brian a salary far in excess of what other Directors were earning and there was considerable resistance from the Board. But what a good investment he proved to be: he literally transformed the company and within weeks was made a Director, responsible for both Sales and Buying.

Investment expansion via Abingworth

Thanks to our computer system taking advantage of high inflation, sales from the Staines warehouse of over £2 million in 1976 were highly profitable.

To celebrate a record year, Dee and I decided that the company should buy a Rolls Royce, which we duly did – a one-year-old Silver Shadow. This was at a time when there

Perks of the job (IGD Visors and Griffin helmets).

were UK Government-imposed currency restrictions in Europe, and the Brits were perceived by the Continentals as being poverty-stricken. The main motivation for buying a Rolls, as ridiculous as it might seem today, was therefore to take it on skiing holidays to France and wave the flag. Of course, we did just that, but it also turned out to be a very useful business tool.

We also decided to open a second branch and settled on an East London location, for two reasons. First, the recently recruited Brian Merry knew the customers in the area, having been based at GKN-Spa's Charlton branch. Secondly, whilst Staines attracted regular business from Cornwall, Wales and even Scotland, customers from Essex, Kent and East London were reluctant to face the tedious journey through London. The M25 was years away.

Opening a new branch required a capital injection, as it could not be financed from cashflow. We looked at our expansion options: the banks were typically unhelpful and told us we were overtrading. However, Ernie introduced us to Peter Dicks, who worked for London-based venture capital company Abingworth Ltd.

From day one we got on extremely well with Abingworth's people. They proved strongly supportive with sound advice and good humour and never interfered in the running of the business. We agreed that the long-term aim would be to build the company to a stage where it could be floated on the stock market. That would allow Abingworth an exit route and us the choices that only money can buy – or so we thought at the time.

Negotiations with Abingworth were as tough as expected: they had a tried and tested formula for doing the best deals, and by comparison Derek and I were corporate virgins. Our final 1977 meeting was at their St James' London office on 3 February. I remember the day well, as it was the first day of my honeymoon with Creech!

By 6:00pm we had finally agreed to sell them a 26 per cent shareholding in GSL, with 60 per cent of funds earmarked for the new Canning Town branch and 40 per cent for Dee and I.

Dee's share more than doubled the return on his original investment and mine was enough for Creech and I to buy a decent house.

The deal allowed Abingworth two seats on the Spice board. Marius Gray, a senior partner with accountants Dixon Wilson, brought a wealth of experience to the party, and Peter Dicks was the other non-exec Director. Outside of business we shared many good times over the next few years.

Up to that stage personal finances were rarely considered. By choice I only drew a modest salary, as the priority was company expansion. The business looked after major expenditure like travel, cars and booze, so we lived well.

Abingworth's involvement changed things.

When discussing bonuses at the end of their bumper first year with us, I told them I didn't need money: I just wanted more time to organise my life and not to be playing perpetual catch-up.

Abingworth suggested I get a chauffeur, as I seemed to be permanently travelling, and so Terry Hackett was recruited. He had taken early retirement from the Traffic Division of Thames Valley Police and having him on call 24/7 transformed my life. He proved the most loyal and trustworthy man one could hope for and he stayed with me until I retired.

In 1977 the export company had had a very good year, with sales approaching £1 million. Due to pressure on space at Staines, Keith moved the export business to a 12,000ft² warehouse on the same estate.

Shortly after Abingworth invested, Ernie Unger took a long stretch of sick leave. As part of our earlier reorganisation, Ernie had arranged that Directors be covered by Permanent Health Insurance. It meant that if any Director was unable to work on medical grounds, the insurance would pay 90 per cent of salary, with no time limit.

Ernie was better organised than I thought: he never returned to work!

Towards the end of 1977, thanks to the Abingworth funds, we opened our second cash & carry in a new 20,000ft² warehouse in Canning Town, East London. Sales took off much faster than budgeted, but so did stock!

Security was a major problem.

We found out the hard way that the 80/20 equation also applies to stock 'shrinkage': staff accounted for 80 per cent of theft, and customers 20 per cent. The following year I called a staff meeting and told them that if the thieving didn't stop, the warehouse would be closed. Furthermore, I would be moving to East London and be present every day.

Within a week Creech found a small flat nearby and from Monday to Friday we made it our base. We didn't have to stay there long, thank God, but the point had been made. A few heads rolled before profit was restored and the problem contained.

Trading in 1978 was booming: with a full year's contribution from Canning Town, profits doubled and sales increased to over £7 million. The RSA holding company, seemingly profitable under Peter Unwin, opened a further

Brother Dee demonstrating FPT fireproof material (and showing no pain!).

12,000ft² cash & carry in Bristol. In addition, in November the RSA Group opened a new 22,000ft² facility in Sheffield.

We now owned a half-share in branches in Leicester, Sheffield, Bristol and Cardiff, in addition to our own Staines and Canning Town operations. All warehouses had computer systems based on the Staines model and it was this facility that made such rapid expansion possible.

Sadly, despite Peter Unwin's total commitment it was becoming apparent that our rela-

Making Griffin helmets irresistible.

tionship with him was not working. His ability to create team spirit was abysmal and he spent very little time on this aspect of his business, whereas it was core to ours. It also got up his nose that he was reporting to Brian Merry – a reversal of their GKN-Spa days. I was the peacemaker, but meetings with Unwin were becoming too acrimonious for my blood.

It was around this time that we recognised the need to strengthen our management team: Charles Tippet was therefore recruited as Chief Accountant, and Jonathan Bailey as Security Manager. Charles, brother of Aylesbury Tappet's Hugo Tippet, was an excellent choice and subsequently became Finance Director. He had the rare gift of clearly explaining and presenting financial information to non-financial people. We relied on him heavily, particularly in later years when the going got really tough. Charles was a keen club racer and completely at one with the company culture.

Jonathan Bailey, who had been a CID Inspector before becoming Thames Valley's Crime Prevention Officer, had highly developed people skills. He was appointed Personnel Director. He was the only man I knew who could fire a member of staff in such a way that they felt grateful.

Following the previous year's manic expansion, 1979 was a year of consolidation. Annual sales from Staines and Canning Town increased to £9 million and net profit exceeded half a million for the first time. Our range of stock continued to increase, but it was the specialised racing lines that differentiated us from our competitors and attracted customers nationally.

Our sole franchises for Linea Sport racewear, Piranha ignition, Griffin helmets, Dzus Fasteners and Fireater extinguishing systems all had national coverage. Our larger customers included Alan Minshaw's Demon Tweeks, Nick Whiting's All Car Equipe and the Burton Performance shops.

Since we had become a one-stop shop, product availability was more important to our customers than price alone. We accepted the inevitable overstocking this necessitated but the target – 99 per cent availability on fast-moving lines and 95 per cent overall – was achieved.

Heavily promoted Trade Days became a quarterly event and we offered strong incentives to attend. Customers had the chance to win anything from a new car to exotic holidays for two.

One Trade Day promotion at the Canning

Dodgy deal salvation

A memorable late '70s cash crisis involved a dodgy Arab in Sudan. Following a successful trial order for Land Rover and Bedford spares from a Khartoum company, the export company received its biggest order ever, worth £250k. Suspicions were aroused when the customer asked for a massive 20 per cent agent's commission to be included in our prices, but the order was too tasty to ignore.

So we asked the Government agency ECGD (Export Credit Guarantee Department) to check out the company for creditworthiness.

To our surprise, they gave the all clear.

After firm confirmation that ECGD would underwrite the risk, we shipped the order with payment due by 90-day sight draft. Predictably, three months later the customer defaulted, so we banged in the claim to ECGD. They responded that, because the customer had disputed the goods' quality, ECGD would not pay until the quality question was resolved. We had failed to spot this in the small print of the ECGD policy. They would not accept that the quality issue was an obvious ploy, despite no complaint being received within the 90 days.

A bad debt of that size would bankrupt the company, so I was despatched to Khartoum to sort it out.

On arrival, I tracked down the customer to a shabby office above a chemists' shop. He was a pockmarked, portly chap in a rather mucky white wrap and turban.

We quickly established that there were no quality issues: the guy admitted he simply couldn't pay.

'No problem,' I said, 'but you must sign this document.' He said he needed to think about it, but a financial incentive might persuade him.

Next morning, I explained I was travelling light on cash, but would be delighted to host an expenses-paid trip to London. He would have the choice of the best British crumpet, stay in five-star hotels and have the time of his life.

As a final gesture of goodwill, I agreed to give him a first-class return ticket to London before I left. After another day of flattery and lying, he finally signed the document, and asked for his air ticket.

'Silly me,' I said, ' the travel agent was closed when I called this morning, but I'll be right back.' Swearing on my mother's grave to return within the hour I left with document in hand.

I checked out of my hotel and headed for the airport – mission achieved. From Heathrow, I drove straight to the ECGD offices in Cardiff and produced his signed disclaimer. I made it clear I would not be leaving without their cheque.

Funnily enough it turned out to be a very profitable sale. Although ECGD only paid out 90 per cent of any claim, none of the commission had been paid, as it was dependent on prompt payment. After financing costs and travel expenses we ended up with a handsome extra profit.

Town branch, when an impressive display of a £5,000 speedboat and trailer could be won via a darts challenge, was especially memorable. For every £100 spent, the customer earned the right to throw three darts. So a £1,000 spend gave ten opportunities to throw a triple 20 and win the boat.

A punter who was not a regular turned up with his 'assistant', who was undoubtedly a pro and on his second attempt threw the required 180. Typical East London! After that the insurance company sent reps to our Trade Days to ensure fair play.

Normally the days would be themed: 'An Orgy at Pontes' (the Roman name for Staines) was particularly successful. For the first time the day's sales exceeded £150,000. All the staff dressed up in Roman style, the wine flowed and trading continued into the night.

During the year we planned the opening of our largest cash & carry yet. Located in Watford, it would be within a mile of what had become our strongest competitor, Maccess, owned by Burmah Oil.

We would be crossing swords with Maccess for the next ten years…

Chapter 14

Le Mans adventures

Charles Ivey RSR Porsche, 1978. Main sponsor's motto? – 'Stop screwing, start riveting'.

Altogether, I drove at Le Mans 14 times with varying degrees of fortune. After the abortive 1964 foray with Lawrencetune in the Deep Sanderson, which had retired in the early hours of the race, I returned in 1970 with Hunky Juncadella's Spanish team, Escuderia Montjuich.

Disappointingly, I did not get to drive the fabulous factory-prepared Ferrari 512S, which I'd qualified in practice, in the race. Hunky found he rather enjoyed driving the Ferrari, so much so that he did more of the early stints than usual… and crashed heavily in the rain at White House just before my

stint. My world fell apart but he didn't seem to care one iota!

My next return to Le Mans was in 1977, when I tried my luck with a converted Lola that Chris Craft shared with owner Alain de Cadenet. I did my three qualifying laps but never felt comfortable in the car, and when I was offered my first stint – at night, in the rain – I declined. Had I driven, it is unlikely the car would have gone on to finish fifth.

The following year was the serious start of my Le Mans assaults.

My company car at the time was a Porsche 911, and that's how I got to know Charles Ivey. Charles had a specialist Porsche workshop off the Fulham Road, near the Hurlingham Club. Success at Le Mans – or even just finishing – was still a burning ambition, so when Charles asked me if I would be interested in driving his RSR, I didn't hesitate.

I suggested to my export business partner, Keith Cundell, that having the Porsche's front wings signwritten 'Gordon Spice (International Spares) Ltd' would be a good investment for a mere £2,000. As a car nut himself, Keith didn't need much persuading and a deal was done.

Co-driver was Jay Rulon-Miller, a six foot three inch larger than life American racer who later became a British citizen. Jay was married to Nan, a tall, drop-dead gorgeous, blonde Texan – the eye-catcher of the paddock. Both are close friends today. The third driver was bespectacled Oz, Larry Perkins, internationally rated driver of Bathurst 1000 fame, a very competitive chap who had raced successfully at every level from Formula Ford upwards.

Me being a short-arse, our difference in height caused major seating problems, but we managed to sort them out before qualifying. As one of the oldest cars in the race, running in the IMSA class, Charles Ivey knew that qualifying would be tough, so he'd fitted a 3.2-litre flat six screamer, borrowed from rallycross ace John Greasley.

On the last evening of practice, Larry and I got into a 'get stuffed' match. Larry would go out and set a quicker time than me. I'd respond with a faster lap – and so it went on. At about 9:00pm, with Larry at the wheel (hurrah!), the engine let go in the biggest possible way, right opposite the pits.

The car was recovered and Charles set about fitting a legal race engine. The 'qually' motor was hidden in the back of Charles' Range Rover under a blanket. Before qualifying times were printed, scrutineers were called

With Maso 'Air, Hair, Lair' Ono of Dome Company, 1979.

and Charles had no problem getting the new engine officially sealed.

We had scraped into the race, but at the expense of a local French hero. Our lap time was unrivalled, even by the legendary works Porsche RSRs of the earlier era! The Frogs smelt a rat.

Our hotel was miles away from the track at Ferte-Bernard, known as 'Farting Bernie'. The restaurant was excellent but the rooms so noisy that we slept in the Rolls in a nearby field. At breakfast next morning, up rocks Charles Ivey, professing not to understand any French, accompanied by two Le Mans scrutineers keen to inspect our qualifying engine. Charles explained that the engine had been sent back to the UK for an urgent rebuild and had the driver mentioned what route they'd be taking to Calais?

The penny dropped, and Charles beat a hasty retreat. It was left to Creech and I to defuse the situation.

The French love Brits who try to speak French – the Maurice Chevalier syndrome in reverse, I suppose. Over coffee Creech and I did our best to convince them of the team's integrity, but they still had their doubts. It was the Rolls Royce that did the trick. The French are nothing if not snobbish and, after producing the Rolls to drive them back to the circuit they were putty in our hands. On the way back I mentioned how short of pit passes we were. On arrival we were given more tickets than an English team has ever seen. Friends for life!

We went well in the race until the gearbox broke. Charles, a brilliant engineer, single-handedly (in the pissing rain) changed the internals it in just over 40 minutes – a time barely five minutes longer than a full team of works mechos.

In the end we finished 14th overall and second in the IMSA class. In 15th place was Craft and de Cadenet's Lola. What a ride!

By far the best season to date of my fortuitously long career as a part-time racing driver was 1978. Endurance racing success at Spa and Le Mans, plus the Diners Club European Championship and the BTCC, earned me the title of Tarmac British & Commonwealth Champion Driver – an award I did not even know existed until the end of the season! The Tarmac Championship of 1972–80 was based on points (20-15-12-10-8-6-4-3-2-1) awarded to any British or Commonwealth driver on results scored in international events. Formula 1 and 24-hour races scored double points.

Its significance only hit me when I found that World Champion James Hunt won the Tarmac title in 1976 with 365 points, and again in 1977 with 238 points. My 282 points in 1978 were enough to beat subsequent World Champion Alan Jones's 238 points, which

Dome Zero: first time out at Silverstone with KG and Chris Craft – note the pull-down roof! (John Gaisford)

must have really cheesed him off, as this was his third year as runner-up! Mind you, Alan won the Tarmac Trophy in 1979 and 1980, and I came second.

I guess the prestige of the Tarmac title contributed to my being asked by The Dome Company of Japan to drive their new Dome Ford-Cosworth Zero RL, a Group 6 sports prototype, at Le Mans in 1979. Initially I turned down the offer, as it was an open car: following my Mallory shunt in 1975, I had agreed with the family (and NatWest Bank!) that I would only drive cars with a roof.

'No problem,' said Dome, 'we will add an aerodynamic roof.'

And they did just that: a unique cantilevered affair that you pulled over your head once you were strapped in. Talk about Japanese ingenuity!

The sweetener was the driver's fee of £3,000, plus 45 per cent of the prize money shared with Chris Craft, a Capri sparring partner. Chris was an established top sports car racer and had done much of Dome's testing and development work in Japan, and was a welcome choice as co-driver. The contract covered seven days testing at Paul Ricard in April, including a 24-hour endurance run, together with the Silverstone 6-hour race as preparation for Le Mans in June. Unavoidably

Frog in the mud

After the Dome retired at Le Mans in 1979, Dee, Creech and I called at the Moët & Chandon hospitality area where Marcus Chambers, the Moët boss, looked after us royally. At around 9:00pm, well the worse for wear, we decided to accompany Marcus to Les Hinaudieres restaurant on the Mulsanne straight for supper. Creech was voted to drive, and we followed Marcus through back lanes and fields to the restaurant in the Rolls.

I immediately fell asleep in the front seat and on arrival at Les H we were stopped at a field gate by a Gendarme with whistle and lit baton who was directing traffic. He had his back to us while we waited, and the Rule Britannia tape happened to finish. As Creech was replacing it with Land of Hope and Glory, her foot came off the brake as she lent across, the Rolls crept forward... and hit the poor Gendarme in the back of his knees.

Down in the mud he went, and the first thing I knew was when Creech lowered the passenger window, and said Gendarme leant in dripping water on my lap from his peaked cap.

Realising there was no steering wheel my side, he asked: 'Qui est le pilot?'; then, rushing round to the driver's side, to Creech: 'Avez vous un permit?'

At that stage it was unwise to speak any French at all. After profuse apologies – amazingly – he waved us on!

Imagine that at Silverstone.

Dome's programme fell behind schedule and the Ricard testing had to be abandoned, but the car eventually turned up exactly one week before the 6 May Silverstone 6-hours.

When I say the car turned up, what I mean is three large crates arrived together with a team of Japanese mechanics. Their job? Assemble all the myriad components to make a racecar.

Le Mans, 1979: warm-up lap behind the pace car, Chris Craft driving. (LAT)

Chief designer Maso Ono, who headed the Dome project, was a charming chap and the only one of them who spoke any English. Maso had a good sense of humour, and was keen to improve his English vocabulary and accent. One evening we were giving him some tips and asked him to repeat slowly the tricky words 'Air, Hair, Lair'. After a few attempts he enunciated it perfectly. (Try it yourself.)

'But what does it mean?' he asked. We explained it was a greeting to which an appropriate response would be 'Hello Maso, how nice to see you.' He was highly amused and from then on his faxes always started 'air, hair, lair'!

Fortunately, experienced team manager Keith Greene had been seconded and this saved the project from turning into a complete shambles. The mechanics worked day and night and by Friday morning they had produced a spectacular looking sports prototype, quite unlike anything seen before. A great credit to all involved.

Aerodynamically, the Dome was an uncompromising state-of-the-art slippery shape. Featuring low downforce, it proved to be the second quickest car down Le Mans's Mulsanne Straight. The problem was the tyres. For political reasons, Japanese Dunlop tyres had to be used, but the chosen compound was so hard that it proved impossible to achieve high enough working temperatures. There was no doubt that a softer compound would have transformed the handling and made the radical Dome very competitive. However, Maso's hands were tied, so we were stuck with probably the fastest, and certainly the most difficult car I have ever raced.

The qualifying sessions for that Silverstone 6-hours were fraught with problems, so I was surprised that we qualified in third place behind the two works Porsches. I can only put that down to Craft's bravery – it certainly wasn't mine. We eventually finished the race in 12th place, after delays with multiple teething problems that surfaced under race conditions. Japanese honour had been upheld.

Come Le Mans a few weeks later, we duly reported at the team hotel, which was way out in the boonies, 50km from the circuit. The number of mechanics to support a now two-car team was only exceeded by the number of Japanese journalists assigned to report on Dome's fortunes. Wherever you turned they were snapping away – there must have been 200 of them.

We had been told that team catering was being taken care of by Cordon Bleu chefs, so Creech was looking forward to a relaxing weekend away from her usual cooking duties. The team had rented a garage at Arnage, where the mechanics slaved away day and night preparing the cars for the big event. However, lack of sleep was hampering their efforts and soon they were wandering around like zombies – not an entirely reassuring scenario for the drivers. We learnt that in Japanese culture the first man to admit fatigue and leave for some sleep would lose face.

Before the first evening qualifying session the caterers had failed to turn up. Maso explained that bread did not go down well with the Japs – they needed rice! So next day it was down to the Carrefour to buy enough rice, tuna and bean shoots to feed 50 mechanics for four days.

Having stripped the supermarket shelves of rice, the locals thought we knew something they didn't... maybe a world rice shortage?

I shall never forget the way our mechs tucked into their bowls of rice – forget about chop sticks. They squatted on the floor, their oily hands a blur as they shovelled rice into their mouths as if they hadn't eaten for a week.

Thereafter, the enormous rice pan in our tiny caravan was permanently boiling away – and Creech became a heroine!

In qualifying, despite being the second-fastest car on the straight, we only qualified 15th on the grid. The problem was speed through the corners, again due to the tyre compound being too hard to reach working temperature. This made the car unpredictable and extremely hard to drive: thoughts of the 24 hours ahead were ominous.

For the race we tossed a coin to decide who would drive first. I won and put Chris in to bat! We talked about parking it against the Armco early on, but this was not necessary, as just before I was due to take over the car ran out of petrol: one of the pumps feeding petrol from the left-hand tank to the fuel pot had failed, and although the tank was a quarter full the other one was empty. I had to keep my helmet on to hide my relief!

The other Dome, driven by Bob Evans and Tony Trimmer, had retired with a blown head gasket ten laps before us, so it was hara-kiri in the Japanese camp.

My first five attempts at Le Mans had produced one finish and four 'did not drives'. Things could only get better.

Opposite: Jay Rulon-Miller's wife, Nan. The hit of the paddock.

About to receive the Tarmac Trophy at the RAC Club in December 1978. (Bill Bates van Hallam)

Chapter 15

Capri salvation

On the saloon car front, meanwhile, I had introduced my friend from New York, Billy Gubelman, to Stan Robinson and a deal was done for Wisharts Garage to run a second Capri for him in 1975. Billy had won the 1972 British Formula Atlantic Championship and was a useful driver. He was also from a megawealthy family, so finance was not a problem.

The 1975 championship was dominated by Chevrolet Camaros, ten of them running in the big class and winning every race. My best results came at Mallory and Oulton, where we were third overall, both twisty circuits where extra power was less of an advantage. Nevertheless, we scored seven class wins in the first nine races with just two non-finishes spoiling our record. The competition came from similar Capris and a couple of Opel Commodores, but I always found the Capri incredibly easy to drive and very forgiving. I had built up a good understanding with Wisharts mechanic Dave Cook, who always interpreted my feedback to make the car faster. Credit for our success must go to Dave and his team: their race preparation was simply the best.

Creech also played an important part in the team's well-being. Before she started catering, team personnel were traditionally given a daily allowance (50p!) to cover circuit refreshments. We stopped this practice and were the first team in touring cars to feed and water the mechanics properly – as is now taken for granted. This was particularly important at endurance events, where it was reassuring to know that a pint and a packet of fags were substituted by good home cooking.

The organisers of the 1975 Avon Tour of Britain had at last found a fair balance between the rally boys and the racers. With Stan back in the navigational hot-seat, we came fourth overall, winning the class.

By the time of my F5000 shunt at Mallory in August, we had done enough to win the (up to) 4,000cc class of the British Championship by a good margin.

In January 1976, before committing to another season I thought it wise to find out whether I would still enjoy racing. F5000 was out of the question – far too painful – and, as mentioned earlier, I'd promised the family (and bank manager) that in future I would only drive cars with a roof.

A race meeting in Guyana, well out of the public eye, satisfied me that I was still competitive, having won races with a locally prepared, Pegasus Hotel-sponsored Mini. So I signed up to drive the Wisharts Capri again, on the understanding that the Spa 600km and 24-hour races be included in the programme. The extra races were made possible by the backing of Wisharts' new sponsor, M&M Plant Hire.

1975 was the last year of the big American bangers, and the RAC introduced a maximum engine capacity of 3.5 litres in 1976 – an excellent decision from our viewpoint as it meant we could score outright wins. It was our best season yet. We enjoyed many victories, only being beaten when I got it wrong or the car failed.

Driving with Pete Clark, we failed to finish the 600km race at Spa due to an accident, details of which elude me. Two months later at the Spa 24 hours, again driving with Pete, we were the first British car home, first in class, and fifth overall. But it was not a trouble-free run, and by the end of the race the car looked more like a Destruction Derby Special than a Group 1 Capri.

For the Wisharts boys, the Belgian sorties were their first time abroad, but with natural County Durham humour they quickly adapted. It wasn't long before fish and chips were out and frogs legs were in. One evening I complained to the restaurant owner that the snails shells were a bit tough – and showed him the crunched up remains as proof. The boys were doubled up as he patiently explained that they weren't meant to be eaten – stupid Anglais!

The 1976 season brought us our second British Saloon Car Championship class win. In the overall standings we came third. Bernard Unett won his class repeatedly with a factory-prepared Chrysler Avenger GT to take the first of his two successive British titles, whilst the runner-up was Win Percy, who would win three BTCC titles, 1980–2.

Since a class win scored the same points as an overall win, it was unlikely that the British Saloon Car Champion would come from the vigorously contested big class. Having driven in the 1,000, 1,300, and 4,000cc classes (before V8s were outlawed) I had no problem with the BTCC scoring system. I knew the tiddlers were trying as hard as anyone, and without the recognition they deserved.

Driving for Stan Robinson I was never paid a driver's fee, and neither did I dream of asking for one. I figured the publicity for the business more than justified the time spent away from the office, which averaged a day a week, plus weekends. However, I was given space on the car to publicise products which GSL distributed.

For 1977 I approached Ford UK's competition manager, the late Peter Ashcroft, for factory support in running a Capri under the GSL banner. Wisharts' resources were overstretched and I needed more control of the race

Wisharts Capri two-wheeler, 1976.

programme than they could reasonably be expected to give.

Ford agreed to supply bodyshells, engines and parts free of charge and Gordon Spice Racing (GSR) would underwrite all running costs. More importantly, John Griffiths, Peter's understudy at Ford, would give support on the technical side and ensure that the right parts were homologated with the FIA (via the RAC). Financially this was a far bigger commitment then the freebies, and would ensure the Capri remained competitive. I also figured that official Ford support would boost credibility with potential sponsors.

It was this turn of events that prompted Pete Clark and Dave Cook's decision to go it alone and form CC Racing Developments at Kirbymoorside in Yorkshire. I helped them set up their company, and this was not a philanthropic gesture: they were without doubt the

best people to prepare my new car. It provided ongoing work for them, and, with far lower overheads than in the South, their charges would be realistic. Above all, they were hungry and keen: the relationship had all the right ingredients.

However, we still needed funds to run the car, and this is where our cash & carry suppliers came in. Michael Christie's Alexander Engineering, our largest supplier of tuning parts, came on board, taking prime space on the Capri. Spectra Chemicals, the car-care division of Burmah Oil, also signed up. With further support from Castrol (unlikely without the Ford connection), we ended up with a healthy budget – enough to be in with a sporting chance of making a profit.

At the time, GSL was in a period of rapid expansion and there were simply never enough hours in the day. So I employed Keith Greene, known by all as KG, to manage the race team and double up as Manager of Specialised Products at Staines.

KG was not the easiest chap to manage but his likeable character, sense of humour and unique turn of phrase overcame all barriers. Over the next five years he became an integral part of our racing success, a personal friend and the best race engineer/team manager any driver could wish for.

Truly, CC Racing brought a new standard of car presentation to Group 1 racing, driven by Dave Cook's perfectionist preparation and KG's unerring eye for detail. We had the best-prepared car in the paddock – and you could tell that by just looking. At that time a new 3-litre Capri retailed for around £4,000, but a Group 1 racer cost over £16,000 excluding engines, which gives some idea of the work involved.

It was not long before CC Racing were commissioned by other teams to build new cars: it was reassuring they would be there for the long term.

We started the 1977 UK season contesting the renamed RAC Saloon Car Championship,

Oulton Park BTCC, 1977: overall win. (Jeff Bloxham)

using the new CC Racing-built Capri II which incorporated all Ford's freebies: the old Wisharts car was rebuilt as a spare.

We had an excellent start to the season, winning the first three races. After sorting out mid-season gearbox problems, we went on to several more wins and podiums. The competition came from Capris driven by the likes of Chris Craft, Tom Walkinshaw, Stuart Graham, Vince Woodman and Jeff Allam. With one race to go before the end of the season, I narrowly led the class from Tom Walkinshaw.

I well remember the last race at Brands. Tom needed to win to take the championship and I had to come no lower than fourth to stop him. As we filled the front row of the grid – with Tom on pole – there was tension in the air. Tom and I respected each other but there was no love lost. Every team pushed the technical rules as far as they dared, but Tom took their interpretation to new levels – and annoyingly got away with it. Our enmity continued through the late '70s into the '80s, when later Tom ran those dreadfully noisy rotary Mazdas followed by the British Leyland works 3.5-litre Rovers.

I got the jump on Walkinshaw off the grid, but first lap into Paddock he barged inside and took us both off. We scrabbled back on with him in front, so second time round into Druids I did the same to him. Every time we spun each other off the rest of the field went streaming by and the heavy contact continued throughout the race. It was great for the spectators and at the end of the race I tailgated him over the line – in about 16th place.

Meanwhile, reports from corner marshals were flowing in to race control about the dangerous driving of two lunatics in Capris.

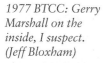

1977 BTCC: Gerry Marshall on the inside, I suspect. (Jeff Bloxham)

Within minutes of the end, over the tannoy came the order: 'Would Tom Walkinshaw and Gordon Spice report to race control immediately.' Before confronting the Stewards, I told Tom that if we wanted to keep our licences we'd better be supportive of each other. At that stage I took my helmet off!

It was the only time I ever benefited from Tom's accomplished bullshit. His range of excuses from 'foot slipped off the brake' to 'didn't see him there' to 'Gordy would never do that deliberately' were most convincing. It became a double act with both of us denying any foul play, and it came as a great relief when we were dismissed with a stern warning – licences intact.

Championship-wise it was job done for Ford, CC Racing and GS – my third successive year as class champion.

From a personal level, the low point of the 1977 season was the Spa 24-hours. We were one of the fastest cars that year and as dawn broke we were leading the race. In typical Ardennes mixed conditions I was about to hand over to Pete Clark and was thinking about tyre choice at the pit stop. It was lack of concentration on the main job that resulted in my clouting the barriers at Malmedy – and instant retirement.

Endurance racing is a total team effort in which the driver plays only a small part, and it's a horrible feeling to have let the team down by such a basic cock-up.

Despite this the 1977 season had been a financial success, and the decision was taken to run a two-car team for 1978.

On our visits to Belgium I had been approached by several local racing drivers with sponsorship proposals involving the thriving Belgian Touring Car Championship, which included the Spa 24-hours. The most serious of these came from Jean-Michel Martin, who had backing from his employer, Belga cigarettes.

The Belga cigarette brand was a Belgian subsidiary of Rothmans. The first meeting with Jean-Michel's boss, Jules Radart, left me convinced they meant business. Jules controlled the Belga promotional budget and had taken JM and his brother, Philippe, under his wing and treated them like sons. He was a most colourful chain-smoking character, a teetotaller who drank prodigious quantities of Coca-Cola. Radart's support of the Martin brothers' careers knew no bounds.

By December 1977 we had agreement to enter a three-car team in Belga livery for next year's Spa 24-hour race. GSR would provide cars and all the backup and the budget was extremely healthy. Jean Michel, Philippe and I would drive separate cars, and GSR would choose co-drivers and reserves.

No lawyers were involved, just a handwritten agreement with a deposit paid, and a handshake: it was the biggest racing deal I had ever done.

A pair of the latest Mk 3 Capris were built from scratch for 1978. GSR established a base in a rented Nissen hut at Silverstone, and KG became full-time team manager based there.

I asked Chris Craft to drive the second Capri, and he agreed on the condition of 'no team orders'. Following a successful career in

Loaded!

The previous years in Belgium I had been befriended by Freddie Semoulin, a short, dark, stocky chap who looked like a friendly baker but had a darker side and was an expert marksman. His mission was to further the career of his brother, Alain, and he certainly had the wherewithal to do it. Alain was an excellent driver, tall, blond and slim – you'd never guess they were brothers. We sold a car to Freddie for Alain to drive in the Belgian Championship, the first round being at Zolder.

In the race I started from pole alongside Alain and we stuck to our plan to block the BMWs behind, and I shadowed him for a few laps before overtaking. He fell back into the clutches of the BMWs, one of which – I'll call him Willy – blatantly nerfed him off to secure second place. Towards the end I lapped Freddy's Capri, and noticed he was driving very slowly, his eyes glued to his mirrors. I thought nothing more about it, but at the end of the race his motive became clear. He had seen what Willy had done to his brother and was waiting for him to overtake. Once Willy had passed he simply drove into him from behind, keeping his foot down until he was well into the boonies.

By the end of the race Alain had recovered to second place and parked alongside as we lined up in Parc Fermé. Freddy, with amazing agility, then leapt from his car, ran across the bonnets of four other cars in the line up, and physically attacked Willy before he'd even had the time to release his belts. He'd seen red mist. Thank God he wasn't carrying his gun!

At the inquiry Freddy was fined heavily, but reckoned it was worth every Franc.

F3 and sports cars, Chris had been driving in the BTCC in the Hammonds Sauce-backed Capri, and I knew he was a competitive and clean racer. We changed from Racing Services to Neil Brown's Bourne-based engine shop in Lincolnshire, and this proved a very good choice. Traditionally we had used Dunlop tyres which we paid for, but, thanks to KG's contacts we signed an exclusive deal with Goodyear which included free tyres and full technical back up. As the sole Goodyear runners, we figured development would give us a competitive advantage.

Ford's Motorcraft became our major sponsor, which guaranteed their position as GSL's biggest parts supplier. Additional support from STP and Castrol was supplemented by *Autocar*'s patronage, which guaranteed great press coverage. We undoubtedly ended up on the healthiest budget of all British-based saloon car teams. And what a season 1978 turned out to be!

In addition to the RAC Tricentrol British Saloon Car Championship, our ambitious programme included selected rounds of the Trophée Diners Club Trans Europe. This ten-race competition covered rounds of the Belgian, French and British National championships, including the Spa and Paul Ricard 24-hour races. The prize fund on offer was the deciding factor – far more generous than anything encountered to date.

The British season was successful for me, and I took six of the twelve Capri victories that year. Chris took a seventh win for GSR and I ended up fourth in the Championship, winning the class. The well-deserved overall winner was Richard Longman – unbeatable in his Mini.

However, these UK adventures paled beside the excitement of the Spa 24-hour race. It was the last race held on the old 14km Francorchamps circuit…

Our (now) four-car Belga driver line-up for Spa was Chris Craft with Alain Corbisier, Jean Michel Martin with Rene Tricot, Philippe Martin with Jean Pierre Jaussaud, and Teddy Pilette with myself. Earlier in the year, with Jules Radart's permission, we had agreed to run a fifth Capri, in full Gitanes livery, for Alain Lierneux, Stuart Rolt and Pete Clark. GSR and CC Racing resources were stretched to the limit, and KG certainly earnt his bread that week!

I had chosen Teddy Pilette as I knew he'd be quick and his strong Belgian following would be good PR. He'd agreed to drive for no fee, but what I didn't know was that he had a long-term sponsorship deal with Gitanes – Belga's main competitor. This only materialised during the race, when we had to stop him being interviewed wearing a Gitanes jacket! After qualifying, Teddy decided he wanted a driver's fee after all, so, rather than risking a major fall-out I said we'd discuss it after the race. The jacket incident was perfect justification for denying him a fee, but he was not a happy bunny.

In qualifying, only Chris and I were running on Goodyears. We both experienced serious delamination tyre problems and had to use Dunlops for our quick qualifying laps. Before the race Goodyear shipped out harder compound tyres, but they were an unknown quantity, which was a bit of a worry.

Pole position went to Vermeulen's 5.7-litre Camaro on 4m 21.3s, but the car was a qualifying special so we were not worried. I was next up on 4m 21.6s, pursued by six other British Capris, all within three seconds. These were followed by a gaggle of BMWs, winners of the race for the past five years, the quickest being a 530i driven by former Lotus F1 driver Reine Wisell.

Hopes were high in the Capri brigade!

At the start, 60 cars took off down the hill towards Eau Rouge. By the end of the first lap I led the race, followed by Craft, John Fitzpatrick, Tricot and Stuart Graham – all in Ford Capris. The driver leading the race after one lap won their weight in sweets – and I was no lightweight – so this was a nice bonus.

After an hour, my engine died at Stavelot and we lost six minutes fixing a fuel pickup problem which put us well down the field. After three hours we had fought back to 11th place and Craft was leading overall. Chris then had a frightening tyre failure at the rapid Burnenville corner and crashed into the Armco before riding it for 50 metres. He sprained his wrist badly and limped back to the pits, but neither he nor the car were fit to continue.

This tyre drama was very worrying. Chris and I were the only Goodyear runners and it was too late to change now, so from then on we changed tyres every pit stop so that the Goodyear techies could evaluate the used ones. By midnight, Teddy and I were up to fourth place, on the same lap as Wisell/Bourgoignie and Vermeersch/Joosen (BMWs), and Martin/Tricot (Capri). Throughout the night we were the fastest car on the circuit: at 1:30am I took the lead and pulled away from Reine Wisell's BMW.

As dawn broke, wrecked cars littering the circuit – four at Malmedy alone – bore witness

1977: Back at the workshop with Spa damage.

Meaty mission!

The July 1978 Spa 24-hours fell on the weekend of a public holiday in Belgium. We only found out on Friday evening that all supermarkets would be closed next day. Buying food for five car crews to last from early Saturday until late Sunday was a major exercise, but we were saved by some local shops remaining open.

At 7:00am Creech set off to find the local butcher. It was a tiny shop with one small counter, and orders were sent up from the basement via a dumb waiter.

The conversation (in French) went like this:

Creech: '30 kilos of sausage, please sir.'

Butcher: 'Surely Madame means three kilos?'
Creech: 'No, I mean 30 kilos.'
Butcher (shouting down lift shaft): 'Henri, 30 kilos sausages… yes I mean THIRTY.'

This continued for some time as she went through the order of chickens, steaks, chops and hamburgers. The regular customers queuing behind were not impressed. After the order for a hundred steaks the butcher plucked up courage to ask how she intended to pay.

When she showed him the cash his smile was a picture. I guess he closed early that Saturday.

Diners Club Trophy, 1978: Alain Semoulin on right-hand side of GS.

to the high rate of attrition during the night. At 5:00am patchy fog descended on the Masta straight but I was on a charge. I could have sworn I wasn't lifting into the blind Masta Kink, but I must have been, because when the fog cleared my lap time reduced by a full second. In the cool of the morning the engine was giving maximum power, delivering fastest lap of the race and a new 3.5-litre record. It was the last year of the old circuit, so the record stands today.

By 9:00am, with six hours to go, we had pulled out a two-lap lead from the Wisell BMW, so we looked in good shape. Then, coming out of flat-out Blanchimont, the left-hand front tyre let go: I hit the Armco at over 140mph. Fifteen hours earlier Chris Craft suffered a similar accident, but I was luckier: damage was limited to broken wheels, suspension damage and creased bodywork along the entire length of the car. Amazingly, Dave Cook and his crew patched up the car and we only

lost seven minutes in the pits, putting us just behind Wisell's leading BMW and two laps ahead of the Joosen 530i. I had just caught and passed Wisell when his engine blew – manna from heaven – leaving us two laps clear of Eddie Joosen's 530i.

At that stage I eased off the pace to rest our overworked engine.

After half an hour of tooling round I noticed the engine overheating, so I pitted with steam coming from the car. I just wanted to cry. The problem was diagnosed as a broken fan coupling – a problem never experienced before, so we had no spare. The boys 'borrowed' one from KG's road car. We lost 12 minutes in the pits, putting us a lap down on the Joosen 530i.

Teddy took over for what was to be his last stint and I went to speak to Belga's Jules Radart. I explained that by taking it easy we could settle for second place or, alternatively, go for the win and risk blowing the engine. He agreed we should go for it: even if we failed,

1978: the Spa 24-hour winning Belga Capri (before the damage).

*1976 Spa 24-hours:
Stan Robinson in
trademark cap.*

the TV coverage Belga had already received was reward enough.

At that stage, I had driven for 14 hours – the maximum allowed by any one driver. Pilette was quicker than me in a F5000 car, but a fair bit slower in a Capri. So KG and Creech (their cooking friend) chatted up the pit marshals: they were eventually persuaded that their records of drivers' seat time were wrong – to the tune of 1 hour 45 minutes.

So when Teddy came in, I got back into the car. With an hour to go the gap to the leading BMW was down to 48 seconds. Much of the dramatic reduction was down to Eddie Joosen's slower co-driver, Dick Vermeersch, who had taken over from Eddie when he ran out of seat time. With 13 minutes to go, an empty tank and a lead of around four minutes, I pitted for two laps' worth of fuel – a tense

time for the boys. With everything crossed I completed the last two laps and arrived at the finishing line to a welcome I will never forget.

It was the most satisfying victory of my career, made all the more special by the team having overcome what seemed insurmountable odds. We'd covered 2,682 miles at an average speed of 111.7mph, been through 108 tyres, spent 30 minutes on unscheduled pit stops, and won by less than three minutes!

The celebrations were wild. The podium scene was something I'll always remember: a sea of Belga dollies with brollies, and massive fan support for the underdogs. For me it was like a dream.

Waiting to appear on the podium, the Ford hierarchy appeared – they were over the moon – and Peter Ashcroft offered me the choice of any Ford road car I wanted. Creech said she'd rather drive a Deux-Chevaux than be seen dead in a Ford, which rather scotched that one. When I later berated her for turning down such a generous offer, she said 'OK, you have the Ford and I'll use the Porsche' – end of dilemma!

BMWs filled the next nine places with the exception of the Clark/Rolt/Lierneux Gitanes Capri, which came fourth. The other Team Belga cars had retired but with genuine sportsmanship their drivers joined in the celebrations.

That evening we were invited to dinner with the Belga bosses in Brussels. I just wanted to go to bed but, running on adrenaline, we made it to the swanky restaurant. After a much-needed drink or three, Jules Radart made it clear we would not be leaving until a deal was agreed for a return to Spa next year.

Before we left we shook hands on a scrawled agreement which committed GSR to running two cars in the eight rounds of the 1979 Belgian Group 1 Championship, and three cars in the Spa 600km and 24-hour races.

Jules's priority was exclusivity with GSR: he assured me the budget would be whatever it took, and on past form I believed him.

Details of the rest of the evening elude me, but I recall the Cheshire-cat smiles on Jean-Michel's and Philippe's faces.

In the Diners Club series, we contested four of the eight rounds, kicking off with an early season win at Zolder and finishing with a victory at Hockenheim. The Spa win, coupled with a win in the Tourist Trophy meeting at Silverstone, was enough to secure first place in the big class and third overall in the championship. The prize money coffers had never been fuller!

The award of the Tarmac British & Commonwealth Champion Driver trophy at the end of 1978, as mentioned in the previous chapter, was a wonderful surprise. It is not every day you discover you have finished ahead of future and past World Champions: it crowned what had been the best year of my life.

1978: Inside Tony Dron in the indecently quick works Dolomite Sprint. (K.J. Sutton)

Chapter 16

Winning times…
and moving on

For 1979, Chris Craft was my team-mate again and we entered two new third generation Capris in the British Championship. Sponsorship continued with *Autocar* and Motorcraft and our Goodyear contract was renewed. The competition was fierce – mainly from other CC-built Capris, the exception being Stuart Graham's car prepared by Ted Grace.

Left to right: Philippe Martin, Jean-Michel Martin and GS.

I enjoyed six of the eleven Capri wins that season, winning the big class for the fifth successive year but still finishing only fourth overall. Happily Tom Walkinshaw, now driving a rotary-engined Mazda RX7, only came second, and the overall champion was Richard Longman, again in a Mini. At some circuits Tom's Mazda was challenging for outright wins and measurement of the RX7's engine

capacity seemed to be beyond the scrutineers' remit – or will. The general paddock view was that Tom was cheating.

The Mazda's speed was hampered by its skinny 4J rims, but at one memorable Brands meeting the car appeared on 4.5J wheels – a major improvement. One of Keith Greene's jobs was to keep abreast of homologation so when Tom produced paperwork showing the wheels were legitimate, KG grabbed them from his hand and refused to give them back. Keith then lodged an objection and the RAC hearing was scheduled for ten days later. We had Walkinshaw at last!

At the hearing in Grosvenor Square, Tom had to admit the homologation papers were forged! We fully expected that Walkinshaw would have his licence suspended, or at least lose championship points. His only defence was that he'd done it as a wind-up and hadn't intended to use them: an extremely weak argument, but delivered in his usual dour but convincing way.

We were flabbergasted when all Tom Walkinshaw received was a reprimand and a £100 fine – less than the cost of a set of tyres. It was now open season on homologation!

The deal I had with Jules Radart the previous October for the two 1979 Spa races and the Belgian series was extremely generous; I still treasure the signed original – handwritten on a tablecloth. Part of the deal was that we should have no involvement with other cigarette brands – so goodbye Teddy Pilette! The separate contract for the Belgian races included Belga buying two new racecars, in addition to hiring our transporter for £10,000. At the end of the season they had an option to buy it for £5,000, which wasn't bad as we'd bought it in 1977 for £6,000.

The lads at CC in Kirbymoorside had a busy winter.

For the 1979 Spa 24-hours we had our strongest driver line-up to date, with Belga cars for the Martin brothers, Chris Craft and Jeff Allam, plus Alain Semoulin sharing with me. I had got to know Alain well and we had earlier driven together at Le Mans in a six-hour race on the Bugatti circuit and enjoyed a particularly satisfying win. That was the first and last race that my Mum ever attended. It surprised me how emotional she was – and so proud of her wayward son!

1979: Fifth at Spa 24-hours – and awarded the Coupe du Roi team prize.

The 1979 Paul Ricard 24-hours.

The team was accompanied by our loyal band of volunteers from the UK. I'll mention just two: Neil Brown, our engine builder, was always on hand to give practical help and advice – he always did a superb job; and Rob Adaway, a regular Silverstone marshal, who assumed responsibility for refuelling all the team cars, a demanding 24-hour task, while his wife Val helped in other areas. These were amongst the many who gave freely of their time with enormous enthusiasm over the years: we were lucky to have them.

This was the first 24-hour race on the new 4.35-mile circuit. Although not as fast as the old track, it was equally challenging and considerably safer. Pole position went to Hans Stuck's BMW with a time of 2m 48.99s, my time of 2m 49.98s being only good enough for seventh spot on the grid! Chris and Jeff were 15th at 2m 52.52s and the competition was so

Australian adventure

In 1983 I was invited by Ozzie Bob Holden to drive with him in the Bathurst Hardy Ferodo 1,000km race – Australia's biggest touring car event. The car was a Toyota Celica which Bob assured me was a winner and was well sponsored by a Melbourne businessmen's club and a local paper, the *Daily Gleaner*. Holden seemed a regular guy so, curious to drive at the iconic Bathurst circuit, a deal was done.

I was taken aback to find that 'businessmen's club' was another way of describing an upmarket massage parlour! The entourage of crumpet which accompanied Bob's team were obviously well prepared, which is more than can be said for the Celica, which was diabolical.

Practice was predictably fraught. At one stage the wretched car broke down in the high gorge before the infamous Conrod straight. Some typical Neanderthal fans, pissed out of their minds by midday, hated anything that wasn't either Holden or Ford, particularly a Jap car with a Brit driver. Oz style, they vented their feelings by pelting the car with empty beer cans.

For the race, knowing the car was unlikely to last an hour, I insisted Bob drive the first stint, and it was a big relief when the engine let go after ten laps.

On the way home I enjoyed a week in Perth on Geoff Jacoby's boat – a welcome contrast to the Bathurst fans' 'hospitality'.

strong that the Martin Bros were not even in the top 20.

After a wet start, the BMW contingent were at it hammer and tongs – you'd have thought it was a ten-lap sprint. Shortly after Alain had handed over to me for my second stint, Beltoise, challenging for the lead in his BMW, had an horrific fiery accident at the legendary Eau Rouge downhill corner, which featured a stream of water across the track. Beltoise was lucky to escape with minor injuries, but in the process he flattened the Armco and three pace cars were out for 90 minutes whilst it was repaired.

I always kept a packet of fags in the ashtray – to save having to cadge from the marshals if I got stuck on the circuit, or felt the urge for one behind a pace car. On this occasion I ran out of ciggies and signed to my pit crew my predicament. Next time round I drove slowly past the pit wall and Creech lobbed a fresh fag pack through the window: panic over!

In the mixed conditions there were accidents aplenty, but we kept our noses clean. By 3:00am (half-distance), despite an unscheduled stop for exhaust repairs (my fault), we were in third place, behind the two BMWs for Eddy Joosen and Bruno Giacomelli. Significantly the Martin brothers, enjoying a trouble-free run, were in fifth spot, and the Craft/Allam car, after a series of niggling delays, held seventh.

At 5:30am our hopes of success were dashed when poor Alain got involved with someone else's accident. Somehow he brought the car back, with what looked like terminal damage. The side window was smashed, the door hanging off and the fuel tank was leaking badly. After replacing the tank and much panel bashing, I rejoined the race well down the order.

Meanwhile, both the leading BMWs hit problems, and with just six hours to go the Martin brothers held a healthy lead over Joosen. For me, it was now shit or bust to catch up, and I set the fastest lap of the race – faster than Stuck's pole time. The cost was probably not worth it as the engine started to sound rough. Neil Brown imposed a 5,800rpm limit to have any chance of finishing.

At this stage I turned down Jules Radart's offer to share the Martin brothers' Capri, for which I was reserve driver. This was an easy decision for two reasons: firstly, the brothers had driven superbly and a win by two Belgian lads would be both well-deserved and politically perfect; secondly, with the Craft/Allam car running just ahead of us, Belga was look-

ing good for the prestigious team prize – the Coupe de Roi – but that would depend on nursing our own car to the end.

By 3:00pm on Sunday the Martins' Capri had the race won, two laps clear of the Joosen BMW and 12 laps clear of Craft/Allam in fourth place. Alain and I came fifth, a lap down on Craft. As the *Motoring News* report summed up: 'Only two BMWs finished in the top ten and only four amongst the twenty finishers. A Spa 24 hours as testing as has ever been seen, long or short circuit. Mind you, only five Capris finished, but they were in the right places!'

It was a brilliant team result, only made possible by impeccable teamwork. Belga had provided the finance, but credit for winning the team prize was down to KG's team management and the pit crew's unstinting efforts.

At a major supper in Brussels that Sunday evening, the celebrations for our GSR team and the Belga people were even more OTT than the previous year, with Jules, Jean-Martin

Letters like this (after the 1979 Paul Ricard 24-hours) make it all worthwhile.

```
Mr.- Mrs. Gordon SPICE
12A Central Trading Estate
STAINES, MIDDLESEX TW18 4UX
--------------------------


Chère Mandy, cher Gordon,

            Je tiens encore à vous remercier pour
l'extrême gentillesse que vous avez eue lors de notre séjour
au Castelet et particulièrement pour toutes les attentions
que vous avez eues à notre égard.

            Bravo et félicitations pour le travail
colossal réalisé par Gordon pour la mise au point parfaite des
voitures et pour l'organisation de toute l'équipe Spice.

            Merci pour cette 2° place qui est
vraiment une victoire sensationnelle !

            La presse belge hier matin était très
élogieuse pour les résultats de notre team.

            J'ai énormément apprécié la façon dont
Mandy a soigné pour le confort de tous les participants.

            En vous réitérant tous mes remerciements,
je vous adresse, chère Mandy, cher Gordon, mes bonnes amitiés.



                        J.A.RADART
                   Administrateur Directeur
```

1981: KG (note the flares!), the Duke of Kent and GS at MOD test track, Pirbright.

and Philippe in seventh heaven. When the restaurant wanted to close, Jules Radart countered with an offer to buy it!

Announcing that Belga had recently become the brand leader in Belgium, Jules publicly insisted that we sign up again for the following year. I argued that two Belga wins on the trot was as lucky as it was exceptional: perhaps we should quit whilst ahead? Jules would have none of it and after dinner my arm was twisted to sign an agreement for 1980, which we did there and then.

A wonderful sellers' market!

When I returned to the office, my first call was from Jean Michel Martin. Would I like to do the Paul Ricard 24-hour race, a round of the French championship scheduled in three weeks time? The Belga budget was not a problem so I agreed to produce a car for the Martin brothers and I. What weekend it turned out to be...

From the moment we arrived, the French were at their anti-Brit best. French Group 1 regulations were similar to ours, but when we secured pole position they deemed our car ineligible. We offered to change whatever they wanted but they failed to come up with anything major. So, after making some minor

changes to humour the bastards, we were allowed to start.

In dry conditions we were the fastest car by miles, but it in the rain our Goodyear wets were no match for the Michelins of the French entries – the gap a massive five seconds per lap! We led the first hour, then the heavens opened. For the next 18 hours the rain rarely let up. The track was awash and we were aquaplaning everywhere. It was sickening watching the BMWs catch up and draw away whilst the three of us struggled just to keep the Capri on track. There was no question of taking a racing line through the corners – a central line gave a better chance of collecting the car before it hit anything.

With two hours to go we were lying fifth when the rain stopped. But it was too late, and our final charge on a dry track failed to stop former French F1 hero Jean-Pierre Beltoise from winning. Under the circumstances our second place was a fine team effort. We all returned to our hotel, wet and knackered but happy.

Next morning, Keith Greene and I returned to the circuit to collect the prize money, normally paid in cash. We thought we had seen it all before the race, but now Brit-baiting hit a new level.

F5000 March 1975. Leading David Purley before an unexpected win at a snowy Oulton Park. (LAT)

After the Oulton Park win, March 1975: (left to right) GS, Creech, Bob Salisbury and Dave Branson (apprentice mechanic).

*Thruxton, 1975: how
the Lola T322 was.*

*After the Mallory Park
shunt in August 1975.*

Battered Wisharts Capri at the Spa 24-hours, 1976. First in class and fifth overall, driving with Pete Clark.

Brands Hatch, 1976: Wisharts Capri leading through Graham Hill bend.

Opposite: Oulton Park, 1977: Gordon Spice Racing's first year as entrant. (Jeff Bloxham)

Left: 1977: newlyweds in team gear.

Below: The 1978 Spa 24-hours winning Belga Capri.

The poster that Belga produced after the 1978 Spa win.

ICORCHAMPS 1978

Preparing for the egg trick!

The moment of impact.

Typical cash & carry promotional leaflets – 1978–85

1979 Thruxton with Richard Longman's BTCC Championship-winning Mini. (LAT)

April 1979 Thruxton. With Vince Woodman in hot pursuit. (LAT)

*September 1979
Thruxton. Same year,
new livery… and
Vince again.
(John Gaisford)*

*1979 Spa 24-hours:
Belga team cars
line up.*

1979 Spa 24-hours. Splashing around in typical Ardennes weather.

1980 Spa 24-hours. The Martin brothers GSR/Belga Capri on its way to their second successive win.

Opposite top: 1979
Spa 24-hours. Belga
team P1, P4 and P5
and Coupe du Roi
team prize.

Opposite bottom:
1980 Thruxton
invitation race.
Result unknown!

Above: Silverstone
1981. Two years later
and still being harassed
by Vince Woodman.
(John Gaisford)

Left: Le Mans, 1980:
the Rondeau Ford
Cosworth M379 –
third overall and first
in GTP with the
Martin brothers.

The beautifully liveried Belga Rondeau Cosworth at Le Mans in 1980.

Above: Le Mans, 1981: the Migault/ Spice Rondeau M379 – third overall.

Right: Le Mans, 1981. Discussing team strategy with Creech between stints.

Opposite top: Le Mans, 1981: taking the flag in formation with the Rondeau of Schlesser/Streiff/ Haran, which came second overall.

Opposite bottom: Silverstone, 1982: the Pescarolo/Spice Rondeau M382 leads the winning Alboretto/Patrese Lancia LC1.

Right: Le Mans, 1982: the Rondeau M382 of Migault/ Lapeyre/ Spice, which retired at 2:00am when leading.

Below: Silverstone, 1982: getting it all wrong… (John Gaisford)

Opposite bottom: … and team-mate Andy Rouse in hot pursuit. (John Gaisford)

Opposite top: Brands Hatch, 1982: leading the pack through Druids – a rare occurrence in my last year driving Capris. (John Gaisford)

Thruxton 1982. Checking the mirror. It's Vince Woodman again… three years later! (John Gaisford)

Le Mans, 1985. Breakfast at Mierré.

Spice-Tiga at Le Mans in 1985 – first in C2 and 14th overall.

The Spice Lamborghini of 1985.

Spice Pontiac at Silverstone in January 1986.

Spice Pontiac at Riverside, California.

*Night practice at
Le Mans in 1986.*

*A Hawaiian Tropic
escort – Le Mans,
1986.*

Fuji, 1986: on the grid in Konami livery.

Fuji, 1986: the Press reception by Konami, which made racecar simulators for amusement arcades.

Fuji, 1987: on the podium with Fermin Velez. Ray Mallock (Ecosse) is on the left.

Fuji, 1987: reception by sponsor Omron, which made medical diagnostic equipment.

Fuji, 1987: knife-catching for the Omron boss.

SE87C on the grid at
Brands Hatch.

SE87C Le Mans
pit stop.

*Mierré, Le Mans,
1980–9.*

*Le Mans, 1988:
Creech explaining to
Eliseo Salazar how to
go faster!*

*Far left: Le Mans,
1988: GS with
Eliseo Salazar.*

*Left: Le Mans, 1988:
Professor Martin –
Jean-Michel's Dad.*

Above: SE88C at
Le Mans.

Above right: GS and
Pierre de Thoisy at
Le Mans, 1988.

Right: SE88C in
normal livery.

SE88C somewhere dark!

SE88C pit stop at Brands Hatch.

Dubai Grand Prix

In January 1982 I helped organise a group of BTCC drivers to race in Dubai at what was billed the Dubai Grand Prix. The race was held in the car park of the Intercontinental Hotel on a temporary circuit protected with Armco barriers. I included Jean-Michel Martin in the jolly and he arranged local sponsorship from Jubilee (a Rothmans cigarette brand).

There was still some advertising space to sell on the car and I was approached by a local Arab to take space on the side of the car for his Financial Services company. We agreed terms but I made it clear there would be no signwriting on the car until the money was handed over.

It was only on the morning of the race that the cash was paid and the signwriting was hardly dry as we lined up on the grid for our race.

I was on pole position with Jean-Michel's Capri alongside, and when the flag dropped I got a good start and was leading into the first right-hander. I had just turned in when the intrepid Jean-Michel crashed into the side of me, taking both of us off and into the sand trap. Instant retirement!

Jean-Michel was mortified, so I pointed out that we weren't there for the prize money, and, with little engine wear in our 300-yard sprint, it had been a very profitable weekend.

The Arab sponsor was none too happy – thank God I'd not taken a cheque!

Opposite: Spice CI SE89C at Le Mans in June 1989 – my last race. (LAT)

Would we take a cheque? – NON.
Could we come back tomorrow? – NON.
Could they send a cheque? – Absolument NON!… and so it went on. Keith was going ape shit and I wasn't far behind. By the time we should have been halfway home the cash mysteriously appeared.

Just what you need after 24 hours of driving round in the pissing rain!

For the 1980 BTCC Andy Rouse became my team-mate and GSR had its best season yet. There were no team orders and Andy was a fierce competitor. In the 50th anniversary of the BTCC in 2008, in the *Motoring News* survey of all drivers since 1958, Andy was voted Top Saloon Car Driver. Jim Clark came third and I was delighted to come 18th – especially as Tom Walkinshaw was only 36th!

Of the ten rounds that year GSR took nine wins, three to Andy and six to me. After a season-long battle I was fourth in the championship on 67 points and Andy was fifth on 64 points. The overall Champion was Win Percy in the dreaded TWR Mazda RX7. It proved to be my sixth and last class victory.

In the Spa 24-hour race GSR took its third successive victory for Belga, by under three minutes, with the Martin brothers sharing the

1981 touring car action – a Mazda sandwich.

With Geoff Jacoby on his boat after Bathurst, 1983.

winning car. It was a cliff-hanger of a race, with BMWs finishing second and third. At 2:00am on Sunday morning Alain Semoulin and I were leading the race before mechanical problems set in, and the team did brilliantly to keep the car going to finish ninth. Andy Rouse, driving with Belgian rising star Thierry Tassin, came seventh after similar setbacks. Only weeks after their successful Le Mans debut with Rondeau, Jean-Michel and Philippe were now national heroes – and Belga showed their appreciation by signing up for the fourth time!

On the home front, the 1981 British Touring Car Championships were again sponsored by the Tricentrol Motor Group. Tom Walkinshaw Racing (TWR) prepared 3.5-litre Rovers,

which became the cars to beat, and the writing was on the wall for the Capris, which had reached the end of their racing development.

A winning Clubman's driver, Philip Martin-Dye, approached us with a sponsorship proposition. Philip was a British Airways pilot with personal backing from a local businessman. My interest was sparked by his connection with BA: to share the Capri's windscreen with 'The world's favourite airline' would be a major coup.

Another approach had come from Mark Thatcher. His mum Maggie was Prime Minister, so taking Thatcher on as a driver might open many doors. We gave him plenty of seat-time at Silverstone pre-season but he never got on the pace. However, the real

Toyota's 24-hour aside

Initially I wasn't that interested when Mike Hughes asked me to drive his Toyota Celica in the Spa 24-hour race in 1984. However, he was offering good pay and the Martin brothers seemed keen, so I signed up. The build-up included a few saloon car races in the UK to sort out the Team Toyota car, which was entered by Hughes of Beaconsfield. Mike Hughes kept a helicopter in a barn in his garden, which I thought was pretty cool, and it was a fun way of going to the races.

For the 24-hour race, Creech was doing the catering and she had strict rules.

On Saturday evening during the race she was serving a hot meal from the motorhome. Unwisely, Hughes pushed in at the front of the queue: he had broken the 'mechanics first' rule. In no uncertain terms Creech despatched the embarrassed boss to the back of the queue. The mechanics loved it!

It was an uneventful race and we won the class, coming fifth overall.

crunch was his arrogance and apparent inability to learn, so, tempting as it was, we let him go. Predictably, he thought I was mad.

Philip was also off the pace, but keen as mustard to learn. After convincing myself that he would get faster, I agreed a sponsorship package with BA in the form of free air travel for the year, and Phil became my team-mate. With continued support from *Autocar* and new sponsor Kamasa Tools, both delighted to be associated with BA, the figures stacked up.

Results-wise, 1981 turned out to be my worst tin-top season since 1974. Chasing more speed, with 'screamer' engines and the like, reliability suffered.

Andy Rouse, now driving his self-prepared Capri, beat me on occasions, as did Vince Woodman in his CC Racing-prepared Esso Capri. Ford wins were rare, and I often had to settle for second place or worse. Martin-Dye never found the pace to be strategically useful and made me appreciate how much Chris Craft and Andy had helped in the past.

Politics took on a new and unpleasant dimension. Frequent protests, often with Tom Walkinshaw at the centre, didn't make for the happiest of seasons. A combination of desperate driving and missed races (after a road accident in Belgium, which we'll get to in the next chapter) resulted in my not featuring in the end-of-season results.

Win Percy won his second championship victory by a country mile. Short of a miracle, prospects for 1982 did not look good.

Since its formation in 1977, GSR had made a healthy contribution to GSL's company coffers every year. This compensated for my feelings of guilt at time spent enjoying myself whilst my colleagues kept their noses to the cash & carry grindstone. I personally only benefited financially when I drove for other teams, and then only when they paid cash.

Over the winter of 1981/2 we built two Capris at our new Silverstone factory, part of a serious effort to compete with the Rovers in the 1982 BTCC. Ford was keen that GSR and Andy Rouse Racing should pool development resources. Renewed Ford support included arranging sponsorship from Shell Oils, and I believe they also put pressure on Andy Rouse to sign up with GSR, so we were back to the 1980 driver pairing.

However, my earlier premonitions came to pass and the TWR 3.5-litre Rovers dominated. Apart from winning at a wet Oulton Park and a few other podiums, it was a disappointing season. Despite no wins at all Andy finished the season third in class and I was fourth. The Championship was won by Win Percy for the third time, this time driving a Team Toyota (GB) Corolla.

With the exciting prospect of a new prototype sports car contract for 1983, it was time to move on. The Capri era had been good to GSR and for me as a driver. Since 1976 I had enjoyed 27 BTCC overall wins (a record at the time), and since 1975 six successive class titles.

Belga's Jules Radart at Spa, 1979.

Chapter 17

Rondeau: Le Mans à la Français

After two years of Spa 24-hour victories, plus winning the Belgian Saloon Car Championship, the bosses at Van der Elst (the subsidiary of Rothmans that owned the Belga brand) were on a high. Belga had become the brand leader and Jules Radart could do no wrong.

Nevertheless, I was surprised when Jean-Michel Martin phoned me to explain that Belga had hired a Rondeau M378 sports car to race at Le Mans in June 1980. Neither of the brothers had driven sports cars before, and to be thrown in the deep end at Le Mans for their debut seemed a little rash. They asked for KG to team manage and me to co-drive. After agreeing terms, we took up the offer.

On the Monday before the race weekend we met up with Jean Rondeau and his team at their factory in Le Mans and our car, in eye-catching livery, looked superb. Jean then took us to the farm where we would stay at Auvers-sous-Montfaucon – an 18km cross-country drive from the circuit. As a local lad you'd expect Jean to know the secrets of the area and Mierré was certainly special.

This working farm, owned by Georges and Bernadette Dubois, had been in Bernadette's family for generations. Despite speaking no English at all (with no intention of trying), they were amusing and attentive hosts. The accommodation facilities were modest with basic facilities, more than compensated for by the

1980: Belga Rondeau M378 at Le Mans. First GTP, third overall. (LAT)

extraordinary ambience of a lakeside setting. Additionally, the easy journey to the track, and good French food – any time night or day – were welcome bonuses. Little did I know it, but Mierré was to become our Le Mans base through most of the '80s.

Next day I was amazed at the way Rondeau's three cars breezed through scrutineering in the town centre. It was a case of, 'you ain't seen nuthin' yet,' for this was French partisanship on a whole new level. Not only were all the officials bending over backwards to be helpful, but they included two Belgians and an Englishman in their largesse! What a contrast to the French bureaucracy so often meted out to the Brits. The popularity of the team was overwhelming and I had never signed so many autographs.

Arriving at the circuit was another eye-opener: we couldn't believe the amount of space directly behind the pits that had been allocated to the Rondeau team. Rondeau fielded three cars, two in Group 6 for Jean Rondeau/Jean-Pierre Jaussaud and Jean Ragnotti/Henri Pescarolo, plus a GTP for Jean Michel, Philippe and myself. The main difference between the classes was weight, Group 6 cars being lighter than GTPs. I was surprised and puzzled to find that I had been nominated as third driver in both Group 6 Rondeaus, but never worked out why. Rondeau's paddock space was occupied by an enormous catering tent and caravans for drivers to rest between stints. Naturally, other teams had to walk miles for these facilities – what a shame!

That evening the team dined at Mierré, full of anticipation for the first official qualifying starting at 6:00pm next day. I warmed to Jean Ragnotti, famous for winning many international rallies for Renault, as well as stunt-driving in films. He was a serious party animal and the only driver enjoying a glass or two whilst the others were all on Evian water. I stuck to rum and coke.

Next morning the drivers all went off for a run – something that would have killed me. Out walking, Creech and I came across Jean-Pierre Jaussaud resting by a stream. He told us he always stopped there to splash himself with water to look like he'd worked up a sweat. Devious old frog!

I get a great kick out of helping young drivers in unfamiliar cars, new circuits and new situations. As I had previously found, the Martin brothers were great students, absorbing information, asking questions and, above all, desperate to do justice to the team. At Le Mans, as in any 24-hour race, every team member plays a critical part. There is a heavy responsibility on the drivers – who quite wrongly get the glory – to put their egos on hold and work towards the common goal of completing the race.

It is not a physically tiring race, but one that requires a high degree of mental discipline.

1981: Otis Rondeau at Le Mans. Second GTP, third overall.

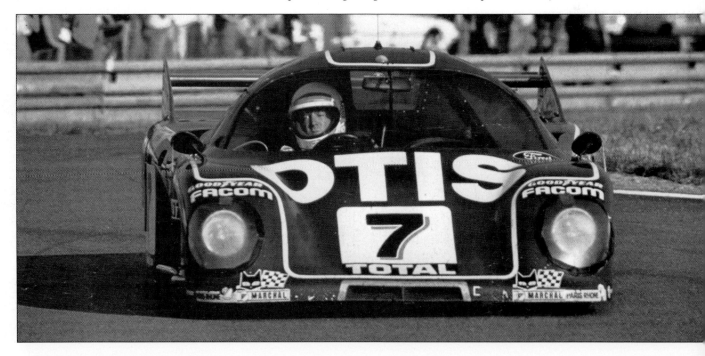

GS, Jean Rondeau and Francois Migault, 1981.

1981: Creech and GS in Rondeau camp.

There are plenty of drivers who can go for 24 hours, but very few with the mechanical sympathy to coax their cars through it. Here are some of the simple rules we all stuck to, with proven results:

If you hit a kerb or run over debris, stop at the pits next time round.

Pit immediately if you suspect problems with the car or you're getting tired.

Check your instruments constantly.

Brush the brakes every lap before the Mulsanne corner: forgetting just once could finish your race!

Once in the rhythm, change gear early; make every gearchange perfect.

Assume every car you lap has not seen you coming.

Drive within your personal limits.

These are tall orders for young drivers, but it's obvious that time lost in a stop is infinitely preferable to being stuck out on the circuit with a terminal problem. (Here endeth the first lesson!)

During the first few days with Rondeau I got the niggling feeling that we were being treated as rental drivers (which we were), and not getting the support that a team car warranted. KG agreed, and after all drivers had qualified in the first of the evening sessions an opportunity came up to do something about it. Around 9:00pm it was still light but raining hard.

'Let's make a point,' I said to KG. 'Set it up for full wet.'

This was something the other two Rondeaus had not done, as no improvements in lap times were likely. After softening suspension, and changing wing settings, brake balance etc, I ventured out to test the set up. It turned out to be spot on. Contrary to my earlier preaching, I started to enjoy myself to the stage where I simply had to go for a banzai lap.

The bemused drivers of the other two Rondeau team cars then decided to have a go. They didn't have the benefit of either KG's experience of wet set up, or mine of wind-up – and it was too late anyway! Our wet time was a full five seconds quicker than their best and the point was made.

Back at Mierré that evening for a late supper, Jean Rondeau brought up the subject of our car's superiority in the wet and asked what we'd done?

As agreed, we all appeared surprised that our times had been faster and I told him we'd left the whole thing to KG, and he'd have to ask him. The discussion that followed broke the ice between the drivers, with Jaussaud and Ragnotti, now convinced that rum and coke was my secret weapon, joining in its consumption with enthusiasm.

We hit the hay at 3:30am.

Thursday evening practice went well and the Martin brothers were comfortable with the car, after overcoming a steep learning curve. We finished 19th out of 55 cars on the grid, a respectable place in the GTP class. In Group 6, Pescarolo/Ragnotti had secured pole position, and Jussaud/Rondeau were fifth fastest, prompting great celebrations in the Rondeau camp.

A thunderstorm at the start resulted in the most evil conditions I have seen at the Sarthe. So bad that everyone was lifting on the straights and lap times were over six minutes. Early accidents eliminated several cars, and wet electrics delayed others. We just plugged on, concentrating on staying out of trouble. Such was the rate of attrition that after Philippe's first stint we were in tenth place.

At the halfway mark we were up to fifth, battling with the Brian Redman/John Fitzpatrick Porsche 935 of Dick Barbour. By 10:00am Sunday morning we were a mind-blowing third overall, leading the GTPs – a position we held to the end. Our conservative race plan had paid rich dividends: we'd only spent 45 minutes in the pits – less than any other car in the race. Everyone, not least Rondeau, recognised much of the achievement was down to KG's expertise and experience. Naturally the Martin brothers were over the moon – third overall and a class win at their first attempt was an unbelievable result. It was great that their Mum and Dad were there to enjoy it too.

Sensationally, our team-mates Rondeau and Jassaud drove to an historic home win. It was the first time ever that a driver had won Le Mans in a car bearing his own name. Two Frenchmen winning in a French car was a dream come true for the fans, and the celebrations were wild. Back at Mierré, it was a night to remember: My memory is a little hazy, but I remember the hangover!

When I met with Rondeau next day, he insisted Keith Greene and I be part of his team next year: we put it down to his extreme euphoria.

1981: Back to Mierré

For Le Mans in 1981 I was extremely chuffed when Jean Rondeau asked me to partner respected driver Francois Migault – proof positive that, despite being a 'Rosbif ', I had been accepted into the driver line-up of a fiercely patriotic French team. A contract was signed with Automobiles Rondeau and KG was again contracted to manage the team. Without KG's

involvement, particularly relating to safety issues, I would not have felt comfortable in signing.

After their giant-killing performance in 1980, sponsorship was on a new level, and Rondeau had entered a five-car team: group 6 cars for Rondeau/Jaussaud, Ragnotti/Jean Louis Lafosse and Henri Pescarolo/Patrick Tambay; GTP cars for Jean Louis Schlesser/Philippe Streiff/Jacky Haran, and Francois Migault and moi.

The city of Le Mans had provided the Rondeau team with a freebie state-of-the-art factory adjoining the circuit, aided, I suspect by his girlfriend, Marjorie Brosse, a lady with useful political influence in the Sarthe region. I therefore should not have been surprised at the disproportionate amount of paddock space that had been allocated to the team.

With drivers, wives and girlfriends staying at Mierré, the place was crowded, but the atmosphere was far more relaxed than the previous year. After practice on the Wednesday and Thursday, several drivers adopted rum drinking, and we ran dry of my week's supply of Captain Morgan. You couldn't buy decent rum in most parts of France in 1981, so, after phoning some friends in Paris, Terry was duly despatched in the Rolls to replenish supplies.

The quick but complicated route from Mierré to the circuit ran cross-country on minor roads, passing through attractive small villages and hamlets where it was rare to see a soul. Even during Le Mans week there was very little traffic. Although we nicknamed Ragnotti 'Pinocchio' on account of his long pointed nose, no one disputed his time of 19 minutes for the Mierré to Le Mans journey. I knew nobody could beat this record: I had been driven by him and scared fart-less.

On the Friday before the race, sponsors and journalists were invited to Mierré, and guests were enjoying pre-lunch drinks by the side of the lake. The approach to the house is down a long straight drive, and who should appear in the distance but Pinocchio travelling at 100mph. He left his braking to the very last minute and stopped with a handbrake turn, his Renault's rear wheels slicing through the edge of the lake causing a massive deluge – all over the guests. Those who had not seen it coming were drenched, and the ladies were not amused. Typical Ragnotti.

My co-driver, Francois Migault, was an ex-BRM F1 driver and a true gentleman. We shared the common interest of finishing the race so neither of us needed to prove who was

*Silverstone 6-hours,
1982: third GTP after
suspension problems.*

quicker. Our beautifully liveried, Otis-sponsored Rondeau M379 was immaculately prepared, overseen by KG.

After qualifying the Group 6 cars of Pescarolo, Jaussaud and Ragnotti were fourth, fifth and tenth on the grid. In our GTP cars we were 15th and the Schlesser car 28th. We'd planned to adopt a similar race strategy to 1980, but early in the race, despite taking things easy, we found ourselves in the leading bunch. Early Saturday evening Thierry Boutsen had a major shunt in his WM at the Mulsanne kink, fatally injuring a marshal. The pace car came out for half an hour whilst the Armco was repaired and debris cleared.

Barely an hour after racing resumed, disaster hit the Rondeau Team. Jean Louis Lafosse hurtled over the barriers at the fastest point of the Mulsanne straight and was killed instantly. The team met to consider withdrawing but, after viewing evidence of damage to Lafosse's front spoiler just before the accident, it was decided to continue.

The four-mile Mulsanne straight, where you sit at over 200mph for more than a minute, provides a short time to rest but a very long time to think. The first few laps after Jean-Louis' accident were the most nervous ones I can ever remember. But dark thoughts had to be put aside, and in an indecently short space of time all the Rondeaus were back on the pace.

With three hours to go Francois and I held a safe second place, well behind the leading Porsche 936 of Jacky Ickx and Derek Bell but well ahead of Schlesser/Streiff in the remaining Rondeau. Infuriatingly, we then had a fuel-feed problem which, despite ages in the pits, we failed to cure. Loss of revs caused a dramatic increase in lap times and at 4:00pm we struggled over the line for a bittersweet 2–3 finish, with Schlesser's Rondeau five laps ahead and the Ivey Kremer Porsche five laps behind.

Having come so close to second place I was very pissed off. Quite rightly Creech was furious, reminding me we should be counting our blessings, which brought home how selfish I was being. Back at Mierré on Sunday evening the mood was sombre as we thought about Jean-Louis' family and what might have been.

Creech wouldn't speak to me for hours.

1982: The start of Group C

Group C regulations replaced Group 6 in 1982. The most significant change by the FIA was a limit on fuel consumption, with 600 litres being allowed for 1,000km or 6-hour races and 2,600 litres for Le Mans. The idea was to encourage manufacturers to concentrate on better engine efficiency, albeit at the expense of power. Significantly, race strategy and tactics became paramount. Full aerodynamic ground effects were allowed and a minimum dry weight of 800kg imposed. These regulations were tweaked over the duration of Group C, but fuel and weight were the bedrocks.

Keith Greene and I signed up with Rondeau for the third time, but this time the Silverstone 6-hour race was included. By Silverstone, in May, the Rondeau team were leading the constructors' championship. I was down to drive the Monza-winning M382 with Henri Pescarolo, whilst Jean Rondeau shared the new and radical M482 with Migault. 'Pesca' was a no-compromise hard racer – the hare of the pack – and recognised as the quickest Rondeau driver. I would have my work cut out to keep up with the former Grand Prix regular.

Silverstone was the first appearance of Porsche's new Group C car, the 956. Destined to dominate endurance racing over the next few years, Jacky Ickx promptly put it on pole. Pesca and I were fifth fastest.

In the race, the vibration from the 3.9-litre Cosworth DFL caused major handling problems, after suspension bolts shook loose during my stint. This was a problem with several DFL-engined cars, including Rondeau's new car, which retired after 60 laps with disintegrating bodywork. After pit delays we finished a disappointing fifth but earned third place points, as old Group 6 cars without fuel restrictions

scored no points. The result was enough to keep the team ahead of Porsche in the constructors' battle. The race showed there was much work to be done on the vibration problems if we were to succeed at Le Mans.

In the weeks before Le Mans I had been suffering from severe chest pains, with all the symptoms of heart problems. After numerous tests, including being wired to a monitor during a race in the Capri, the doctors were no wiser, except for finding my heart in excellent shape. It turned out to be fortuitous that old doctor friend Michael 'Spike' Milligan joined us at Le Mans for the big race.

As expected, the Rondeau Team cars flew through Tuesday's scrutineering in the main square at Le Mans. The partisan officials, focussing their interpretation of the technical regulations on the British entries, ruled that the roofline on the Aston Martins was too low. This was ingeniously overcome by fitting a small Plexiglas dome above the cockpit – on which some wag painted 'TAXI'.

The Rondeau Team entered three Group C M382s for Rondeau/Ragnotti, Pescarolo/Jaussaud and Migault/Spice. I was particularly pleased to be paired with Migault – we had become good friends and enjoyed working together. In qualifying we were pleasantly surprised to be the fastest Rondeau, in 16th place, with the other two Rondeaus 22nd and 38th on the grid. Our lowly position was on

Rondeau M382 at Le Mans, 1982. Retired at 2:00am when leading.

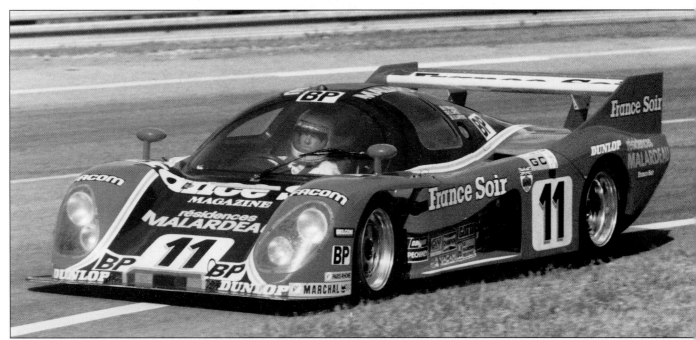

Belgium, 1981: my Porsche 911 after coming second to an oak tree!

A fully aerobatic Porsche

Le Mans 1981 was memorable for the off-track action, which did not start on a happy note. I was due to attend a press conference in Paris announcing the Otis (lifts) sponsorship of the Rondeau that I was down to drive with Francois Migault. My schedule meant driving directly from a Capri race in Holland to Paris.

En route for Paris, I was passing through the Ardennes mountains near Spa: it was a sunny morning, the roads were dry and I was tooling along at about 90mph. Driving down a long straight hill, between snow banks, I saw that the dip at the bottom was full of water – trapped in by snow either side and hidden from sight until the last moment by overhanging trees. I braked hard but it was all too late.

The Porsche hit the water, aquaplaned across the road, hit a snowbank and overturned. Still travelling at speed, the 911 snapped through a telegraph pole before coming to rest on its roof, wrapped around an oak tree like a banana.

I struggled up the bank to the road in a dazed state and by a stroke of luck the first person to arrive was a lady driving her son, who was a Spa fan. She kindly drove me to a nearby clinic, where my ribs were X-rayed and strapped up and my head was shaved to remove glass from my scalp.

I phoned Creech to let Rondeau know I would not be attending the press conference and to arrange for Terry Hackett to take me and the wrecked Porsche home.

Back in the UK I received a bill for over £100 from the Belgian authorities for the replacement telegraph pole, which I thought was pretty impressive. My best business suit was recovered from the boot of the Porsche and it appeared undamaged. However, when the car had been upside down acid had leaked from the batteries and dissolved the nylon stitching.

When I put on the jacket for the first time, both arms fell off.

account of the turbocharged cars (Porsches and Lancias) turning up their wicks for a quick lap. This was something they couldn't do in the race without running out of fuel, so we weren't too worried.

In the race, the new Porsche 956s filled the front of the grid and rushed off into the distance. However, after the first hour, when I handed over to Migault, we were in first place, due entirely to early fuel stops by the faster cars. After two hours we were still in the lead, with the Jaussaud Rondeau in sixth place, whilst the Pescarolo car was near the back with every problem under the sun.

At 2:00am in the morning, when I was due take over from Migault, Jean Rondeau asked me 'Voulez vous faire un double?'

I thought he was asking if I'd like a double rum and coke, so I explained that as much as I'd like one I didn't drink whilst driving. He seemed surprised when I declined and it was Creech who had to explain he'd been asking me to do a double stint.

After ten hours things were still going well and we held a steady third place behind the 956s of Ickx/Derek Bell and Jochen Mass/Vern Schuppan. Just before the end of my double stint I was delighted to see 'P1' on the pit board – we'd finally cracked it! The car was running perfectly in the lead. I went to bed thinking about the winner's speech in 12 hours' time.

It was a rude awakening when Creech came to the caravan a little later with the devastating news that our car was out with engine failure. It turned out that the rubber mounted ignition pickup on the flywheel had failed, due to a faulty batch of material on the latest DFV engines. Pescarolo had retired earlier with the same problem, and the same fault had hit the Ragnotti car.

I consoled myself with a large Croque Monsieur, the French equivalent of Welsh rarebit, and returned in a foul mood to Mierré with Creech.

After an hour in bed I woke with bad chest pains. Unlike in the past, they did not go away, so Spike was called: suspecting heart problems, he advised hospital ASAP. He had arrived at Le Mans by private plane so I was flown to Southampton General Hospital, where Spike was a resident lecturer. Again, tests showed the heart was fine: a dodgy gall bladder was diagnosed and plans were made to remove it at the end of the season.

In October, in an otherwise healthy state, I checked into the Princess Margaret Hospital in Windsor for the minor op. I should have been out in a week but after five days, following a load of blood transfusions, I was feeling at death's door and swelling up as if pregnant.

During the second operation – witnessed, at Creech's insistence, by a second surgeon (called Dr Luck!) – they discovered an artery had been cut and I'd been losing blood faster than they could top it up. When I was strong enough I was taken to St Thomas' hospital in London, where one of my nurses was Jonathan Palmer's lovely fiancée Jill. Jonathan was a leading F1 driver at the time and went on to be a highly respected C1 Porsche driver. It was a pleasant turn of events to be nursed by a current hero's future wife, and my recovery was far too fast.

Le Mans podium, 1980 – a French victory! Drivers (left to right) Philippe Martin, GS, Jean-Michel Martin, Jean Rondeau and Jean-Pierre Jussaud. (LAT)

Chapter 18

Tougher times and memorable conventions

In March 1980 our new 30,000ft^2 Watford warehouse opened. The timing could not have been worse as the UK economy was entering a recession, which had a severe affect on the motor trade. We now had three outlets, but sales only marginally increased at £9.5 million.

During the year it became apparent that the RSA Group was in deep trouble, so we took over Peter Unwin's shares in the holding company. That meant the Leicester, Sheffield, Bristol and Cardiff businesses became fully-owned subsidiaries of GSL. The negotiations with Unwin were fraught, but we held the whip hand as his warehouses were losing money and ours were not. The timing was risky, but this acquisition provided the company with a spread of prime locations – unlikely without a recession's trading conditions.

GSL trading profits slumped: in hindsight we made inadequate provision for heavy losses in RSA pre-takeover, so we ended up with a profit of £25,000.

Tough times indeed, but worse was to come.

Early in 1981, the restructuring of the old RSA Group, now trading under the GSL banner, was complete, and new technology enabled us to connect all the warehouses to our Staines computer. It was a groundbreaking task and the integrated system was operational by late 1981.

During the big downturn in business morale was low and I never worked so hard. I visited each warehouse every week, as it was impor-

tant to keep everyone motivated. I set the staff and managers short-term targets, listened to their moans, and praised them for successes. I spent most time at the checkouts – the pulse of the business – talking to customers, establishing stock availability, and listening to their moans too. Tuesdays it would be Canning Town and Watford, followed by a late night at Leicester – ending in a pub session with staff to find out what was really going on. Wednesdays were devoted to Leicester and Sheffield followed by a late-night drive to Cardiff or Bristol, where I'd meet one of the managers for a briefing over a nightcap. After late-night trading on Thursday I'd return home for a day in the office – racing permitting – on Friday.

This routine went on for about two years until trading picked up and we began to see light at the end of the tunnel. After that, one of the Directors took 'special responsibility' for each warehouse – a task they rather enjoyed and which I should have thought of before!

In the financial year to October 1981, on sales from seven branches of £15 million, we were hit with a loss of almost £0.6 million, most of which was attributable to reorganisation costs and losses in the old RSA Group. Although the company's revenue reserves were much reduced most of the problems had been sorted and we were in good shape for any upturn in the economy.

Our plans for a Stock Market flotation had gone out the window – you need at least four years of profits to be taken remotely seriously.

Abingworth's support through these difficult times was exemplary and, whilst they kept us focused on the important issues, they never gave the feeling that they regretted their 1977 investment.

The export company ticked along during this period under Keith Cundell's able if conservative management, but I thought the business should be growing faster Although on a personal level we were good chums, this difference of opinion led to Keith wanting to go it alone and I had no problem with this.

It was difficult to put a value on our 50 per cent stake, so I brought into play a formula I had used before when buying out partnerships. It simplifies negotiations and, more importantly, leaves both parties feeling a fair deal has been struck. I offered Keith a price for his shareholding, giving him the option of either accepting the offer, or buying me out at the same price.

Frankly, I was relieved when he agreed to buy our shares as the cash would be useful in rebuilding GSL's depleted assets, and we would be released from our joint bank guarantee.

Keith lined up two backers, Mick Cave of Austin A40 '60s racing fame and a partner in stockbrokers Kitcat & Aitken. The deal was done with goodwill all round and GS (International Spares) Ltd became simply International Spares Ltd. Over the next ten years Keith's company remained an important customer, mainly on the racing equipment side. His business prospered and in 2007 he sold out and retired.

During 1982 we took the difficult decision to close three of the old RSA branches: Sheffield because it was still losing money, and Cardiff and Bristol because their profit contribution didn't justify the management time spent on them. At a closing-down party at Sheffield, customers were given strong incentives to start shopping at the Leicester branch. Similarly, we managed to transfer sales from Bristol and Cardiff to Staines.

Not before time, business at our four remaining branches was improving. Despite the closures, sales to October 1982 were £15 million, and after writing off closure costs the company broke even. This, of course, was a vast improvement over the previous year. Our venture with Peter Unwin had cost the company close to £1 million over three years, not to mention a load of aggro. The good news was that we'd retained the best four branches and the company was back on track.

The mystery of HIAWS

By now our group's purchasing power was significant. However, I felt manufacturers' representatives tended to treat Spice group buyers with unwholesome respect, and they tended to become too big for their boots. It really annoyed me when they kept sales reps waiting for appointments, usually in the reception area outside my office. I soon put a stop to that by seeing the rep myself and, if their product was any good, placing an order. This was unprofessional and buggered up the buying budgets but the point was made and soon reps were seen on time.

I couldn't do anything about the private 'hospitality' that the buyers enjoyed, but I could act on the vast quantity of booze they received at Christmas: it was shared in a Christmas staff raffle. When a buyer was fired for receiving his booze at home the message got through.

Looking back, I admit to double standards when it came to leaning on suppliers for racing sponsorship – justified in my mind by good company publicity. This led me to thinking about customer loyalty incentives, which Ford Motor Company was particularly good at.

A highly effective incentive was that if you hit your sales target, Ford rewarded you with an expenses-paid holiday for two (billed as a Convention) to an exotic foreign location. Creech and I were invited for the racing celebrity bit, regardless of Motorcraft sales targets. Along with Ford dealers from the UK and Europe, we enjoyed lavish hospitality in Thailand, South America and the Caribbean. The Convention element of the holiday was minimal, but it created customer loyalty which Ford obviously found cost-effective.

I asked the lateral-thinking Brian Merry to come up with a similar scheme for our customers, but one that didn't cost the company any money. Of course, Brian went one better and came up with a brilliant idea which not only built loyalty but was the most profitable promotion we ever did. It was only after our flotation in 1987 that the promotion was dropped, for fear of 'benefits in kind' reprisals from Inland Revenue.

HIAWS was so innovative that it warrants detailing.

HIAWS – short for Have It Away With Spice – was basically a holiday savings club, one made possible by our major customers being owner-managers and appreciative of tax-free perks. The title of the promotion was not lost on them.

HIAWS parties were thrown at each warehouse, presentations made and customers signed up. Customers were then charged every month for an agreed number of Convention Units, shown randomly on their computerised invoice as a 'Conv Unit'. The number of £20 units depended on how many people they planned to take to our Convention. This money paid for their holiday.

The rules were that customers had to pay at least two visits a month to their home warehouse, and spend a minimum amount on the 'Supplier of the Month's' product. If they failed to do either, they were excluded from the promotion and any money accumulated was refunded. These two rules were strictly enforced, but there was another financial incentive that made dropping out extremely rare.

The other element, which is where our profit derived, was the involvement of manufacturers. Each month we approached one or more major suppliers to become 'Supplier of the Month'. The condition of being granted such status was that they would give an extra ten per cent discount over our best trading terms: this would apply to the initial order, orders throughout the month, and a final order at the end of the month. This extra discount would only be passed on, in a novel way, to customers on the HIAWS scheme.

The attraction to the supplier was that the orders were far bigger than normal and their products got top billing in our promotional literature. The huge extra profit this generated for us – in a business where margins were notoriously tight – derived from the ten per cent we did not pass on. Additionally, the final order would be for up to three months' stock, on which the company kept the extra ten per cent.

It was the best thing since roaring inflation!

Just before the holiday started, the ten per cent discount earned by HIAWS members, and faithfully recorded by the computer, was returned in whatever form the customer wished. So they had plenty of spending money and their commitment to the 'Supplier of the Month' was guaranteed. Suppliers were delighted with the increased sales, and the company's cashflow was highly positive.

Most significantly, we had found an entertaining and bullet-proof way to ensure customer loyalty.

Derek was in charge of organising the conventions, which was a logistical nightmare, but there were other perks, like checking out the venues for suitability, and we used the promotion as a reward for managers to accompany the delegates. Halfway through the holiday, next year's HIAWS scheme would be presented and that was the Convention bit done.

I don't remember one customer not signing up before coming home.

The stories of those holidays could fill this book, and several spring to mind.

We had booked our party into the ultra-exclusive Glitter Bay Hotel, then Barbados's newest hotel, adjoining Sandy Lane on the West Coast. Mini Mokes were hired for all delegates and beach barbecues and round the island treasure hunts organised. For two weeks the tranquility of the hotel was shattered.

'Fancy a nice cuppa then, Fred?' shrieked from a balcony by a wife in curlers to a man in knotted hanky, jarred the refined ambience of Glitter Bay. So did late-night Hokey-Cokeys with 'tired and emotional' guests ending up in the pool fully dressed.

On leaving, I enquired about a return visit next year. The manager's face said it all!

One year we took our HIAWS customers to Thailand. In the grounds of the Pattya Beach Hotel was a bowling alley, which became popular with guests. The reason for its popularity soon became apparent – above the alley was a massage parlour.

Creech and I visited one day and from the selection of girls, scantily clothed behind glass, Creech chose for me number 21 – a pretty little thing named Tuka-tu. I chose another one for her and we had our massages in adjoining cubicles. At the end Tuka-tu asked if I would like some 'fucky-fucky?' – an option available at extra cost.

I explained that, with the wife next door, this was not a good idea.

'Your wife velly plitty,' she said, 'she no mind.' That certainly summed up a difference in cultures!

One of our bachelor guests on the same Thailand trip, I'll call him Dave, was keen to find a girl. Dave had heard that some of the prettiest 'females' were men in drag, and that it was hard to tell the difference. Women are reputedly more perceptive in such matters, so he asked Creech to select a companion: thereafter Dave spent most of the time in his room.

The Coverdale philosophy

While I was sitting in my office in 1981, feeling cheesed off with some stupid problem, Len Bridge (ex-Lawrencetune) called in for a chat. I explained my frustration at spending too much time in meetings, and always playing catch-up.

Len was then a counsellor for the Coverdale Organisation, a management training company with a difference. I'd never been on any business course but he overcame my scepticism by offering me a free trial.

A date was booked and it turned out to be the week after Creech and I had collected our adopted son, Patrick, from Winchester hospital. Despite a perfect excuse to postpone, Creech insisted I went.

I turned up at the New Forest hotel, not expecting to get much out of the Coverdale course but willing to try. How wrong I was!

Coverdale changed my thinking about good management and it would not be an exaggeration to say it changed my life. Subsequently all GSL Directors were sent on the course and this was soon extended to managers.

The Coverdale philosophy had a strong Christian element, based on several basic principles which are blindingly obvious, but often forgotten in the heat of business:

Every individual has a skill to contribute. Identify and use it.
Listening is more important than talking. Establish understanding and support for
    WHTBD (What Has To Be Done).
Take a systematic approach to WHTBD.

Review the WHTBD process regularly.
    Build on success – learn from failure.
Take time to thoroughly prepare for
    meetings.
Put a timescale on meetings.
Give 'ownership' to those delegated
    with a task.
Appoint an observer – they will become
    effective participants.

On my first training course the delegates ranged from supermarket supervisors to top executives. The mixture of talents demonstrated the power of Coverdale principles, which were further validated in competitive inter-group tasks.

For the first task, we were divided into small groups and told: 'You have ten minutes to arrange these packs of cards in maximum disorder.' That was all.

Heated debate followed as to what constituted 'maximum disorder'. After ten minutes many of the group felt alienated, few were listening and some had not even opened their cards. Obviously there was no right answer, but the point had been made. By the end of the week, harder tasks produced high quality results, irrespective of the mix of delegates.

By the end of the course I was hooked and religiously adopted the principles, in private life and business. It bored my colleagues rigid… until they had been on the course too.

As Coverdale training spread through the company, we became a more effective team, communication was vastly improved and – best of all – Board meetings were limited to one hour!

On the last night Dave failed to appear at our gala dinner. So Creech, using a telephone at the table with guests listening in, phoned his room. The conversation went like this…

Creech: 'Leception here, you have lady in loom?'

Dave: 'Yes, it's her last night here.'

The hotel made an extra charge for twin occupancy, so Creech tortured Dave a little more…

Creech: 'You have cledit card – lumber please?'

Dave: 'Busy right now, I'll let you have it later.'

Creech: 'So solly, hotel lules, manager says must have lumber now.'

Cursing and paper shuffling and Dave eventually comes back to the phone.

Dave: 'Number is 7843 4084 1142.'

Creech: 'I lepeat to you – 7843 4084 742.'

Dave: 'No, its not 742, it's eleven – one one – four two.'

Creech: 'So solly, lumber is 1142 7843 4084.'

Dave, now on the boil: 'No, its 7843...'
And so on.

Creech kept Dave on the phone for what must have seemed a lifetime. He only cottoned on when the laughter from our tables became uncontrollable as 'Reception' asked him when we could expect his company at the gala?

In the financial year to September 1983, despite sales increasing by only £1 million, a profit of £340,000 was achieved, mostly due to the HIAWS promotion. Net assets increased to just under £1 million and the business was in good shape to resume its flotation plans.

Coverdale training (see the panel) had improved the efficiency of the Spice board in a dramatic way. Operationally, brother Dee remained in charge of specialised products and the HIAWS promotion, Roger Henwood continued responsibility for computers, and the redoubtable Brian Merry for buying and sales. Jonathan Bailey looked after staff training and security, and Charles Tippet was responsible for accounting and financial planning.

My main job was keeping them all happy – and checking their expenses!

Our middle management was developing well and we had some highly committed and talented men. Andy Criddle, Marketing Manager, was responsible for sales and promotional literature: despite some serious mocking of our competitors he managed to keep us out of the law courts. Sales Manager John Power was a great motivator of the sales staff, leading by example and rarely behind a desk. Ron Ford, Group Buyer, developed into an experienced and approachable professional, respected by suppliers. With our newfound profitability, we could at last properly reward these chaps, but it was the 'ownership' of their own domains that was the biggest motivator.

The Staines warehouse still accounted for over half of trading profits, with Canning Town and Watford producing 20 per cent each. Leicester was still the weakest branch and plans were made to introduce a distribution side, offering delivery of a range of leisure products (garden furniture, BBQs and so on) to garages and other multiples.

Building towards a Public flotation, the share option scheme, introduced in the late '70s, became a big motivator, but it was the priority of making the company business a fun place to work that bred extraordinary staff loyalty.

For me, these were the halcyon years. Business was thriving, Creech and I had a young son, and a whole new era of motor racing was about to open up.

Chapter 19

We are the Champions!

In 1982, on behalf of Gordon Spice Racing, I signed a contract with Ford Motor Company to compete in the 1983 FIA Group C Sports Prototype Championship. A completely new Group C racing car with aerodynamic ground effects would be built, powered by a 3.9-litre DFL Cosworth engine. Cosworth Engineering were contracted to develop a turbocharged version of the engine to compete with the Porsche 956s in the top C1 class. I believe the first-year budget was over $20 million, the majority earmarked for engine development.

February 1983: the new Tony Southgate-designed Ford Group C Sports Prototype prior to testing at Paul Ricard, France. (LAT)

Above: 1983: Neil Crang's original Group C Tiga-Chevrolet at Brands.

Above right: 1985: The Jaeger/Listerine/Waspeze/Cannon/Holts/Redex/Mobil Spice Tiga-DFV in tasteful livery!

Right: 1984: The Spice Tiga at Le Mans (now with Cosworth DFV power).

Drivers were former Swiss F1 racer Mark Surer and myself. The first year's programme covered six races, with a full assault on the World Endurance Championship (WEC) in 1984. Team manager was Keith Greene (himself an ex-Formula 1 driver), who Ford recognised as the best man for the job.

The first car, designed by Tony Southgate and built by John Thompson in Northampton, was delivered to GSR in December 1982 and taken to the warmer climes of the Paul Ricard circuit in the South of France for shakedown tests.

We arrived at Paul Ricard in February 1983 – I had come directly from skiing in Chamonix, so was as fit as I had ever been. Mark Surer, with Formula 1 experience of ground effect, did the initial testing and there were very few teething problems. When it came to my turn, never having driven a full ground effect car, I was miles off the pace and didn't understand why.

Henri Pescarolo, who was testing the new Rondeau, came to the rescue when he sidled up and asked 'Gordon, avez-vous une prob-lème?' It turned out he too was off the pace so we went to the fast corner at the end of the straight and watched the other cars. Mark was going through almost flat, briefly lifting where we had been braking and changing gear!

Next time out I plucked up courage, defied logic, and tried the same thing. Sure enough, the car didn't fly off into the boonies, it stuck like the proverbial to a blanket, and the faster you went the greater the suck. Finding the limit was the next trick to learn but this was easy compared with the experience of discovering unbelievable levels of grip for the first time. Within a day I was on the pace, but next day I had a very stiff neck and it looked as if I would finally be forced to start training (for which see the 'Physical fitness' sidebar).

By the end of the week we were consistently quicker than the Porsche 956s, which were the benchmark, despite running with a normally aspirated DFV. When lightly turbocharged to produce an extra 100bhp it would really fly.

Shortly after returning home it was off to Barbados with customers on a HIAWS bash. It

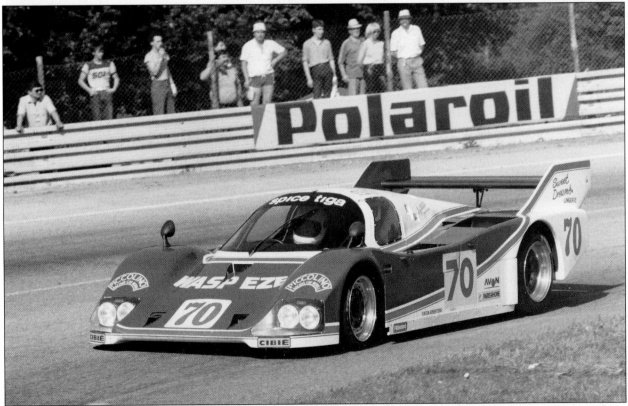

almost spoilt the holiday when a telegram arrived from Peter Ashcroft, Ford's Competition Manager: the contract had been cancelled and would I report to Boreham immediately.

Ford in the States had instigated a change of policy and my ally Karl Ludvigsen, Vice President of Ford Europe and the instigator of the Group C sports car programme, had resigned. The net result was that the Group C effort was cancelled, as well as the Escort RS 1700T rally programme, despite both projects being at advanced stages.

My attempts to buy the (now two) C100 Mk3 rolling chassis were unsuccessful – they were history as far as Ford were concerned.

One went into a crusher and the other was converted to a crowd-pleasing Ford Transit 'funny car'.

As expected, Ford behaved honourably and GSR was paid off (including my £30k driver fee!) and the machines and equipment, a sizeable investment, became the property of GSR. All the team personnel were handsomely paid off, and snapped up by other racing teams. The Silverstone race shop and equipment were mothballed whilst I looked for a new sponsor.

For the 1983 season Neil Crang, a wealthy Swiss-based Australian, had commissioned Tiga to build a C1 sports car using a 5-litre Chevrolet engine. Neil was a backer of Tiga Cars, founded by New Zealander and former

Pit stop at Hockenheim, 1985.

F1 and F5000 driver Howden Ganley. I drove that Tiga-V8 at the Brands Hatch WEC round with Neil, but we only came 14th. It was obvious that it would never be competitive in C1.

Over the winter of 1983/4, with Howden's agreement we took Crang's Tiga chassis, modified it to take a 3-litre Cosworth DFV V8 and made it eligible to run in the C2 class. We also changed the bodywork to suit. At the front we copied the lines of the Porsche 956, and despite the hotchpotch it turned out to be a good-looking sports car. Crucially, it was fundamentally stable and responded to suspension and aerodynamic changes.

We named it a Spice-Tiga.

It's a strange life: the biggest disappointment of my racing career led directly to the start of Spice Engineering Limited (SEL). Without the cancellation of the Ford contract it never would have happened.

For the 1984 season, before SEL was formed, we raced under the Gordon Spice Racing banner. The team received sponsorship from Waspeze and other pharmaceutical brands owned by Ray Bellm, and the Spice-Tiga was driven by Neil Crang, Ray and myself. That 1984 season we raced at the Silverstone 1,000km (retired) and Le Mans 24-hours (retired) before going on to five consecutive C2 victories in WEC rounds at the Nürburgring, Brands Hatch, Spa-Francorchamps, Imola and Sandown Park (Melbourne). Had there been a C2 championship that year, we'd have won it hands down.

In detail, our season took off after a tardy start. First time out at the Silverstone 1,000km we retired after 117 laps. The car was fast enough, but we needed more test mileage to sort out reliability.

For Le Mans we took over glorious Mierré, as Jean Rondeau no longer had a team, preferring to compete as a driver. The party of 40 included the Bellm, Crang and Spice clans, all of whom were accommodated, wined and dined for the week.

The race was won by Pescarolo and Klaus Ludwig, with Rondeau/Paul Jr coming second, both in 956 Porsches. It was the year that 'Driller' Sheldon (a dentist) got badly burnt writing off a Nimrod Aston Martin at the Mulsanne kink, the debris causing their teammates' Nimrod to also crash. We were going well until Crang hit the barriers at Tertre Rouge after only 70 laps, so he was none too popular!

Nevertheless, socially it was a vintage year, Group C's equivalent of Royal Ascot.

Our first success was at the Nürburgring 1,000km where we won Group C Junior, and then went on to win at Brands Hatch and Spa, the car running like clockwork. But the Imola weekend is the one I remember well.

Creech and I had flown to Geneva to see the Crang's new and very flash lakeside house, complete with 50-foot waterfall running through the middle. From there we drove to

1985: (left to right) Almo Capelli, John Cafaro (GM), Brian Folley, Tony Fall (GM), GS, Keith Cundell and Peter Dicks (Abingworth).

Left to right: Charles Skipwith, GS, Beth Cafaro and Pierre de Thoisy.

Mugello in Neil's Audi Quattro. Victory celebrations after the race made it unwise to drive back to Geneva so we decided to stay on at our hotel. Unfortunately they were fully booked due to F1 testing next day, so Creech, being the most sober, was voted to drive back to Geneva. She had never driven a left-hand-drive car before, and certainly not one where the cockpit resembled that of a Boeing 747.

Egging her along on a three-lane highway we clipped wing mirrors with an oncoming car, and I told her to continue flat out. A little later we came to traffic lights, so I told her to turn right so we would hide in case the other car came back. I had not spotted a deep roadside ditch. Down we went into it and got stuck, despite four-wheel drive. Minutes later the driver of the other car came back! As we were negotiating compensation the police turned up: now we were in deep shit.

Disloyally we identified Creech as the driver. When the cops asked 'Why you no stop?' she burst into tears, clutched her tummy, and choked 'bambino'. She was wearing loose

dungarees and it could have been true, but it was news to me! The older of the two cops consoled her with a bear-hug embrace and the driver of the other car became the villain. After handing over a few million lira for the wing mirror, peace was made, and everyone helped push the Audi back onto the road. Creech was racked with guilt, but her quick-thinking had defused a very difficult situation.

But the evening held still more. When we hit the Autoroute, traffic came to a sudden halt with no sign of movement ahead. Neil, who had continued drinking rum and coke in the back with Di, decided to get out for a pee, still clutching his bottle. The traffic still showed no signs of moving.

When I went to search for Crang I found him a few cars back in a Fiat Uno with a young lady, whose name was Anna. From the rocking of the car, he was obviously busy so I left him to it. Di had passed out, and 20 minutes later the traffic started moving. We took off, leaving Neil behind. After a few miles, headlight flashing from the Uno told us Anna was taking the

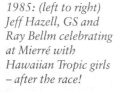

1985: (left to right) Jeff Hazell, GS and Ray Bellm celebrating at Mierré with Hawaiian Tropic girls – after the race!

Lake Como turn-off. We took pity on Neil, who was about to get hell from Di, and picked him up.

The legend of 'Anna from Lake Como' goes down in the annals of Men Behaving Badly.

The last race of the 1984 season was at Australia's Sandown Park, a circuit surrounded by the premier horseracing course in Melbourne. Ray was busy elsewhere so Crang drove with me in his hometown. Arriving late Thursday and leaving early Monday was a bit tiresome but the race went well and we scored our fifth consecutive class win.

After the race, with both of us feeling good, I took the opportunity to resolve a long-standing dispute with Crang over his contribution to the racing. With the company's Unlisted Securities Market flotation on the horizon failure to settle matters could have been a showstopper, and Crang knew this. We came to an agreement and my annoyance at being screwed was more than compensated by the relief of one less USM hurdle to jump – and it made the trip worthwhile.

The 1985 endurance racing season was a memorable one for Spice Engineering. It brought two FIA World titles in the C2 class and attracted a major car manufacturer. The FIA had introduced a secondary championship for both constructors and drivers within the WEC. This new C2 class replaced the previous Junior category and was comparatively affordable, attracting entries from Ecurie Ecosse, Alba-Carma (Italy), Tiga, ADA, Gebhardt, Ceekar and URD-BMW.

Ray Bellm had secured prestigious sponsorship from Jaeger – we were certainly the best-dressed team – and the car's livery was eye-catching. Jeff Hazel tied up useful Mobil sponsorship and my contribution came from Holt Lloyds and Cannon Car mats, both important cash & carry suppliers. Ray's Listerine and Waspeze brands also featured and his Dad's Piccolino model-making company appeared occasionally.

Over the winter a new chassis was built with lighter bodywork and major changes to the original Tiga chassis. The first race at the picturesque Italian Mugello track (now owned by Ferrari) was interesting. We were well in the lead and conserving fuel with just ten laps left when the car coughed, obviously running out of fuel. I pitted on fumes and Jeff Hazel told me we'd used our fuel allocation, and that was that.

Ready for lunch at Mierré.

At my insistence the car was topped up – we'd argue the toss later.

Luckily we'd pitted early in the race for a minor problem and topped up the fuel at the same time. It gave credibility to Jeff's argument that we had not started with a full tank – it was all part of our race strategy! Officials could not prove their case and our class victory (seventh overall) was reluctantly allowed. To stop anyone else using this somewhat unlikely excuse, all teams were advised that, henceforth, it would be assumed all cars had started with full tanks.

If that was lucky for us, two weeks later at Monza was even better – with no cheating. After a strong challenge from Ecurie Ecosse, our fuel level was marginal and after 125 laps we were forced to slow right down to finish. Imagine our joy when, 34 laps before the scheduled distance was complete, a tree blew down across the track and the race was red-flagged.

Undoubtedly arch-rival Ecurie Ecosse would have beaten us and there was little love lost between our teams, both suspecting the other of skulduggery. It was only thanks to gale force winds that we recorded our seventh consecutive win.

*Punting at Mierré
with son Patrick
(aged 3) in 1984.*

1985 Le Mans

At Le Mans in June, we returned to Mierré, where we'd invited John Callies, competition chief of General Motors' Pontiac Division, to join us. Other guests included John Cafaro, top GM stylist, and his lovely wife Beth. It was a memorable trip for them as it was the week Beth became pregnant with their first child. Joining us at work and at play the GM people entered into the spirit and we got to know them well – they were excellent company.

Sharing the driving was underrated Irishman Mark Galvin, who brought sponsorship with him. It's always a risk bringing in a new driver but he was a true gentleman, fitted in well, and proved to be fast and sensible. The coup of the week was last-minute sponsorship from Hawaiian Tropic. The money was not great but the bevy of stunning young American beauty contest winners who accompanied the car at every opportunity guaranteed maximum exposure.

Although we only qualified on the 14th row of the grid the bikini-clad girls attracted more photographers than the front six rows combined!

The race went well and after eight hours we led the class; then a long pit stop dropped us to fifth. At 3:00am I hit a (deaf?) fox but, after the bodywork had been repaired, we ran trouble free. By midday, after a steady trundle, we were back in the class lead and maintained it to the end. Out of the 29 finishers – more than usual – we were 14th overall and won the class by ten laps from Ian Harrower's Gebhardt. It was both a timely win and a fine show of teamwork in front of our GM guests. A major milestone.

The following month, the Hockenheim round became a race of attrition. Towards the end, when we looked unbeatable, I pitted to save fuel. Unbelievably, the wretched car wouldn't restart for the last few laps, handing C2 victory to Ecurie Ecosse. How they must have laughed!

Physical fitness

In endurance racing the time spent behind the wheel can be several hours at a stretch. A 24-hour race gives the equivalent seat time of at least six F1 Grand Prix, all in a noisy and incredibly hot cockpit.

Throughout my driving career I never found it necessary to visit a gym or go running to keep fit: I have a strong aversion to both disciplines.

The advent of Group C ground-effect cars forced a change in that. Now it was necessary, pre-season, to strengthen the neck muscles to counter high G forces in the corners. Failure to work on your fitness resulted in a floppy neck and considerable pain after surprisingly few laps. It only happened to me once, but never again.

The exercise I adopted was to put a race helmet on, lie on my side, and raise and lower my head to the floor. Do this practical exercise on both sides for a prolonged period without any discomfort, and you knew your neck was up to the job (and a full collar-size larger).

My forearms also needed strengthening, as the steering is heavy on ground-effect sports prototypes. The exercise I found most effective was using spring-loaded handgrips which you compress and relax. When you could keep that up for hours, without tiring, your arms were strong enough.

After the season started, the regularity of both testing and racing was quite enough to maintain a decent level of fitness.

First production Pontiac-Spice-Fiero at Silverstone 'straight out the box' prior to shipping to the USA in January 1986.

1986: Pontiac-Fiero first race at Riverside, California.

At the Mosport round in Canada we qualified seventh overall and first in class but we knew that fuel consumption would be a problem, and so it proved. In fuel-saving mode we kept in touch with the Finetti/Finotto's Alba, which led for the first hour. Then tragedy struck. Manfred Winklehock, driving a Porsche 962 with Surer, went through the catch fencing at Turn 2 and hit a concrete wall, trapping him in the car. The pace car was out for an hour, during which we saved enough fuel to go for it. We charged for the rest of the race, finishing fifth overall and class winners.

There were no celebrations – we knew Manfred's accident was a bad one. He had been flown to hospital but died next day.

With Winklehock's death fresh in everyone's mind, the next round at Spa-Francorchamps started ominously. Early in practice Jonathan Palmer, in Richard Lloyd's Porsche 956, hit the barrier and was trapped. It was a horrific accident, and Jonathan was lucky to escape with only concussion and broken legs.

But things got worse. Halfway through the race Stefan Bellof, probably the fastest man in sports cars and a promising talent in the Tyrrell Grand Prix team, tried an ambitious move on Jacky Ickx's similar Porsche. Stefan ended up head-on in the barriers at Eau Rouge. The pace car controlled the race for an hour. Shortly after the field was released, news came through that Bellof had died. Nobody had the stomach for racing: after five hours the team managers unanimously decided to stop the race. The Bellof tragedy completely overshadowed both

Lancia's first win over the dominant Porsches, and our class win.

Those two deaths at consecutive race meetings brought home the dangers of motor racing: something I rarely thought about.

With the GM deal for 1986 signed, and the workshop time it would involve, we decided not to go to Fuji in Japan or Selangor in Malaysia for the last two rounds. Our last race of the 1985 season became Brands Hatch. My company had laid on tickets and hospitality for Spice employees so I was particularly keen to do well in front of the home crowd.

The weekend started well and we were fastest in qualifying by a country mile. In the race we were out after only 12 laps with terminal suspension failure. We'd had nothing like this all season, and, sod's law, it had to happen at home!

Still, it had been a good season overall, with Spice Engineering Ltd (SEL) winning the C2

Team title by a healthy margin from Ecurie Ecosse. Ray Bellm and I took the C2 Drivers World Championship: at 45 years old, I was very proud of my first World title!

Commercially, the highlight was securing a megabuck deal with GM-Pontiac to design, build and run a new sports prototype in the Camel Lights class of the American IMSA series. During final negotiations we offered GM-Pontiac two choices. The first option was that they pay all development costs and the technology would be exclusive to GM in the USA. The second less expensive option was that SEL be allowed to run Cosworth and other engines in the same chassis, with sole marketing rights for new cars worldwide.

Looking back, it was the making of SEL when Pontiac went for the second option, on the condition that for 1986 the cars be named Spice Fiero. To us this was a compliment, not a problem!

Le Mans 24-hours, 1986.

Spice-Fiero leads Rondeau M379 of Noel Del Bello and Bruno Sotty at Le Mans.

1986: Transatlantic expansion

Between October 1985 and April 1986 the workforce was flat out at our Silverstone base on the new Spice Fiero. It demanded frequent visits from Pontiac's John Callies and John Cafaro. The car had to be styled to resemble the Pontiac Fiero (GM's plastic-bodied 2.8-litre sports car) and a balance struck between GM corporate styling and racing aerodynamics. Wind tunnel testing of quarter scale models was carried out in the Southampton University wind tunnel and the final shape appeared both recognisable and striking, with the lowest drag coefficient of any sports prototype to date.

Critically, talented Graham Humphrys had designed a user-friendly sports car suitable for privateers. It was easy to service and repair, and

at £170k for a rolling chassis (less engine), far less money than the competition. It was cleverly designed to take a wide variety of engines with only small changes to the honeycomb aluminium monocoque. Over their six year lifespan, 50 Spice chassis were built, and engines included Cosworth, GM range, Judd, Hart, Honda, Lamborghini and Ferrari.

For the 1986 season Ecurie Ecosse fielded a two-car team, powered by Austin Rover's Metro V6 rally hardware, and our intense rivalry increased. Other competition included the C2 Argo-Zakspeed of Dutch rallycross ace Martin Schanche, and the two Gebhardt-Cosworths of Frank Jelinski and Ian Harrower – all potential class winners.

For the first outing of the new Fiero-shaped Spice-Cosworth, at the Monza 1,000km in May, Ray and I adopted a conservative fuel strategy which allowed both Gebhardts and

Driver comforts

In closed sports cars, the cockpit temperature is often over 50°C for long periods. There are two reasons for this: firstly, the chassis acts as a heat sink for the engine which sits a few inches behind your back, so some internal aluminium panels became too hot to touch; secondly, it is technically difficult to achieve effective airflow through the cockpit without compromising aerodynamics… or blowing the doors off!

Sweating can induce serious dehydration and it is essential to constantly drink whilst driving. A switch on the dashboard activates a pump which forces fluid from a cool box into your mouth via a plastic tube: taking on fluid every lap becomes an automatic habit.

In addition, discomfort caused by high cockpit temperatures can adversely affect driver performance, and this can be reduced by using a cool suit. This is a body jacket and balaclava worn next to the skin that has inbuilt capillary tubes, through which a super-cool antifreeze is pumped (by another switch). I didn't use a body jacket, as I found it was only effective at the beginning of a stint, when it was least needed.

However, I found the balaclava was a real godsend when used sparingly. If the pump was left on, after the initial cooling, then the benefit was minimal as it became your norm. However, if used sparingly – maybe for five seconds every few laps – not only was the cooling effect dramatic, but it would last a whole stint.

For me, it became part of the mind games one plays whilst driving. I'd set personal targets and use my cool hood as a reward when they'd been achieved.

Pit stop at Spa Francorchamps, 1986.

1985: the Lamborghini Spice Tiga – ran once at Kyalami, South Africa, and came second.

the Argo to draw well ahead. We thought our fuel-saving strategy had worked when towards the end the Harrower/Clements Gebhardt ran out of fuel and we overtook the Argo, which was struggling with the same problem; but contrary to our calculations the Jelinski/Dickens Gebhardt just made it to the finish (running on fumes) and we had to settle for second place.

Still, it was a good result for a maiden race. However, celebrating on Sunday evening at our hotel in Monza, where most teams were staying, I became involved in a conversation which nearly resulted in dire consequences.

At the bar, I mentioned to one of the team bosses that I was worried about changes in the power base at the FIA, and my conviction that these did not bode well for the future of sports car racing. I was surprised at how many team managers and principals agreed. The conversation led to the possibility of breaking ranks with the FIA and creating an independent more aggressively promoted championship. Contact numbers were exchanged and it was left that we would meet at a Heathrow hotel the following week with a view to making a plan.

When I arrived back at the office on Tuesday morning, waiting in reception was an old mate from F5000 days whom I hadn't seen for ten years. He was not the jolly chap I used to know, but I took him to my office thinking it would be fun to catch up on old times. However he made it clear he had no time for social niceties and went straight to the point.

Fred (name changed): 'Gordon, my boss (name omitted) didn't like what you were saying at Monza on Sunday. In fact he's quite angry.'

Me: 'So sorry, Fred, but I only said what I believe and several people agreed. And by the way, f...k your boss.'

Fred: 'You have a five-year-old son, Patrick, don't you?'

Me: 'Yes... but so what?'

Fred: 'At Virginia Water pre-prep isn't he?'

Me: 'Yes... but what are you getting at?'

Fred, very coldly: 'You wouldn't want anything to happen to him would you?'

... And without a further word, he stood up and left.

I was totally gob-smacked, and sat in shock as his words sunk in. The threat was chilling and hit the most vulnerable spot: certainly not one I was prepared to put to the test. In other words, I chickened out and cancelled the Heathrow meeting. It was scant comfort to later be proved right, but the incident was proof that the politics of motor racing can be as dangerous as the sport itself.

Le Mans 1986 at Mierré was the usual frantic week-long bash and the party included my whole family. Georges Dubois, that year's local mayor, took Patrick (aged five) off in his tractor and then produced a Polaroid of him driving it on his own! Georges had put the tractor in low gear, leapt off leaving Patrick at the wheel, took the photo and then jumped back on.

Georges was over 70 years old and Creech was furious.

Jean-Michel Martin, now an experienced endurance man, joined the team as third driver. Qualifying went suspiciously well and we concentrated on finding the right balance between straightline speed and fuel economy.

We were well in contention for the first 12 hours, swapping the lead with the Ecosse, but then the pace car appeared and stayed out for two hours. Jo Gartner, in the Kremer 962 Porsche, fatally hit the barriers on the long straight from Tertre Rouge, breaking his neck. He was a popular chap in the ascendancy of his career, and the Kremer brothers withdrew their other car.

Shortly after the racing started again, our clutch, which was becoming increasingly spongy, virtually gave up the ghost. Leaving the pits was a gear-crunching exercise and we expected the gearbox to expire at any time. For the last few pit stops the only way to leave was to find first gear, jack up the rear wheels, clear the crowd, start the engine and give it enough revs to keep going when it was dropped off the jack! Initially the pit marshals weren't too happy, but they soon caught the never-say-die spirit.

Against all the odds the crew kept the car circulating to the end: we were the last classified finisher, in 19th position and 6th in class. We completed exactly 100 laps less than the winning factory Porsche of Derek Bell and Hans Stuck!

Anyone who has competed at Le Mans will confirm that the most satisfying thing is to finish. From the celebrations afterwards, onlookers could be forgiven for thinking we'd won!

The Nürburgring 1,000km saw the Eifel mountains at their worst. Such wet conditions bordered on impossible and several cars crashed out early on. The crawling pace of the safety car, combined with zero visibility, caused a further horrific accident: unsighted in the rooster tails of spray, C1 cars ploughed into the back of the pack at speed. I was standing near the scene opposite the pits and the eerie sound of crashing cars, which you could not see, was something I'll never forget. The race was red-flagged and the remaining cars sent to Parc Fermé.

Amazingly there were no major injuries. The German organisers at ADAC decided to continue, with the two parts scored on aggregate. During the three-hour break we – in company with others – repaired our car. This was illegal and several teams used it as an excuse to withdraw, but the organisers – bless 'em – stuck to their guns. This dramatic race was won by Mike Thackwell and Pescarolo: it was the new Sauber Mercedes' only win of the season. We came third behind Ecosse and Gebhardt.

The August meeting at Jerez coincided with son Patrick's bucket-and-spade holiday with Creech in Spain. Ray and his Dad had arranged to pick us up from Gerona in their plane. The night before we'd been go-karting with friends and I'd been involved in a major pile up. I felt no pain at the time – can't think why – but on Friday morning awoke with all the symptoms of cracked ribs.

I was in agony, but on the flight to Jerez Tony Bellm came to the rescue with a concoction of pain relievers: by Saturday's qualifying I could move again.

On Sunday's 360km Supersprint race, I took the start stuffed with painkillers, leaving Ray to do the hard work. We netted a class win and fifth overall, and next day I returned to the beach.

For the penultimate round at Spa, Ecosse – with support from Austin Rover – brought in the quick Belgian driver Mark Duez to partner Ray Mallock. In the race, attempting to pass Will Hoy in Hugh Chamberlain's pole-setting Tiga-Hart, I had my first race spin of the season. Towards the end, attempts to catch the leading Ecosse with Duez at the wheel came to

Top GM stylist John Cafaro, with Captain Morgan on hand!

John Cafaro's original sketch of the Pontiac Spice-Fiero, drawn on a paper tablecloth at Le Mans in 1985.

nought, and we had to settle for second place.

The Spa result was enough to secure the 1986 Drivers' Championship, but ADA were leading the Teams' contest on 54 points; we had 53 points, and Ecosse were on 50 points.

Originally we'd planned not to go to Fuji for the last round in October, but a sponsorship deal with Japanese medical instruments firm Omron, organised by ex-Dome friends at Hyashi Racing, made the trip viable. And what a busy trip it turned out to be: the egg trick was performed at numerous press parties and we all became accomplished karaoke singers!

Finding the way around Japan was a nightmare with all road signs in the local hieroglyphics, not to mention Hertz's infuriating tamper-proof speed alarm buzzer that came in ear-piercingly at 50mph. Traffic jams in Tokyo made it far quicker to walk anywhere and three-tier motorways running at ten-storey height through the city did little to help.

In the race we were easily the fastest car but dogged by more punctures than we had suffered all season: the techies put it down to exceptional surface temperatures. Ecosse's third successive win earned them a well-deserved C2 Team Championship, beating us by two points.

Meanwhile, back at the factory orders were starting to roll in for new cars, based on the 1986 design, from both the States and Europe. Premises were taken in Atlanta to run our works IMSA cars and service customer cars,

and Julian Randles, an ex-Theodore F1 man, was put in charge of the operation. And what an excellent job he did, creating a highly motivated and professional outfit whilst never forgetting the importance of the fun factor. Most of the mechanics were ex-pats and, boy, did they know how to party.

In the IMSA series, Camel Lights was a class within GTP: similar to C2 but with a maximum engine capacity of 3 litres and a minimum weight of 1,800lb. The first car delivered, using GM's 330bhp four-cylinder engine, weighed in at 1,650lb and had to be ballasted, but it was competitive straight out of the box, winning in only its third race.

The regular Fiero driver was Bob Earl, who was top class, winning several races in his first season. He was also driving in the GTU class, so when the classes were combined in the same race, or Bob needed a co-driver for a long race, Ray or I would fly out and fill in. Bob and I led our first race at Riverside by over a lap at half distance and then electrical gremlins robbed us of victory. Ray and Bob later went on to win at Charlotte by a convincing six laps.

Pontiac didn't win Camel Lights that year but we'd done enough to be signed up for 1987. Meantime, the Atlanta factory was flat out assembling customer and team cars, with components shipped out from Silverstone.

The future of Spice USA looked bright, as did the company's prospects in the City.

Chapter 20

The road to market

The year to September 1984 was another good one for our company. Again sales increased by a modest £1 million to £16.2 million, but profits rose to £475,000. Due to losses rolled forward from the bad years, we were still not paying Corporation Tax, and net assets rose to £1.4 million.

As was related in the preceding chapter, towards the end of the year Spice Engineering Ltd was formed from the ashes of a cancelled Ford racing contract. Ray Bellm, who had proved to be no mean sports car driver, bought into the assets of what had been GS Racing and became a 50 per cent shareholder. Equally important, Ray's business acumen made a major contribution to SEL's future success.

Another record year in 1985 saw sales of £18.8 million and a corresponding increase in profit. Higher sales were due to a buoyant marketplace, and higher margins largely down to the HIAWS promotion. After a slow start, the distribution business looked promising and both the Leicester and Watford warehouses came into their own. By the end of the year we were delivering to 360 garage forecourts and 38 out-of-town supermarkets. With the increasingly higher specification of new cars the traditional accessory market was stagnant, so it was essential to introduce new products to sustain growth.

Charles Tippet and I spent much of our time preparing for entry to the Unlisted Securities Market by way of a share placing. This involved finding a suitable broker to sponsor the placing, appointing a financial PR firm, changing accountants to one of the big five, and countless City meetings. Managers spent time with the City 'grey suits' who visited the warehouses to see the business in action for themselves.

The chemistry between our advisors and ourselves was an important element. After the usual beauty parades we settled for brokers Capel, Cure, Myers (CCM) to sponsor the float and what a good choice it turned out to be. Even by City standards they were a no-nonsense, heavy-drinking bunch who worked hard and played even harder. Bob Lederman was the Partner in charge and, by amazing coincidence, Tim Worlledge, one of Creech's favourite cousins, was appointed to look after us.

The opulence of the City, the amount of champagne consumed and the vibrant atmosphere were real eye-openers – heady times indeed. The plan was to float on the USM in September 1985, subject to a clean bill of health by Reporting Accountants Coopers & Lybrand.

Spice Engineering, following a lucrative contract with General Motors' Pontiac Division, was running profitably, and winning the C2 class in the 1985 FIA World Endurance Championship had attracted orders for new cars. I was therefore not on the back foot when our motor racing involvement was questioned by the City – it could be justified on purely financial grounds. Entertaining our City folk at race meetings helped convert the doubters.

As D-Day to market flotation approached, an inordinate amount of time was spent with CCM preparing the share placing prospectus. Meetings went on for hours, involving brokers, accountants, lawyers and financial PR people. Every word was agonised over, with the professionals (charging by the hour) determined to justify their exorbitant fees. Coverdale it was not!

I was becoming increasingly concerned by not having any idea of the likely share price. I was told that the price would depend on 'market conditions' at the time and it would be the last decision to be made, which gave me an uneasy feeling. Just ten days to go before the big day, the prospectus was finally put to bed. Then disaster struck.

The London Stock Exchange conduct their own security checks on key personnel involved in any flotation. The bombshell hit when a telex arrived from the Exchange claiming that David Roberts, the Group's Financial Controller, had criminal form.

No one could believe it – if it was true the float would have to be aborted. We were only persuaded when a courier arrived at Staines with a newspaper cutting showing David Roberts being led from Court, freshly convicted of fraud!

February 1986: for the record and signed by Brian Winterflood, a leading stockbroker on the Unlisted Securities Market.

Roberts was a respected member of the management team: approachable, good with people and a competent accountant. I personally held Roberts in high regard and had him earmarked as a potential future MD. How wrong I was…

It transpired that Roberts had adopted the identity of a qualified accountant who had the same date of birth and was of similar appearance, but had emigrated to South Africa several years earlier. Before employing him, Jonathan Bailey had done the usual Criminal Records Office and Institute of Accountancy checks and his references were impeccable.

On confronting Roberts he came clean. So clean, in fact, that he admitted nicking over £80,000 from the company, which we'd never have known about – unbelievably, he'd done it during the weeks before flotation when Head Office was crawling with accountants! He was suspended and sent home, and Charles Tippet and his team set about trying to find the missing funds.

After two days, they were no closer to finding the money than when they started, so, despite the damage to Charles' professional pride, I insisted they ask Roberts how he had done it? We knew that he sometimes called in temporary help for tasks like bank reconciliation. What we did not know was that one helper was his father-in-law and the other a friend – both in cahoots. The scam was Roberts writing company cheques to bogus suppliers, not recording them in the books, and rolling forward the money as accruals in the bank reconciliation. Very simple, and, with the volume of money going through our bank account, very hard to rumble.

The float had to be postponed to 'some time next year'. Coopers and Lybrand undertook a thorough investigation (more expense), mainly to establish the integrity of our accounting systems, as if they hadn't done so already! Even today their report makes fascinating reading: referring to the bank reconciliation, they dismissively cover their backsides by stating 'We have not pursued this matter as the precise arithmetic is not material.'

Fair enough, I suppose… the report only ran to 60 pages!

Recently Roberts had been seen driving a Porsche 928, which he claimed had been lent to him by an overseas friend but was actually paid for with his ill-gotten gains. He'd used the rest of the money for a deposit on a new flat in Windsor, where he was living. Naturally we had to make provision in the accounts for the

1st. DAY DEALINGS
on
Unlisted Securities Market
(U.S.M.)

CONGRATULATIONS

Date: 20th FEB 86
COUNTY BISGOOD LIMITED
COPTHALL HOUSE,
48 COPTHALL AVENUE,
LONDON EC2R 7DN.

A classic cash till

Before going public, it was decided to change the name of the company from Gordon Spice Limited to Spice plc. When we went to register the new name we were told it could not be done, as the name Spice had been registered and paid for. After tracking down the owner, who specialised in registering names, I went to see him at his home in North London.

I explained that we were trying to move our small company upmarket and Spice Ltd would give us a snappier image than the old name. No mention was made of the plc plan, and we finally settled on a price of £1,000, subject to his partner's agreement. Time was not on our side and I needed to do a deal there and then, so I persuaded him to take a cheque and he'd phone me next day to confirm his partner's consent. I was not entirely happy because he could still change his mind.

On leaving, I noticed in his hall an attractive 1930s all-singing all-dancing brass cash register. After establishing it was for sale (he was that sort of chap), some good-humoured haggling followed and I ended up giving him a cheque for £500. My thinking was that if he ratted on the Spice name deal I would stop the cheque and end up with a free trophy.

To this day kids still enjoy playing on my Jewish Piano.

missing money and that, as I'll now explain, turned out to be the upside of this sorry saga.

Originally, based on projected profits of £580,000 (to year ending 30 Sept 1985, allowing for the fraud), 2.9 million 5p shares were to be offered at a price of 70p each. With issued capital of 7.75 million shares this would have given the company a market capitalisation of £5.4 million, representing a price/earnings ratio of a modest 9:1.

However, before the accounts were signed off in December the whole £80,000 had been recovered, and this unexpected windfall dropped straight to the bottom line. After allowing provision for the ongoing 'rainy day' fund, for year ended September 1985 we announced a profit of £650,000. The City was ecstatic!

When we finally floated in February 1986, with a share price of 80p, the market capitalisation was £6.2 million. That healthy £800,000 increase was some consolation for the costs and aggro that Roberts had put us through.

After the hype of the build up, the last minute postponement was a big downer. It was too late to cancel our planned 'Spice Spectacular' promotion celebrating the flotation, so this went ahead. The highlight of the day was flying customers in eight small helicopters, decorated in company livery, from Denham airport to the London Barrier and back, following the river Thames.

It was a popular promotion with over 200 customers, plus what seemed like half the staff, qualifying for the ride. As far as the float was concerned, customers were unaffected and in the build up to Christmas that year the tills were red hot.

In January 1986 it was back to the grindstone, with more prospectus meetings, more late nights and more costs. This time I did not have brother Dee's comforting presence, as he was going through a difficult patch in his personal life and had taken leave of absence. As a major shareholder the City would not allow him to resign, contending it would undermine investor confidence.

Early in the morning on the 20 February 1986, 13 of us sat around a grand table in our best suits, armed with our best pens, signing countless copies of the final papers. Dee, dressed for the South of France, turned up to make his contribution, and the sober mood of the occasion was lifted when he scrawled his outsize signature on each document using the thickest red felt-tip pen I have ever seen!

We went off to the Stock Exchange to watch the first day of Spice plc share dealings. The majority of shares had been pre-placed with institutional investors but trading was brisk and the price closed at 86p. I had considered the 80p striking price to be too low, expecting them at least to break the £1 mark, but again the City were right. My disappointment was short-lived as I took heart from my newfound wealth...

Chapter 21

A spooky sponsor
and other tales

For the 1987 season, Ray Bellm decided to take a break to concentrate on his pharmaceutical business and there was fierce competition for his seat in the team car. We were looking not only for a fast reliable driver, but one with a decent budget – a somewhat rare combination! After testing several contenders we settled on Spaniard Fermin Velez and we drove together throughout the season. Fermin was an amazing little chap, only five feet four inches tall,

Spice SE87C at Monza – Fermin Velez driving.

extremely fit, non-smoking, non-drinking and seriously intense. He could never work out why I was normally a bit quicker, my best time always set on the second lap of qualifying, when the tyres were at optimum temperature. He was never sure whether to believe that I tried harder, working off a hangover.

Fermin was always accompanied by his manager, Raimon Duran, a cheerful, chubby and sociable character, devoted to Fermin's

Le Mans, 1987: first in C2 and sixth overall!

Le Mans scrutineering, 1987: Philippe de Henning, GS and Fermin Velez.

career. Fermin went on to a successful sports car career in the USA where, as a leading driver in the IMSA series, Raimon's early nurturing paid dividends. Raimon and Fermin were complete opposites, but without Raimon's pushiness I suspect the shy Fermin would never have made it. My partnership with Fermin worked well and we became good friends.

The season started with a supersprint race at Jarama where, in Danone livery (Fermin's sponsor), we romped to a class win. A week later at the Jerez 1,000km we won again, achieving the team's best-ever result of fourth overall. These two races saw Fermin becoming a firm favourite with Spanish fans, and at the end of the season he was voted Spain's 'Sportsman of the Year'.

Monza in April marked the first appearance of Hugh Chamberlain's team, with Nick Adams and Costas Los driving their new Spice-Hart SE87C. Early in the race they challenged for the lead – there was no doubt about the pace of the car – until their turbo blew, but it was an encouraging debut. I spun away the lead at Lesmo, but a fine last stint by Fermin saved the day, and we took the class win after a late chase by David Leslie in the Ecosse. Hugh Chamberlain, one of sports cars' true gentle-

men, stayed loyal to the Spice marque for the next three years, winning the C2 class in 1989, with Adams and Velez sharing the honours.

In C1, Tom Walkinshaw's re-engineered Jaguar XJR8s had taken over Porsche's dominance by winning the first four rounds of the 1987 season.

1987 Le Mans

The 1987 Le Mans 24-hours produced a spookily strange scenario for our team. It started with an approach to Jeff Hazell by Frenchman Philippe de Henning to be the main sponsor of SEL at Le Mans. He had come up with an innovative idea for raising serious sponsorship. He had persuaded six organisations to put up (say) £50,000 each, and there would be a draw to establish who would win the main sponsor title. The winner, whose livery the car would bear, would be obliged to offer corporate hospitality to X number of guests for each of the five non-winners. The five would have logos on the car and recognition in press releases, but their contribution would be capped at £50k. We would only know the winner a month before the race.

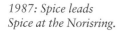

1987: Spice leads Spice at the Norisring.

We were sold on the scheme and took de Henning's deposit.

Then the bombshell. Dianetics, the face of Ron L. Hubbard's Church of Scientology, had won the draw. Unfortunately, only days before, the cult had been featured on a well publicised BBC TV documentary and the revelations had been damning. Financially SEL were committed, so we phoned our regular sponsors to explain the dilemma. It proved not to be the problem we'd expected and they were happy that we carry their logos.

At Tuesday's scrutineering, the Scientologists turned out in full force, handing out team jackets and hats in the Dianetics colours, yellow and black. They had a fetish about black and Philippe, who was staying at Mierré, even had black underwear! Driving in practice you couldn't help noticing the groups of black-clad supporters all around the circuit, waving and cheering whenever the car went by.

It was all most weird, but they were friendly people who did not bother us once we'd made it clear we were not potential converts.

Practice went well, and we qualified 25th overall, second in C2 just behind Chamberlain's Spice-Hart entry.

Thankfully, unlike with Hawaiian Tropic we attracted little attention on the grid and settled into the race, sticking to our usual conservative race plan. By 10:00pm, we were up to 15th overall, trading the class lead with Ecosse, and at half distance (4:00am) we were 10th overall, three places adrift of the Ecosse. Philippe was off the pace so Fermin and I double-stinted through the night.

At the 18-hour mark we took the class lead and incredibly found ourselves in sixth position overall, with only four Porsches and the remaining Cheever/Lammers Jaguar in front. Egged on by the enthusiastic Dianetics tribe, who hadn't moved from their spots for 24 hours, we held sixth till the end of the race.

Stuck/Bell won in a Porsche, the Jaguar was fifth and ours was the best result ever for a C2 car at Le Mans.

Each year the Le Mans Chamber of Commerce award the Montenay-Econergy Trophy, worth 150,000 French francs to the first three cars in the Index of Performance. No one understood how it worked and we had always assumed it was a typical French thing, destined to be won by a French team. However, we had been proved wrong the previous year when we had won it coming last.

C2 Spice leads Stuck/Bell Porsche 962 at the Norisring!

1987 Guild Award

In October 1987 I received a telephone call from someone claiming to be a journalist and committee member of the Guild of Motoring Writers. He told me I had been shortlisted for their 1987 'Driver of the Year' award. My immediate reaction was that this was a wind-up by a friend, but he eventually convinced me it was true. He asked me if I'd be free on Thursday 3 December to attend the awards dinner? So, to give me time to think, I said I'd check my diary and call him back. The last thing I needed was to be a bridesmaid at such a dinner.

When I called back I told him that I was supposed to be racing in Guyana the following weekend, but if I'd won I'd postpone my flight and attend the dinner. If I hadn't won, they would have to go ahead without me. There was a long silence, enough to think maybe I'd pushed my luck too far. Then, to my utter amazement, he told me I had been chosen, but swore me to secrecy and told me to be suitably surprised when the moment came.

This gave me time to find out more about it and I discovered in the Guild's annual Year Book, *Who's Who in the Motor Industry*, that the citation read: 'Awarded annually to the driver of any nationality who, in any make of car, or in any event (or events), shows such skill, courage, initiative or endurance – or a combination of any of theses qualities – as to single him or her out, in the opinion of the Guild, as Driver of the Year.'

Bloody hell!

An illustrated lap of Brands in a Group C car. It was used for a Spice staff outing and we were beaten by Ecosse!

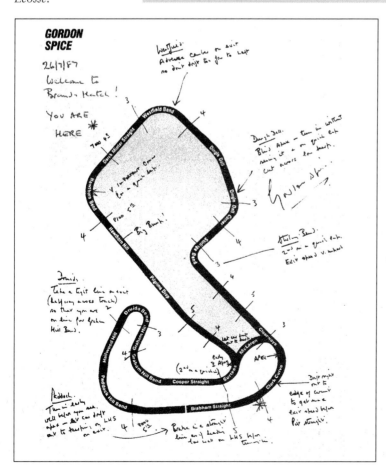

This year we were pipped to the post by the Ecosse, which had come eighth overall at an average speed of 188kph against our average of 190kph. Interesting to see C2 cars filling the first four places.

A week later I received a copy of the Dianetics book with a letter from the President of the Church of Scientology International, one Heber C. Jentzsch. The dedication read: 'For your personal library to commemorate this fine outreach on your part'. I found it worked better than sleeping pills.

My lasting memory of the Nuremberg round in Germany was of the late Brian Kreisky. Brian, who owned Videovision and attended all WSPC rounds, was a popular and outrageous character who claimed to be an Iranian Jew. Standing on the same impressive edifice where Hitler had reviewed his troops 45 years before, Brian performed his theatrical Führer act in front of the bemused German fans. Highly politically incorrect – only Brian could have got away with it!

At the Brands Hatch 1,000km in July, after Fermin came in with a healthy lead for the final handover the car wouldn't start, and we lost the lead to Ecosse whilst the battery was changed. It was their second win of the season in front of the home crowd. Most annoying.

At the Nürburgring a month later, starter motor gremlins hit again on the last pit stop.

The stewards spotted our push start in the pit lane, resulting in disqualification. It was the only race of the season where we failed to score points.

Wins at Nuremberg and Spa had secured Fermin his first FIA C2 Drivers' title, and me my third. But the Team's C2 title was still unresolved, due to Ecurie Ecosse running two cars for the season. So we had to go to Fuji for the last round…

At Fuji, to quote Janos Wimpffen's definitive work on sports car racing: 'The Spice duo led the entire way in a rather anticlimactic finish to the last title to be decided for 1987.' And that's exactly how it was. We had scored eight class victories, winning the Teams' Cup by 13 points and the Drivers' by 28.

Team morale was at an all-time high.

In the USA, where SEL had produced cars for Pontiac to run in three IMSA categories, the season had started well with a win in the Daytona 24-hour race, followed by second in the Miami 3-hours and third in the Sebring 12-hours. This was followed by eight wins from 13 races ranging from 300km to 500 miles, and was sufficient to give Pontiac the Camel Lights championship. It was the first time a US car-maker had won an IMSA Manufacturers' title and – being the blue-eyed boys – we signed up to do it again in 1988.

One of the spin-offs of the US success was that orders for IMSA-spec cars rolled in, not only for Pontiac Fiero-powered cars, but for V6s and V8s from GM. Monocoques and components were shipped from Silverstone and assembled at the Atlanta factory, bodywork being made locally. Additionally, we ran a three-car 'works' team for 1988, with prestigious sponsors like Minolta, AT&T and Entech.

The operation of the US team, with Julian Randles in control, brought a new standard in presentation of both cars and team. No team member was allowed on the grid without freshly laundered team gear every time, and car preparation areas were carpeted and spotless. Other teams followed but it was the Brits who showed them how.

Whenever I visited the US there was always one journalist who singled me out at the circuits, asking technical questions I could rarely answer. He doggedly came back time after time and said he was writing a book on the history of sports car racing: I could never remember his name and thought little more

Parade lap at Le Mans, 1988: GS, Ray Bellm and Pierre de Thoisy.

Le Mans, 1988: new Spice SE88C – first in C2 and 13th overall.

about it. In 1999 he produced a two-volume history entitled *Time and Two Seats – Five Decades of Long Distance Racing*. It runs to 2,250 pages detailing every major sports car endurance race from 1953 to 1998. Without it I would have been lost trying to recall what happened and where.

Thank you, Janos Wimpffen!

From mid-1987, Graham Humphrys somehow found time to work on a major development of the original Fiero race car, and produced drawings for the SE88C Spice. No major modifications were made to the modular monocoque which had been engineered to take up to 700bhp, but without styling constraints there were major developments aerodynamically. These included improved effect tunnels under the car, and a more compact cockpit, allowing better airflow to the centrally mounted rear wing, which now fed its loads into the chassis rather than the body. The new package included improved brake ducting and larger discs as an update kit for customer cars.

We were on a roll and totally focused on producing faster cars. SEL monopolised the graveyard shift at Southampton University's wind tunnel for several weeks before the design was finalised. Development costs were well over half a million pounds, which was greater than a full season's racing budget. Most racing teams' culture is driven by the pursuit of better performance, and financial realities tend to

take second place. This is why so many small manufacturers fail to make old age, and we were falling into the trap.

1988

Following several approaches by drivers with access to serious sponsorship it was decided to run a two-car works team in 1988. Thorkild Thyrring, an ambitious Dane and the best self-promoter I have met, was paired up with Almo Coppelli, a charismatic and quick Italian. Thorkild always kept his financial end up, but by halfway through the season it was only Almo's promises – and charm – that kept him in the seat.

I was pleased when Ray decided to share the other car with me; the German Supercup, which he'd won the previous year, had kept his interest alive and his businesses were going well. Wish I could have said the same for mine!

Jeff Hazell, with an expanding SEL business to manage and plans for C1 next year, recruited Mick Franklin as Team Manager and an excellent choice he proved to be. His Formula 1 career ran from 1980 to 1987 and included being race engineer for Reggazoni, Jones, Mansell, Rosberg and Patrese. Ray and I bagged him to engineer our car, leaving Jeff to the second car. It was the right decision and Mick played a significant role in our good fortune.

The season kicked off with an 800km race at Jerez, where the strong C2 entry, including five Spices, outnumbered the C1s. Chamberlain had entered a new SE88C for Claude Ballot-Lena and Jean Louis Ricci (of the French perfume family), and his 1987 car for Nick Adams and Graham Duxberry. In addition, Costas Los, who had bought last year's Spice, was entered with Philippe de Henning as co-driver: at least the Dianetics cash was still in the SEL family. In Jerez, we won the class from Costas Los, with the other works car of Thyrring/Coppelli retiring with throttle problems.

A week later at the Jarama Supersprint, Ray and I finished first again (seventh overall) after de Henning had squandered second place in Costas's car. Spice chassis filled the next three places in a C2 whitewash in the order Ricci, Thyrring and Adams. But the Martin Schanche/Will Hoy Argo had shown real pace early on, so it was no time for complacency.

At the Silverstone 1,000km there was home-crowd pressure on Jaguar to win, although Jean Louis Schlesser putting the Sauber-Mercedes on pole did not bode well. As it transpired, Jaguar's Cheever and Brundle took the overall win with the two Saubers just behind.

In C2 Spices, Costas Los had replaced Philippe de Henning with Wayne Taylor, a talented young South African who went on to drive many of our cars and became an IMSA champion. At Silverstone, Ray and I were delayed with electrical problems, as were Taylor and Los, so we ended up second in class behind Thyrring and Coppelli. It was a good team result and gave confidence to the newcomers that winning races was not our sole prerogative.

1988 Le Mans

This year Jeff Hazell had invited Eliseo Salazar, the ex-F1 Chilean driver who he knew from his Williams days, to share the second car with Thorkild and Almo. Jeff always rated Salazar highly and expected him to blow off us part-timers. Ray and I shared with Frenchman Pierre de Thoisy, who bought serious Rexona (soap) sponsorship with him. Pierre was a charming chap who enjoyed the social side as much as us. Having crashed Walter Brun's Porsche 962 out of last year's race, we hoped Pierre had learnt his lesson. As it turned out he drove consistently all weekend.

Practice went well and Ray and I had a quiet laugh when we qualified with a time of 3m 37s against the Chilean hero's time of 3m 41s – maybe we'd get some respect from now on! This put us second in class behind Chamberlain's Hart-powered SE87C driven by

Spice SE88C at Le Mans in 1988 with Ray Bellm at the wheel. (LAT)

Nick Adams on a time of 3m 30s with the wick turned up. We reckoned the race pace would be around the 3m 45s mark, so we weren't too worried.

Up front, the two Sauber Mercedes were withdrawn when Klaus Neidzwiedz's tyre exploded in the Mulsanne kink at well over 200mph, and he was lucky to be alive. Everyone sympathised with Peter Sauber's decision, recalling that the last time a Mercedes had run at Le Mans (in 1955) had been the occasion of the worst tragedy in motor racing history.

We stuck to our usual race plan, focusing on giving the car an easy ride and minimum time in the pits. Most drivers have no problem with driving for 24 hours, and with a long rest on the Mulsanne Straight every lap – albeit at 220mph – it is one of the less demanding circuits. It's the mechanics who are the real heroes. For them there is no let up, mentally or physically, for they know that one mistake can end in retirement, or worse...

After a tense battle, the Lammers/Dumfries Jaguar took a historic victory, finishing on the same lap as the Stuck/Bell Porsche. After a steady run we came 13th overall, winning C2 by over 200 miles. The Salazar car came 25th but a late engine blow-up meant it was not classified as a finisher.

July marked the first race at Brno, billed as 'The Czechoslovakian Grand Prix', and our weekend did not start well. We had flown to Vienna, hired a car and crossed the Czech border, overlooked by menacing, fully-manned guard towers, reminding us this was still an Iron Curtain country. On arriving in the beautiful city of Brno, we stopped alongside a parked police car to ask for directions to our hotel.

'Passports please,' was the response, so we dutifully handed them over.

Next question: 'Do you have dollars?'

'No, we have no dollars – how do we find Hotel Vilja?' It soon became clear we'd be off to the slammer if we didn't pay a stiff fine for parking illegally whilst talking to them! No passports, no argument, so we paid up – no receipt, of course. This was one of their many ways of fleecing tourists, who were easily identified by their hire cars.

In the evening the hotel bar was overrun with the largest selection of eye-watering crumpet imaginable – all keen to practise their English. Thorkild was not interested but the smooth Almo was in his element. Having accompanied one of these lovelies home to the suburbs one evening, Almo appeared at breakfast next morning very much the worse for wear. Returning in the small hours, he had been stopped no less than six times by the police. It was only thanks to the last lot, who happened to be racing fans and escorted him home, that he made it at all, stony broke at 4:00am! For the first time, Thorkild was quicker in qualifying.

On race day the crowd was enormous, most of them walking to the circuit, and they were introduced to sports cars with a cliffhanger of a race. I took the start in fuel-saving mode and Ray took the class lead (seventh overall) three laps from the end when the Coppelli car ran short of fuel, as did Los. Five Spices started and five finished, filling the top C2 places in the order Bellm, Coppelli, Los, Ricci and Adams. In C1 the Sauber-Merc of Mass/Schlesser just pipped the TWR Jags.

At Brands Hatch in July there was an early session behind the pace car, following one of the C2 cars taking out the Sauber in a colossal accident. Ray and I were delayed by electrical problems halfway through, but with no fuel constraints we drove flat out, passing our teammates towards the end to finish fourth overall. Our sixth win of the season was enough to secure the 1988 Team C2 World Championship for Spice Engineering and the Drivers' title for

1987: receiving the Guild award from Lord Strathcarron.

1987 Guild Award Speech

'Good evening, my Lords, Ladies and gentlemen. I am not being allowed to let this moment pass without saying a few words – something far more frightening than driving any racing car.

'When I was told about this evening, which I must admit I thought was a wind-up, I bought a copy of your annual Year Book. Being a typical racing driver, I immediately turned to the section entitled "World's top racing driver" to see if I was included – surprisingly I was.

'Among the 164 entries – I counted them – I noticed I was not the oldest driver listed – there are several American "ole boys" who give me great hope for the future. However, I have to admit to being older than Derek Bell – that is if he is telling the truth.

'So I guess those of you who voted for me did so on the basis of the "endurance" part of the citation.

'When I won my first F5000 race at Oulton Park – it also turned out to be my last – the race report in the *Daily Mail* referred to "Veteran driver, Gordon Spice". That was in 1975.

'Correct me if I'm wrong, Lord Montague, but a veteran car is one built prior to 1905; a vintage car is one built between 1905 and 1931; anything after 1931 is known as a post-vintage thoroughbred – as long as it has the pedigree!

'I therefore have a serious request to make of members of the Guild: please do not refer to me as either veteran or vintage, and only as post-vintage thoroughbred, if you think I have the breeding.

'My rise to the dizzy heights of tonight could hardly be called meteoric. I remember my first season – 1962, it was

– at the end of which my CV read, races entered: 6; qualified to start: 4; race starts achieved: 2; race finishes: 0.

'Naturally I blamed the car – at least I had learnt something about being a racing driver – but secretly I began to wonder if the old adage was true "If at first you don't succeed, failure may be your style."

'Twenty-five years later, how things have changed:

'Wearing racing overalls is no longer seen as posing.

'Tents have been replaced by flash motorhomes.

'But most important of all, I've found a formula where the chap who uses least fuel has the best chance of becoming a World Champion!

'It's been said that behind every successful man stands an astonished woman. My wife, Mandy, happens to be that woman and because she's here tonight, and all the other people who've helped me are not, I'd like to acknowledge the support she has given me over the past 14 years – in both my racing and business careers.

'That support has taken many forms:

'Cooking for 48 hours for 50 mechanics.

'Chatting up the Press, sponsors, stockbrokers and bank managers.

'Prising me out of the bar the night before practice.

'And all in addition to being a housewife and a Mum.

'Anyway, I know that she, along with the Spice Engineering Team, would wish to join me in thanking the Guild for this award – a terrific boost for C2 sports car racing and a very great personal honour.'

Ray and I. I just wished Spice plc was going as well – but more of that anon.

At the Nürburgring 1,000km the ADAC made it a two-part race, one being run at night. It turned out to be a crazy idea as the circuit was simply not prepared for night racing: drivers could see neither the kerbs nor the flags and the pace car had to be sent out to end the practice session. In appalling race conditions,

Ray was leading when he was unlucky enough to hit a spinning Ricci: we retired with engine problems after 75 laps.

After the Sunday day race, won on aggregate by the Sauber, the C2 honours went to the Tiga of the happy-go-lucky Italian Kelmar team. Everyone was delighted for their drivers, Vito Veniata and Pasquale Barberio, who embodied the true spirit of racing.

2007 Guild awards (in the company of real heroes!).

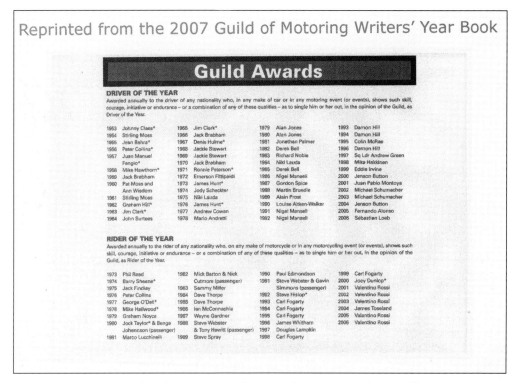

Reprinted from the 2007 Guild of Motoring Writers' Year Book

At Spa in September the Thyrring/Coppeli car enjoyed its second win of the season, and we came second. It was Almo's last race for the team and we were sad to lose him. His sponsorship had run out, and he was replaced by Eliseo Salazar for the last two races.

At Fuji in November, Ray and I were again out of luck with a rare engine failure, four hours into the race when leading. The Cheever/Brundle Jaguar had another win. After a trouble-free run Thorkild and Eliseo took C2 class honours.

The last race, at Sandown Park, saw the end of our dry spell since the Nürburgring. C2 cars outnumbered C1 by eleven to seven. After qualifying fifth overall, our best result ever, we also finished fifth with an easy class win.

It had been a stunning season, with ten SEL Team wins out of twelve races, Ray and I taking seven of them and the second car three. Our team had taken its third Team title, Ray his third Drivers' Championship, and it was my fourth. In that drivers' contest, Thorkild came second, Almo third. Hugh Chamberlain's team were runners-up in C2. We couldn't have asked for more.

In C1, Martin Brundle took the Drivers' title, and in the Manufacturers' Championship Tom Walkinshaw's Jaguar team won from Sauber (Mercedes), Joest (Porsche) and Brun (Porsche), with SEL in fifth spot.

On the way home from Melbourne, I stopped off in Perth to spend a week on the boat of my old mate from the 1950s, Geoff Jacoby. He always spent the Oz summer on his classic timber launch, moored in a bay at Rottnest Island, ten miles off the Perth coast. Nelleck Jol, his long-time Dutch partner, was an amazing lady. An accomplished gymnast who represented Australia in the Olympics, she had pioneered the first gym academies in Australia. Well into her 60s, she still swam at least a mile and ran four miles everyday. We feasted daily on lobster and fish – all caught by Nelleck.

Partying every evening with the other 'boaties' was a great way to unwind before facing the business problems that I knew awaited.

At the beginning of 1988 Spice USA moved to a new purpose-built 10,000ft^2 factory in Atlanta, enabling them to provide full chassis repair and body shop facilities. Providing an instant spare parts service at all circuits to six IMSA teams proved to be a logistical nightmare, but Julian's humour and the commitment of his dedicated team overcame all.

In Camel Lights the team enjoyed an amazing season, with 11 pole positions in 15 races. In the 5-litre GTP class customer cars were showing great potential and Spice chassis now outnumbered all other makes in the IMSA Championship.

Chapter 22

The City road to crisis

Shortly after our 1986 USM listing, in best company tradition we threw a 'thank you' party for all advisors (with partners) involved in the flotation. We booked rooms at Cliveden, Buckinghamshire's grand mansion backdrop to the Profumo scandal of the '60s. Cliveden had only recently opened as a hotel, but delivered a slap-up dinner in their magnificent dining room: goodwill abounded late into the night. Next day I had a vague recollection of someone mentioning that City expectations were for future company growth of at least 30 per cent a year. They must have been joking – or drunk.

Shortly after, the subject was raised again, this time seriously. I asked why this significant revelation had not been mentioned before the float? There was much procrastination but no answer, but at least I held the high moral ground. I explained in some detail that it had taken us 20 years to build a company turnover of £20 million a year and on course to make £1 million profit. I knew that achieving sales of £80 million and profits of £4 million in a five-year timescale was well beyond my ability.

I suggested that they might like to find a new MD? I would understand, no offence taken. I didn't want to appear too keen, but the more I thought about it the more attractive the idea became: far less hassle and more time for racing! A plan was made, a recruitment agency briefed, and the hunt for a new MD with experience in acquisitions began.

The search proved a time-consuming exercise and involved the whole Board. It was impossible to get a total consensus, but eventually the list of candidates was whittled down to a shortlist of two.

Our final choice, 'Kevin', was not as personable as the other finalist but had a better history.

He was known to the City, had an excellent record in larger companies and his references checked out well. Before making a final offer, I spent hours with Kevin, as did my board colleagues, showing how the company worked and agreeing priorities for his first few weeks.

He was a confident negotiator – witness his package of a three-year rolling contract at very high salary. Quite outrageous I thought, but the City were keen.

Kevin's first day at work, 12 January 1987, is implanted in my memory. I moved out of my office, to let it be seen that he really was taking on my role, and moved down the passage into brother Dee's quarters. The very first thing he did was to install a coffee machine in his office. I was not impressed, as this was a cultural change and our tea lady was central to HO bush telegraph. If he'd asked for a cocktail cabinet that would have been more understandable.

We had agreed that Kevin's first week would be spent getting to know staff, customers and key suppliers, as well as gaining a feel for the business. Not a bit of it. He shut himself up in the office, only appearing to complain about the state of my filing system. After two days I insisted that he stick to the agreed plan, but the warning signs were there... and foolishly I ignored them.

After an unimpressive start, Kevin came into his own. He was demanding but fair, and very much better organised than me. On announcing his appointment in the City the share price shot up to £1.38, but I didn't take offence at the implication, since I still had a 24 per cent shareholding.

The most demanding role as Chairman was keeping the peace, but I had more time to spend on motor racing and no longer felt guilty about it.

In the year to 30 September 1986, my last full year at the helm, the company showed a pre-tax profit of over £1 million on sales of £20 million.

Kevin's presentations to brokers and potential investors were full of fire and enthusiasm: the City loved him and the share price rocketed. He even had me convinced that 30 per cent annual growth would be a doddle. However, I was flabbergasted when, after an upbeat forecast of 1987 profits and announcing plans for a National Distribution Centre, the share price hit £2.45! I found it incomprehensible.

Spice plc – looking good in March 1987.

Dee and I always acted together in the sale of our shares and would have happily sold all our shares at that price, but the City had us in golden handcuffs, so we had to be content with less. Shortly after the float, with the company apparently healthy, Dee's resignation was accepted without any adverse investor reactions.

During 1986 plans were made to open a National Distribution Centre (NDC), which would supply garage forecourts and supermarkets, as well as our own cash & carries. It was an ambitious plan but seemed the solution to meeting growth targets.

By early 1987 a suitably central location was selected, adjacent to the M1 in Luton. It just happened to be a stone's throw from MD Kevin's Dunstable home. The warehouse offered a new 50,000ft^2 facility at Woodside Park. The eaves height of 30ft allowed storage of 80,000ft^2, and it was purpose-built for national distribution. A state-of-the-art warehouse, it featured random computer-controlled stock location and virtually automatic order picking, with branches and key customers linked by computer for ordering.

It was a mammoth task and it cost £1.2 million to fit-out the warehouse with floor to ceiling racking, new computers, new offices, and the myriad items of equipment needed. Break-even point would be sales of £40 million, not an unrealistic target if it all worked out. With hindsight, too many eyes were taken off the ball and the core business suffered badly.

Results for the year ended September '87 showed a profit of £1.26 million on sales of £22.6 million. So the City was happy, the share price healthy and Kevin had met his target. I had a nasty gut feeling about these results, but motor racing kept me busy – particularly the American operation – and there seemed no point in having a dog and barking yourself. I was pleased that Spice Engineering had shown a profit of £120,000 to June 1988, which made a useful contribution to the plc's results; even more pleased when the financial press at last acknowledged it.

Meanwhile, we were negotiating to buy Alpha Discount Spares, a successful Leeds-based cash & carry. Following the closure of our Sheffield branch, Alpha would re-establish a presence in the North. I was persuaded the extra £8 million turnover would make a significant contribution to NDC's target, which

COMPANY PROFILE 3

Spice plc

SPICE PLC
Buy @ 138p

We reckon that this motor parts and accessories group is determined to increase its share of a massive market. Through both organic and acquired growth we forecast that it will expand substantially in the next year or so and reckon that its shares are ready to reflect that potential. They are an immediate buy.

Buy Rating 10   TARGET PRICE 200p

In a trade report published 18 months ago the annual turnover at retail prices of the automotive aftermarket was put at £2,064 million. That figure was made up by £1,260 million on replacement parts (excluding tyres and exhausts), £525 million on accessories, tools, and in-car entertainment, and finally £279 million on car-care and chemicals.

The automotive aftermarket is a large and growing one as motorists continue to show an increasing willingness to tackle repairs and maintenance themselves in order to reduce service costs.

There are over 16 million cars on the road in the UK, of which about 86% are over two years old and some 50% are over six years old. The private motorist with a car over two years old is the typical customer for Gordon Spice's company.

Set up way back in 1965 his Spice group has since developed into being the country's largest independently owned cash and carry supply of motor accessories, replacement parts and other related products. It operates four cash and carry warehouses providing one stop shopping for trade customers. It also operates a distribution service to multiple retail outlets. The group's success to date has been built upon the availability and close control of a wide range of products, currently over 20,000 items.

It sources its own supplies from over 400 manufacturers, distributors and importers and, wherever feasible, there are two or three suppliers for each product range.

It has a very wide customer base numbering more than 4,000 clients. High Street accessory and spares shops account for over 56% of its sales, whilst garages with shops or repair/ service facilities represent a further 15%. The balance is made up of sales to fleet users, van factors, motor factors, body repair shops, main agents and other specialist outlets. It carries on a very sales orientated marketing campaign to all of its account holders by way of mailshots and special promotions.

Full use is made of the group's comprehensive computer facility which provides a detailed analysis of individual customer spending patterns, regularity of visits, purchases by product group and current sales trends. This data assists management in evaluating changes in spending

The Unipart sponsored Lamborghini Countach QVX built by Spice Engineering, a 40% owned interest of Spice, that after start up losses should be profitable this year as it progresses the development of new cars for the Pontiac division of General Motors and picks up more export orders.

patterns and product demand enabling sales opportunities to be maximised by both the sales teams within the warehouses and the field sales force.

Over the five years prior to coming onto the USM a year ago group sales had risen from £12.1m in 1981 to £18.8m in the year to end September 1985. In the same period a loss of £49,000 in 1981 was turned into a pre-tax profit of £648,000 by 1985.

A couple of months ago the company announced its results for 1986 and they were good. They saw sales improve 8% to £20.3m and pre-tax profits jump 55% to £1,006,000. Earnings per share increased 27% to 9.5p to 12.1p whilst net assets jumped from £1.9m to £3.5m, some 48p per share.

The company still has some unutilised tax losses, the greater part of which is derived from stock relief from earlier periods, and that reduced the tax charge last year and will do so again this year.

In the latest Report & Accounts chief executive Gordon Spice, 46 years old and owner of 24.5% of the equity, states that "with a strengthened board and a proven middle management team in place, we are not only developing the core business, but actively seeking acquisitions which fit our medium and long term strategic plans. During 1986, time has been spent identifying

target companies and during 1987 these will continue to be pursued."

In other words we may very well soon see an acquisition or two that will boost the group's spread and profits as well as organic growth. With an ungeared balance sheet, backed by £1.2m cash in the bank and an improving share price we suggest that Gordon Spice should move fairly soon in his expansive aims.

The average rating for the motor components sector is 15.5 times historic which would put the shares of Spice straight up to 187p, compared to their currently low rating of 138p, just 11.4 times historic earnings.

We suggest that the shares of the Spice group are ready for a strong upwards run fairly soon as the market begins to anticipate early action, so buy some now.

Fact Sheet   SPICE
FT Motors (Components)
There are three market makers dealing in up to 5,000 shares on a 5p spread.
Came to the USM in February 1986 by way of a Placing by brokers Capel-Cure Myers of 2,886,750 shares @ 80p each.
Issued capital: 7,790,000 ordinary 9p shares
Current market capitalisation: £10,695,000
Board and family interests control 3,388,593 shares, representing 43.7% of the equity.
Company's brokers: Capel-Cure Myers (01 236 5080)
Company's address: 12a Central Trading Estate, Staines, Middlesex TW18 4UX

SPICE Performance				
Year to 30th Sept	Turnover £000's	Pre-tax £000's	Earnings per share	PE ratio
1983	15.4	340	5.2	26.5
1984	16.2	480	7.3	18.9
1985	18.8	650	9.5	14.5
1986	20.3	1,000	12.1	11.4
1987 Est	23.0	1,300	15.0	9.2

made sense. In January 1988 we paid £2.8 million for Alpha: £800,000 in cash, £1 million in convertible loan notes, and the balance in plc shares. As if this wasn't enough, a new cash & carry was planned for Birmingham, with NDC in mind again.

More critically, Kevin was beginning to make what I considered unreasonable demands on Charles Tippet's hard-pressed finance department. Despite my best peace-keeping efforts, this led to Charles's resignation and he left in January 1988. Kevin recruited David Evans as the new FD, making much of his past career, which included being FD of the fast expanding McDonald's chain.

Evans was a grey character, and I never took to him.

The year to September 1988 was disastrous: a cosmetic profit of only £23,000 despite sales increasing to £28.7 million. To avoid a public loss, I knew that the contingency fund had been raided. Unless the new NDC came to the rescue, the future looked grim. It was ironic that Spice Engineering, hitherto a source of suspicion in the City, returned a net profit of £48,000 – hallelujah!

An important profit contribution had traditionally come from the Have It Away With Spice convention-holiday promotion, abandoned when we floated in 1987. This followed strong advice from the City that HIAWS was sailing too close to the wind with Inland Revenue for a plc involvement. We missed the 'conventions' as much as our customers did – the end of an era.

In May 1988, Brian Merry, who had given his all to the company, now gave 12 months' notice of his resignation. Brian had become disenchanted with the increasing financial priorities and he had little in common with Kevin. Brian was not an easy man to manage, but on previous occasions we had worked out our differences. This time there was no turning back, and Brian Merry left in April 1989, working his guts out to the end.

I realised my hands-off approach with Kevin was becoming dangerous and found it impossible to change things without usurping his authority. I tried very hard but the long and the short of it was that he had to go. His resignation was finally agreed in November '88. Infuriatingly, due to his employment contract, he was on full pay until he found another job; he seemed in no hurry. He was a financial drain for a further six months, but worse than that,

I was now back to square one and out of my depth.

Motor racing was put firmly on the back burner: I was not a happy bunny.

By January 1989, it became clear David Evans had lost control of the finances and I no longer accepted his excuses. His departure was no loss at all but, following so soon after Kevin's departure it did not go down well in the City. The dire position of the company was only fully revealed after Evans had gone. After much persuasion, Charles Tippet returned on a consultancy basis to try to sort out the mess.

In the meantime, the NDC project was going from bad to worse. The initial £4 million of stock arrived and was stored in the random

Spice plc – looking dodgy in March 1989.

COUNTY NATWEST
WOODMAC

Spice

| USM Smaller Companies | UK | 20th March 1989 |

Rights issue rescue

Price: 60p
Action: Hold
Long Term: Neutral

The new MD has a lot to do; the National Distribution Centre has occupied a significant amount of management time and the core business has been neglected

Years to Sept	Pre-tax Profits £'000	Av No of Shares m	EPS Stated Tax p	Tax Rate %	Net Div p	P/E Stated Tax	P/E Rel	Gross Yield %	Yield Rel
1988	23	8.21	0.5	—	1.2	120.0	890	2.7	67
1989F	(1,400)	12.32	(11.4)	—	1.2	—	—	2.7	62
1990F	700	15.56	4.5	—	1.2	13.3	115	2.7	57

- Spice distributes and wholesales automotive products through a series of six cash and carries and a central distribution centre at Dunstable.

- Spice has recently announced a 5 for 6 rights issue to raise £3.0m net of expenses. The money will be applied to the group's debt burden and will reduce gearing to 34%.

- In the year to September 1987 the group reported pre-tax profits of £1.26m; however, the management time spent on developing the National Distribution Centre meant the core business was neglected and profits slumped to £23,000 in 1988.

- A new managing director, Richard Fleming, has bought into the group, via the rights issue. He and his two partners could end up with 28.6% of the enlarged equity.

- There is a great deal to be accomplished at Spice and evidence of the changes implemented in 1989 will not be seen until the first half of the next financial year.

- The current share price is being supported by the city's confidence in Richard Fleming and an element of bid speculation.

Penny Freer 01-382 1000   Sales Team 01-600 0238

♣ The NatWest Investment Bank Group

Conference laughter

In February 1988 I was invited to address the *Financial Times* London Motor Conference, something I would normally avoid, as public speaking doesn't come naturally. For public relations reasons I accepted, and had plenty of time to prepare during whiteouts on a ski holiday. The brief was 'Whither the Aftermarket?'

After the usual waffle I finished by predicting that Government legislation would soon make it mandatory that new vehicles be fitted with a device to prevent drink-driving.

This would take the form of a gizmo on the dashboard, with a hole into which you'd have to blow before the engine would start.

I ended 'Of course, it will be jailable offence to blow into someone else's hole', which raised a few laughs.

Twenty years later I was amused to read in *Reader's Digest* that just such a device, called an Alcohol Interlock, is now being fitted to commercial vehicles in Sweden, and will be compulsory on all buses and lorries from 2010 and new cars from 2012.

locations, in high racking accessible only by forklift trucks. Sadly, the computer lost track, and when orders arrived it showed either no stock or the wrong location. To cap it all, the computer refused to invoice stock that had been found manually, because it said we had no such items! Similarly, the reordering of stock, based on historical sales, was a nightmare. Within weeks business at the branches reduced dramatically. Availability reduced from 98 per to 55 per cent, and we lost major customers hand over fist. Our competitors had a field day.

Top distribution experts were called in at enormous expense, but they usually reverted to the 'not invented here' syndrome. Before we had no business left at all, branches started reordering directly from suppliers and we were left with the worst cashflow crisis imaginable.

Company morale was at an all time low.

Following Kevin's departure, on returning to the office from Australia in December 1988 I found waiting on the doorstep a stranger named Richard Fleming. He explained he had been following our recent problems and he'd like to help. I began to take him seriously when he offered to invest £1 million of his own money, adding that his partners would be prepared to underwrite a Rights Issue for considerably more. One of his conditions was that I should have no further involvement, and I had no problem with that!

Fleming had a reputation as a high flyer: he was a Director of Doctus plc, a quoted management consultancy group known in the City for their success in reviving blue chip companies.

With his partners' blessing Fleming planned to resign from Doctus and become MD of Spice plc. I put his proposition to our advisors, but they were adamant that for the sake of investor confidence I must stay on as Chairman. I reluctantly agreed to do so in a non-executive role.

The relationship between Richard and I blew hot and cold. Sometimes he was brilliant and other times a complete dork. He had a management style the likes of which I had never encountered. Of his intellect there was no doubt but his behaviour swung from sickly patronising to egotistic lunatic. He had no talent for basic trading and spent a disproportionate amount of time on computer modelling and 'what if' theories. All major decisions were taken with the minimum of consultation, then, having got rid of the 'old management', he delegated the work to staff who were simply not up to the job. He thought that increasing their salaries would make them perform better, and even I knew this never worked.

I noticed Richard's dark curly hair was supported by the company paying £60 a time for his frequent visits to the barber. Small fry compared with the leasing costs of his Bentley.

In February 1989 the Rights Issue happened: very much Richard's domain. It was well subscribed and, at 45p per share, raised a vital £3 million. The Board was now down to Richard Fleming (MD), Jonathan Bailey (personnel), Brian Merry (due to leave in April), and Abingworth's Marius Gray.

The following month the 1988 results were announced, showing a loss of £1.4 million. The fact it came as no surprise did little to alleviate the ignominy. My dear Mum unexpectedly died in the Cayman Islands in February that year, which gave me the kick I needed and put my life in true perspective.

Restructuring was now the name of the game. Richard recognised the potential of the NDC, and courageously rejected the option of closing it down, which would have been the simple way to return the group to profitability. Critically, he assumed responsibility for making NDC fully operative. To reduce overheads HO at Staines was closed and key staff transferred to Dunstable. The warehouses were renamed Spice Supercentres, the idea being that they would supply retailers for cash or on credit, either collected or delivered. I strongly disagreed as it was abandoning the core cash & carry business, but Fleming called the shots.

Critically, the group's business changed from 70 per cent cash sales with debtors of only three days, to 30 per cent cash with debtors of 45 days. Allied to interest rates rising by five per cent over the period, it was a recipe for disaster.

The writing was on the wall for the company I'd founded, so I bought the plc's half-share of Spice Engineering Ltd. I did this to ensure that SEL would be safe and not dragged down should the plc go bust.

Despite Fleming's best efforts and the resources that were thrown at it, NDC never fulfilled expectations. Even experts from Halfords, which had overcome similar difficulties, failed to get to the root of the problems. In October 1989 the NDC lease was sold to a French company, Legrand Electric, the stock transferred to the branches, and the National Distribution Centre closed.

The Rights Issue £3 million soon ran out and a second rights issue was implemented. This required my selling a chunk of shares for a pittance, but in my demoralised state I didn't really care. I recall that a further £4 million was raised, but that didn't last long either. It was a ghastly year, most of it spent in City meetings at which I had little say.

I had simply had enough.

My resignation was at last accepted, and I mentally wrote off my remaining million shares: it turned out they would soon be worthless anyway!

I had always planned to retire at 50, influenced by my Dad who'd died aged 52. Although it was dissatisfying not to go out on a high, at the time I felt remarkably detached

Businessman	Company	Car
Lord Rayner	Marks & Spencer	(work) Rolls Royce Silver Spur (personal) Mercedes 230TE
John Egan	Jaguar	Daimler 3.6
Gordon Spice	Spice	Porsche 911 turbo
Danys Henderson	ICI	Daimler 3.6
Sir John Read	TSB	Ford Scorpio
Richard Branson	Virgin	Bristol 411
Terence Conran	Storehouse	BMW 7
Anita Roddick	Body Shop	Rover Sterling
Lord Weinstock	GEC	Ford Granada
Sir Ralph Halpern	Burton	Aston Martin V8

What the top executives drive

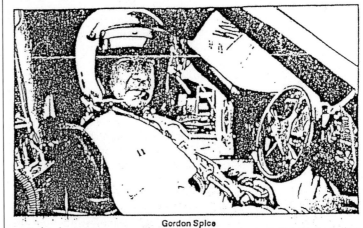

Gordon Spice

John Egan

and relieved that the hassle was over.

On top of all these woes, the consumer markets took a steep downturn, with rivals Maccess posting a loss of £8 million the following year, mainly due to closure costs. In July 1989, a month after I'd retired from racing, Spice shares were suspended after posting a six-month loss of more than £4 million.

Negotiations to sell the group to Dana Corporation, owners of Monza cash & carries

April 1988 Investors Chronicle survey. My 'top executive' status was short-lived!

Reflections on becoming plc

Readers who have been involved in a growing business will have experienced the endless demand for more working capital. Ensuring the company is properly funded takes priority over drawing a large salary. For the first ten years in business, I only looked at my private bank statements when the bank phoned, and there was certainly no time for financial planning.

After my divorce from Birdie in 1973 I ended up without a house or any personal money and had to raid company funds to pay the final settlement. However, I kept the businesses, which were all in good shape, but for the first time began to think about building some personal wealth.

Thinking through the options, I decided the best way would be to develop the company to a size that could be floated on the Stock Exchange. My father had done just that with Gill and Duffus, and it had worked well for him. I had the support of my co-directors and key managers in working towards that objective. It took longer than planned, but Abingworth's entry a few years later took care of my immediate cash needs, and was a key step in the plan to go public.

When Gordon Spice Limited became Spice plc via the Unlisted Stock Market in 1987, I became wealthier than I had ever imagined. Looking back, I was also extremely naïve as to how the City works. Post flotation, I was still the largest shareholder by miles and I thought I would retain control. The reality was that in future the City would call the shots.

In becoming a Fat Cat. I'd lost the balls to fight City expectations, which centred around rapid growth that I couldn't deliver. I took the easy option, which suited my motor racing passion, and left the company's direction in the hands of the City and 'professional' management.

For this reason, the company's demise was very much down to me.

Shortly after the new MD 'Kevin' was appointed in 1988, the Spice plc share price virtually trebled, appearing to justify the decision. It was typical of the City that this was based entirely on expectation and had nothing to do with Kevin's actual performance in the job. Similar to modern politics, presentation took precedence over substance, and Kevin was a top man on that front.

Within a year the planned expansion had failed and profitability had gone out of the window. At that stage I didn't have the experience to rescue the situation, hence the acceptance of white knight Richard Fleming. To be honest, with money in the bank I'd also lost the fire in my belly... Strangely, despite having given the business first priority for over 25 years, I took its ultimate failure quite pragmatically.

It was not the emotional crisis that I'd expected, and by far the worst aspect was letting down so many loyal employees.

and Brown Brothers, broke down. I am told that in a final cash-raising effort, Alpha was sold via a management buy out (MBO). In December the Birmingham branch was sold to Car Bar. Similarly, Watford was sold to Maccess, and Leicester to Abbey Park Motor Spares.

When the bank appointed a Receiver, only the two original and most profitable Spice branches remained: Staines and Canning Town. In February 1990, Canning Town was sold to Charles Tippet in a MBO backed by 3i plc; in July the Staines lease expired and Charles bought the stock. I was unaware of this later history and must thank Charles for his help on this.

Despite my memory lapses, I remember the one thing I got out of the financial meltdown. A large quantity of Swedish Brunzyl wood shelving, originally bought for the Windsor warehouse in 1968, had been chucked out of Staines when it closed. I still use that old timber to make pine furniture, a happy reminder of carefree days at Windsor in the '60s.

Chapter 23

Racing to retirement

For 1989 the FIA initiated major rule changes for Group C racing, outlawing turbocharged cars from 1991, when 3.5-litre normally aspirated engines would be obligatory. Some thought they saw the growing popularity of Group C as a threat to Formula 1, others went along with the official explanation that they were trying to improve the series and reduce costs. Whichever theory you believe, following a meteoric rise in the 1980s it is indisputable that 1989 was the start of Group C's rapid decline. Significantly, the FIA had previously shown little interest in sports cars racing; now they were paying it very close attention.

The change coincided (er-um?) with Formula 1 switching from 3 litres or 1.5-litre turbo, to 3.5-litre normally aspirated engines. The rationale was to attract more major manufacturers to the series, but the reality was that the extra cost was beyond the reach of privateers. The further nail in Group C's coffin was the phasing out of the C2 class. Since the new specification was closer to C2 than C1, most teams converted to C1 during 1989. As a result, C2 was prematurely cancelled for 1990.

Another significant part of the new package was the introduction of a $250,000 fine for every non-appearance of teams that had entered the championship. It was obvious who would be the beneficiary of any such fine! This resulted in the underfunded teams resorting to all kinds of ruses to avoid the fine – it was cheaper to pay the freight and have the car fail at scrutineering than to pay the fine. Even the points system was changed to that of F1, with 9-6-4-3-2-1 for the top six positions.

In the interim, there was no fuel restriction for the 3.5-litre cars, unlike the turbo brigade which had their minimum weight increased to 900kg. The final deadly move, which struck at the heart of endurance racing, was reducing race distance to 480km, with the exception of Le Mans. The 1990–1 seasons were unique in that it was the first time since 1953 that the world's premier sports car championship was reduced to one class. This was supposedly to increase the appeal to TV audiences, but by the end of 1992 several manufacturers had pulled out, and the field was reduced to single figures. In 1993 the renamed Sportscar World Championship (as opposed to the WSPC) was abandoned.

The 1989 rule changes were on the table well in advance and many thought the new regulations would play into the hands of the likes of Spice Engineering, for it was relatively simple to change from a 3.3 Cosworth DFL engine to the 3.5-litre DFZ and run with the same chassis. In reality, the 'Cossy' was getting long in the tooth: it would not be long before the manufacturers came up with better and far more expensive alternatives – as in F1.

At the beginning of the year I was up to my eyes – and out of my depth – trying to salvage Spice plc. My unwritten agreement with Ray Bellm was that all team drivers would bring enough sponsorship to the team to run their own car for the season, and up to now I had used my business clout to secure my share. By 1989 I was looking for entirely different favours from suppliers, and had neither the time nor the heart to find sponsorship. It was out of the question to expect SEL to fund my seat and it would go against my own long-held principles to pay for it myself. The result was that my seat would be filled by a driver with sponsorship.

Excepting Le Mans, I would not be driving this year.

The rapid expansion of SEL and the USA operation, despite a thriving customer base, had brought inevitable cashflow problems. We were no longer contracted to GM, so all development costs – which were considerable – were now down to the company, and it made a big difference. To bolster the coffers, a 25 per cent shareholding in SEL was sold to Jean Louis Ricci, who intended to run a C1 chassis.

I was not involved with the driver line-up for our cars, but the works entry was initially Ray sharing a car with Costas Los. A second SEL car went to Thorkild Thyrring and Wayne Taylor – the latter again proving to be both quick and well funded.

Spices were well represented in 1989 C2 with Hugh Chamberlain's two-car team which included Nick Adams and Fermin Velez. France Prototeam ran a car for Almo Coppelli amongst others, Richard Piper's PC Automotive ran one for himself and Olindo Jacobelli. Philippe de Henning was back with Los's old team, GP Motorsports. Sunseeker designer Don Shead bought a Spice to drive with his son James – and very well they did too.

Pierre Lombardi's French team bought the total to seven Spices.

Without going into detail, suffice it to say that the new car never reached its full potential. One reason was that with the pressure of delivering new GTP cars to the States, pre-season testing was inadequate. Critically, the new DFZ engine, which was higher revving than the DFL, was prone to extreme vibrations. This led to multiple component failures – frequently on the electrical side – and poor reliability throughout the season. The car was quick enough but was usually beaten by the Mercs and the Jags and a few fourth places were its best results. It didn't help that some of the team drivers ran out of funding, which meant taking drivers whose wallets were greater than their talent.

At Donington Park, a circuit where expectations were high, Wayne Taylor drove superbly, and pulled away from Mark Blundell's Nissan and Baldi's Merc. Ironically, he was the first to pit for fuel and shortly after electrical problems led to retirement. This was particularly disappointing as we were wooing

Le Mans, 1989: the Spice Engineering cars with team personnel at scrutineering. (LAT)

a large Japanese corporation for sponsorship in 1990 and had laid on accommodation, helicopters and circuit hospitality for their executives – at a cost of around £10,000.

Under such circumstances I was none too pleased when I found the ubiquitous Jackie Stewart in our hospitality tent, handing out Paul Stewart Racing cards and posing for photos with the top guest. He disappeared when I threatened him with the bill, but the damage was done.

At the end of the season the SEL team was fifth in the C1 Marques championship. We were behind Mercedes, Porsche, Jaguar and Nissan, but ahead of Aston Martin, Toyota and Mazda.

The good news was that in C2, Spices took the first four places in the Team Cup, with Hugh Chamberlain winning from Don Shead's team. Nick Adams and Fermin Velez ran away with the Drivers' Championship.

The first time I sat in the new Spice C1 was at Silverstone, for a shakedown test before Le Mans. After spinning three times on three consecutive laps, at exactly the same spot,

heads were starting to shake – and so was mine. The problem was eventually sorted and I had at least driven a few laps, but I felt far from comfortable in the car.

In April we had been approached by John Gorsline to secure a third seat at Le Mans for his protégé driver, Lynn St James. John was a broker, the biggest insurer of professional racing drivers anywhere. John persuaded Jeff that Lynn was up to the job, and the sponsorship she brought clinched the deal. We had not met Lynn at this stage, but from John's glowing references it seemed likely that she would blow us all off (driving, of course).

Bernadette's welcome at Mierré was as warm as ever and we were joined by the two Americans for another gastronomic week. Lynn turned out to be a sensible driver, a fair bit slower than Ray and I (what a relief!). At scrutineering, we once again did a deal with Hawaiian Tropic – mainly due to Gorsline's tenacity. Whatever the result, the team could enjoy the glamour and the sponsors the publicity.

Ray qualified the car at 3m 32s, fastest of the 3.5-litre C1 brigade, a full six seconds clear

Le Mans, 1989: a routine pit stop. (LAT)

of Tim Harvey who was quickest in the Thyrring/Taylor car. Practice was fraught with handling problems due to new tyre compounds, and our straightline speed was disappointing. Vibrations permitting, things could only get better for the race.

Come race day, early delays put us down to midfield and at 6:30am on Sunday morning I finished my stint and handed over to Ray. I mentioned that the engine was not achieving maximum revs and felt 'tight' and that he should watch the instruments. When Ray joined me at breakfast at around 7:00am I was not that surprised to see him. Ray had found the same problem getting worse, and there was no way the car would last another ten hours. So, rather than risk an expensive engine failure, the car was withdrawn.

Before Ray joined us, I mentioned to Creech that this would be my last race and, having had no prior discussion, she was surprised but very pleased. I'd always vowed that if another driver was quicker than me, in the same car and in the same conditions, I would retire. That had just happened, and the fact that I had not felt relaxed in the car all weekend made it an easy decision to take.

No official announcement was made – only those within the team were told – but I was quick to quash the rumour that I had retired because Lynn was quicker. What a cheek!

In the USA, a Spice-Buick SE88P won the 1989 Camel Lights series, with privateer Scott Schubot driving, and the other six customer cars ran competitively through the season. In GTP, the factory ran Bob Earl initially in a Spice-Pontiac SE89P and latterly in a SE89 V8 Chevrolet chassis. They were the only US-engined cars in class and ended the season behind the works Nissans and Jags.

1990

The plan for 1990 was to run a two-car team in the WSPC, and this was dependent on a £1 million sponsorship deal with Mexican driver Bernard Jourdain. He was known to Jeff and Julian through the USA operation, and as a rookie in the CART series had gained a high reputation. Ray had shared his car with him at Mexico City for the last race of 1989, so he was a known entity.

After the contract was signed, but before any money was paid, Jourdain was allowed to drive the now GM-supported Spice-Chevrolet SE90P at the Daytona 24-hours. In March at the Sebring 12-hours, after paying a token deposit and with a promise of the balance within days, Jourdain was again allowed to drive the same car, running as high as third in the race.

Bernard Jourdain was certainly quick, but, despite many promises, no further funds appeared.

Ray having decided to take the season off, Fermin Velez had been signed to drive one of the factory cars with Jourdain. Depending on sponsorship, drivers for the second car included Tim Harvey, Bruno Giacomelli, Eliseo Salazar and Wayne Taylor. To cut a long story short, the million from Jourdain never materialised, the reason given being that he'd been injured in a big accident at Indy 500 qualifying. With the wisdom of hindsight, that was the time we should have insisted on reducing our race programme and concentrated on the commercial side. Jeff Hazell would have none of it.

Despite Ray's and my opposition, Jeff pressed ahead, arguing that the $250,000 fine for every non-appearance justified continuing.

The cost of running DFZ engines doubled the budget needed compared with C2, and three major blowups at Dijon didn't help matters. Some good results were achieved – enough to come fourth in the Teams' Championship – but without the Jourdain money the team was unsustainable.

Before the end of the season Ray and I decided to call it a day. Jeff Hazell had the cheque book and was out of control. So, whilst he was away in Japan pursuing a 'sure thing' sponsorship deal, we put the company into voluntary liquidation. The way the company was heading we risked the bank calling in our joint guarantees: with Spice plc going down the tube I couldn't risk that.

After the Receiver had sold the company's assets, it was pleasing that the Bank and all our creditors were paid in full. The company was bought by a large Japanese Corporation and a few months later several of its directors ended up in jail! After that I lost track, but despite many changes of ownership there was no company revival.

However, it says something for the appeal and design of the cars that they are still much sought-after to this day. At least 12 Spice cars are competing regularly and have enjoyed overall wins in Historic Group C races – something we never managed to do!

Chapter 24

Retiring becomes a busy business

The story of how we came to live on a river island began when Creech and I started a life together at Rambler Cottage back in 1974. When we married in 1977, the sale of Gordon Spice Ltd shares to Abingworth provided the money to buy a decent house. At that time gazumping was rampant and we lost our first choice, a riverside house near Maidenhead, to BBC sports commentator Frank Bough. How we hated him!

From an ad on the front page of the *Sunday Times* we came across a unique place called Weir Point, situated on the Thames between Windsor and Runnymede. It was so cheap that I had trouble persuading Creech to even look at it. When she did, she found Weir Point to be a rather ugly, jerry-built flat-roofed bungalow, but we both fell in love with the location. Weir Point stood on an isolated one-acre plot on the tip of Ham Island, surrounded by the Thames and approached through fields via a long bumpy track. It featured a large weir at the bottom of the garden, which could be heard but not seen. Used as a weekend retreat, the seller was the widow of Liberal MP D'Arcy Conyers.

In 1978, at £28,000 it was the bargain of the year, but our friends and family thought we were mad to buy such a dump.

Having failed to sell Rambler Cottage for £20,000, before going to Le Mans to drive Charles Ivey's Porsche we left the cottage keys with the Weir Point estate agent. We returned a week later to a firm offer of £38,000 for Rambler Cottage with more buyers lined up, hoping to gazump!

After moving in to Weir Point, I suspected planning permission for a replacement house would be difficult so employed an architect and planning expert to do the legwork. When their fees reached £12,000, with no result in sight, I fired them.

Unbelievably, the Royal Borough of Windsor & Maidenhead's planning department took the official view that no permissions would be given as they wanted the area to revert to one of 'natural rural beauty.' Furthermore, if residence was not maintained it would be subject to a demolition order!

So we set about 'improving' the bungalow. We started by pulling half of it down and moved into the other half with a tarpaulin dividing the two. Having rebuilt the first half on more or less the same footprint, a Stop Order was served before we had a chance to move in. The Council claimed we needed planning permission for what we had done and if the original walls of the other half were not left standing, they would make us pull the lot down.

I explained to the planners that it was the only house we had. If we weren't allowed to finish it we'd be forced to seek Council accommodation of a similar size. During negotiations, I offered to timber-clad the bungalow, thus enhancing the 'natural rural beauty' of the plot. This was the turning point and seemed to give the officials the equivalent of a planning orgasm. The Stop Order was lifted and I resisted the temptation to paint it pink with large purple spots.

This was the first round of a battle with the planners that continues to this day on other Ham Island properties that I subsequently bought.

In 1999 we bought another home on the island (in which we still live) and sold Weir Point, for around £1 million, to a chap who was a solicitor and forgot to mention he was also a serious property developer. Within a year he'd

somehow got permission to demolish the house and replace it with a Holiday Inn look-alike! Before he sold Weir Point in 2004 and moved on, he'd developed the two plots adjoining his house as well, but we've got used to the 'Wentworth look' on that end of the island.

Retirement did not last long, much to Creech's relief, as the novelty of free time for woodworking, boating and holidays soon wore off. So when Peter Martin, a computer expert and friend, introduced me to a young struggling electronics engineer, I got involved in the electronics business.

A part-time interest soon became full-time and before long I was commuting daily to offices in Chiswick, having formed Telcom Telemetry Ltd (TTL) in partnership with Pete, developing new communications technologies.

The business was not an instant success and I found myself relying on information I did not understand, in a market about which I knew nothing. I was about to pull the plug when the business changed dramatically following Peter's visit to his native South Africa. He'd come across the Invention Company in Johannesburg which had gone bust developing a device, called Send-It, which eliminated the need for hardwiring between PCs and printers. This was groundbreaking technology with a big future.

The company had successfully developed wireless telemetry and it was being used by major banks and universities in South Africa.

The device comprised two small boxes, no larger than a pack of fags, one of which plugged into the back of the PC, the other to the printer. Encrypted radio waves travelled between the two up to 100ft – through walls and any other obstructions – eliminating the need for cables. The Receiver's deadline for selling the company was in four days so we immediately flew to Joburg.

The reason the Invention Company was in receivership quickly became clear. The inventor and founder was enjoying the lifestyle of a millionaire and although he was incredibly clever, his business skills were zero. Recognising that it would require at least £1 million to develop and market the product in the UK, I telephoned Peter Dicks at Abingworth but he was away: I knew the idea was right up their street.

Confident of Abingworth's backing, we bought the company (and its liabilities) for one Rand. I returned to the UK and Pete stayed on to close down the company, only retaining the R&D side.

Timing is everything, and it was a major setback when I found Abingworth were out of IT and we'd have to find the money elsewhere.

Opposite: Weir Point in 1981.

Opposite below: Weir Point in 1978.

Below: Weir Point in 1988.

Our current home,
Bear Shack, in 1998.

I spent the next few months between Johannesburg, where R&D continued, and London, doing the rounds of venture capitalists. Pete and I travelled the country doing demos of this amazing device, which everyone wanted to buy. Peter was so confident in Send-It that he sold his lovely house near Kyalami and we both continued investing.

Within a year we had spent over £200,000 getting the necessary UK Radio Communications Agency's approvals. This was more than either of us could afford, let alone the costs of going into production. Despite business plans justifying finance of between £500,000 and £5 million, tailored to the potential source, we failed to get backing. Reluctantly, we decided to cut our losses and walk away. It was small consolation that within two years the groundbreaking telemetry that Pete had found had become common technology in the computer world.

The pioneer is often the first to leave with an arrow in his back!

The TTL venture showed the dangers of investing in a business about which you know sweet FA. So when brother Dee asked for help in selling cocoa shell to the horticultural market – another thing I knew nothing about – I was naturally hesitant.

However, after a meeting with Dee and Jane – his second Ozzie wife, and a lady of strong character – I agreed to do the sales job on the basis of commission only, but with no managerial involvement. Their partnership, based in the Isle of Wight, bought raw cocoa shell (a by-product of chocolate manufacturing) and sold it under the brand name Sunshine of Africa (S of A) as a garden mulch to garden centres. It was an excellent product, well accepted, but they had to commit to buying a minimum quantity every month throughout the year. Sales were below target, meaning that the old aircraft hanger near York, where bulky raw cocoa shell was bagged and shipped, was bursting at the seams.

Commission only was a good arrangement for them as sales costs were fixed, and good for me too: the more I sold the more I earned. I set about the task with enthusiasm. After three months sales had tripled and the cocoa mountain reduced. It was hard work, but fun.

I was then invited to become a partner in Sunshine of Africa so I bought a 40 per cent stake for £50,000, took charge of sales and gave up my lucrative commission. My suggestion to

Bear Shack in 2001 (ugly thanks to planners!).

turn the operation into a limited liability company was turned down and it remained a partnership. Manufacturers' agents, whom I knew from my travels, were recruited to sell on commission, and within weeks we had complete UK coverage.

Business boomed, but imitation being the sincerest form of flattery, it wasn't long before competitors appeared. The dangerous ones were established suppliers, who simply added their own brand of cocoa shell to existing ranges. Our company's prosperity would depend on monopolising all sources of cocoa shell in Europe, and this was my next task. It wasn't until I toured all the coca bean processors in Europe, establishing their shell production volumes, that I realised this was well beyond our capacity.

We would need a substantial partner.

Before its use in gardens, cocoa shell was traditionally ground up and used to add bulk to animal feeds. Comparatively, Sunshine of Africa added enormous value to this cheap raw product. The biggest supplier to the animal feed market was a company in Holland, which I approached. I offered them a ten per cent share in the profits of our partnership, and exclusive marketing rights to Sunshine of

Africa in the Benelux countries. In exchange they would guarantee to buy all excess production of EEC cocoa shell – something they were well capable of doing. We established the Heads of Agreement, and I told them I'd return with my partners to formalise the deal.

A week later, Jane, Dee and I met our future partners at their office in Eindhoven. The meeting went well – or so I thought. However, when we got back to our hotel, Jane announced that she would not do business with them as the MD fancied her – and it was a rotten deal anyway!

I was furious that we were back to square one, having failed to eliminate our competitors and wasted one helluva lot of time. Worse than that, there was not another company around with the clout to make such a commitment. It was the beginning of the end of Sunshine of Africa's prosperity.

I made my displeasure known. Even so, I was taken aback to receive a fax a week later saying that Dee and Jane were not comfortable with our partnership, and would like me to go.

The business was now highly profitable, with annual sales of £1 million and rising. After taking advice on partnership law, I offered to buy their 60 per cent share for a substantial

Night service!

In 1993, over supper one evening Charles Ivey mentioned that he'd sold half his Porsche business in Fulham and bought an Alfa Romeo dealership in East Sheen, West London. The business had not gone well, and his house was on the line. I was between building projects at the time and offered to look at the business and come up with some recommendations.

The service department was very profitable, especially when Charles spent his time there. The parts division washed its face, but new car sales were loss-making. Giving up the franchise was not an option, because Alfas were then notoriously unreliable and warranty claims represented a significant and profitable part of the service work. It was agreed that Charles would work fulltime in the workshop and I would oversee car sales.

To ease pressure from the bank, I posed as a potential buyer for the business, which kept them at bay whilst sorting out the cashflow. I came up with

the idea of 24-hour servicing to boost profits with a minimal increase in overheads. Starting with two eight-hour shifts there was the potential of doubling the servicing income. The merit of the scheme was that fixed overheads like rent, rates, insurance and depreciation were unaffected, and the only extra costs would be overtime rates for late-shift workers.

Allowing for a 50 per cent increase in mechanics' hourly pay, the figures stacked up. The mechanics welcomed the idea, and the problem was finding day staff! To widen the potential market, the service was available to all car makes, with an option of a collection service within five miles. Leaflets were distributed, a PR campaign implemented, and we received excellent coverage in the national press.

The night servicing idea took off far quicker than expected and the business became profitable once more. I never understood why more garages didn't copy the idea.

1993: Charles Ivey overnight car servicing.

What The Papers Say.

The following are quotations from the press about Charles Ivey's overnight servicing.

THE TIMES
26 November 1993

The Daily Telegraph
6 December 1993

Daily Express
19 November 1993

THE SUN
7 December 1993

Barnes, Mortlake & Sheen Times
19 November 1993

"...take the pain out of waiting"

"Night-time servicing keeps car drivers on the road"

"At your service"

"Brilliant idea and so simple... I bet a lot more garages follow the lead... set to revolutionise car servicing... overnight servicing at daytime prices"

"The value of the idea is beyond doubt"

What the papers said.

sum. Alternatively they could buy me out at an equivalent rate.

I didn't mind which way it went but, having made my offer, the price was not negotiable. They decided to buy me out. It was a disappointing end to the partnership, but at least I'd recovered my TTL losses – and tax free.

Property beckons

It was my tax situation with Inland Revenue that forced me into the property market. By the early '90s I had accumulated agreed Capital Losses on my personal tax account well over £1 million. Whenever I had taken a business loss in the past, I always ensured it was recorded and the figures mounted up: SEL, Spice plc, TTL and several other ventures all contributed. This meant I could make equivalent capital gains without paying any Capital Gains Tax, providing certain criteria were met. The big question was: how?

I discovered that as a property developer these losses were not offsettable, but as a long-term investor in rental properties they were. To test the theory, in 1996 I developed a property on Ham Island which I'd owned since 1987 and Pete Martin had been renting. I replaced the modest wooden bungalow with a

much grander house. The property that had cost £50,000 in 1987 suddenly became a £400,000 asset. I sold the house and the substantial profit proved tax-free. I had found a new hobby!

In 1985, a neighbour from hell moved into a house close to us at Weir Point. He was an unpleasant man and operated 20 hot dog vans and trailers which he parked in the fields adjoining his house: illegal and unsightly. Those fields were jointly owned by the ex-owner of Weir Point and another lady who lived nearby. Neither wanted to cross this aggressive neighbour, so they agreed to sell me the ten-acre field and the access track, which Hot Dog Man was using illegally. It was £25,000 that I could not afford, but I bit the bullet and bought them.

Those fields were the best investment I ever made.

After sorting out the parking problem, another neighbour, an old lady reputed to be a white witch, put a curse on Mr Hot Dog by informing Customs & Excise of his dodgy business. HDM's house was repossessed to repay unpaid VAT. I bought it from HM Customs by sealed bid, but that's an unrepeatable story.

There were eight holiday homes on the north side of Ham Island, all adjoining the fields I'd bought, and all with riverside

1998: Chris Schofield (standing second from left) and Mers (seated).

frontage. Their plots, however, were quite narrow, which limited their development potential. The fields are part of a listed ancient monument – Berkshire Monument No 79 (Site of Edward the Confessor's Palace). If I could get permission from English Heritage to move the track 30 yards into the fields, and incorporate the extra space within the plots, it would add significant development value.

I started by trying to get the fields de-listed, but EH were adamant that they were historically too important. Over the next few months I wrote many letters badgering for permission to move the track, and on the rare occasions I got a reply, they never said 'no' and they never said 'yes.' So there was hope yet.

After a year my patience was wearing thin so I visited EH. I think it was out of embarrassment at their lack of response that they eventually agreed I could move the track. The condition was that the soil must not be disturbed beyond the depth of a plough's furrow and fence posts must be driven in, rather than dug. Suddenly those fields were looking very cheap!

Now, whenever any of the properties came up for sale I could afford to make the best offer. On top of that, if I happened to be outbid I still owned the land needed to make development viable. This was put to the test when a few years later the new owner of Weir Point wanted

to develop the two adjoining plots. The price he paid for the two ransom strips was akin to winning the lottery.

Thanks to Hot Dog Man, all eight of the properties have been developed with the exception of one I bought in 1999, where a dispute with the planners is ongoing! Of the six riverside houses I've built, we've sold three and kept the others. Happy to tell, my tax losses have all been used up.

When I took Creech on her first ski holiday in 1975, we drove into Zurs as the ski lifts closed. Looking up the slopes we could see an empty ski lift with the T-bars high in the air. Her first reaction: 'If you think I'm going up there, forget skiing!' I explained how T-bars worked and next morning she checked in for her first ski lesson. Her instructor's English was limited to 'Bend ze knees.'

At her first attempt on a lift she fell off, and the next person up piled into her. As she lay on the ground, in fits of laughter and unable to move, she was relieved to find she had locked skis with an English speaker.

And that's how we met the Schofields.

Chris and Mers Schofield came from Southern Rhodesia, renamed Zimbabwe in 1980. During the holiday we got to know them well. When the UK had imposed sanctions on Rhodesia's Smith Government, prior to independence, Chris was a frequent visitor to the UK and based himself at my office. The deals he was doing were fascinating, and I was sworn to secrecy. Over the next 30 years Chris became my best friend.

A few years later, following a HIAWS safari in Kenya, we flew down to Zimbabwe to visit the Schofields. Chris was a wonderful host and we were taken aback at the awesome beauty of that country and the warmness of the people.

We fell in love with Zimbabwe, the wildlife, and particularly the gentle people. Unlike South Africa there was no racial tension and respect between blacks and whites was genuine. There was some poverty but no hunger in the breadbowl of Africa. Chris was a leading businessmen and his Radar Group owned a diverse range of businesses from brickfields to builders' merchants. The lifestyle was that of colonial times, and pleasurably addictive.

Over the years, on frequent visits to Zim we made many friends and decided it would be a great place to live during the winter months. A forgotten insurance policy matured in 1996 and with the proceeds we bought a house. There were Z$15 to a UK pound then and property was dirt cheap. We settled for a house overlooking Lake Chivero, 15 miles outside Harare and adjoining a national game park.

Starting with Mugabe's land-grab, things have progressively got worse. The unpleasantness of living in a police state has driven out both blacks and whites, and most of our friends have left.

In 2002, Chris Schofield met with officials at the UK Foreign and Commonwealth Office, with a simple plan involving Government help in ending the dictatorship of the ruling Zanu-PF party. Chris knew it would only take a small task force to restore democracy and end the people's misery. The vast majority would support such action, the only opposition coming from the minority under Mugabe's patronage.

Questions were raised in parliament, backsides covered by sending us Hansard reports to prove it, but no action was taken. After several meetings, the Zimbabwe desk of the FCO reported to Chris that no direct action would be taken as there was 'no political mileage' in it. How different would it have been if Zimbabwe had oil?

The view over Lake Chivero from our house in Zimbabwe.

Chapter 25

The road home from Zimbabwe

Creech and I have kept our house in Zimbabwe, hoping to return when things get better. Rather than leaving our 4x4 Isuzu there I decided to drive it back to the UK. The decision was taken late on a Friday night but next morning it still seemed a good idea and Creech agreed. She would not be accompanying me – camping is not her scene – but the trip had her full support.

Edward Carter, a recently retired pilot with British Airways, volunteered to join me. Being an old car buff he's a practical 'hands on' chap and his expertise in navigation would be invaluable.

Chris Schofield's youngest daughter, Kim, who lives in Johannesburg, collected the Isuzu from Harare and her local garage prepared the car for our marathon. A dual 12V electrical system was fitted, mainly to power the drinks fridge. Other modifications, such as heavier springs, quick-lift jacks and additional tanks,

Sudan, February 2004: crossing the Nile at Dongola.

were obvious. A crate of spares and giveaways (baksheesh) was air-freighted to Joburg and the RAC supplied a Carnet de Passage for the vehicle. If the carnet was not returned with all the right stamps at the end of the trip, the substantial deposit would be forfeited.

Three months was insufficient time for organising all the visas but we left in January 2004: any later and we'd have hit the rainy season. The route planned was via Zimbabwe, Zambia, Tanzania, Kenya, Ethiopia, Sudan, Egypt and Libya, returning to Europe from Tunisia by ferry. But it did not quite work out that way!

After a week in Joburg with Kim, buying stuff for the trip, we set off for Harare, loaded to the gunnels with spare wheels, jerrycans, emergency supplies and camping gear. It looked the real McCoy.

It was a relief when we left Zimbabwe, Carnet stamped and without the anticipated aggro from the police. Northwards through Zambia and Tanzania, Ed and I shared the driving equally for the whole trip. To avoid hitting wandering natives in the dark, we never drove after sunset.

Near Moshi in Northern Tanzania we stayed the night near Ed's family coffee plantation, overshadowed by Mount Kilimanjaro. Ed was mortified at the state of the land of his childhood: deforestation by the locals had caused massive hillside erosion and no crops grew any more. Surprisingly, Ed's family's plantation home was in comparatively good order, untouched by the locals who knew his family had put a curse on it when they left 40 years ago!

When stopped at police roadblocks and borders we discovered that cigarettes were the best peacemaker. When a 20 pack was prof-

Sudan: negotiating for a camel...

... or so I thought!

fered it would be grabbed and pocketed. We soon learnt to keep a supply of near-empty packs at hand.

In Johannesburg, Kim's boyfriend had mentioned that he owned a Safari hotel at Ngoro Ngoro near the Kenya-Tanzania border. He'd invited us to stay as his guests, so that was our next destination.

Ngoro Ngoro is a national park within a 20km-wide crater only accessible by a steep track in a 4x4, with our stunning hotel perched on the top and the base 1,000ft below. Completely unspoilt, with a lake in the middle, the crater's steep sides kept the animals captive. I've never seen such numerous, and varied, wildlife. You name it, the crater had it.

After phoning Creech on our wedding anniversary, we left for Kenya. Entry into Kenya was remarkably easy but we ended up hiring a taxi to lead us to our Nairobi camp-site. The camp was very civilised, close to the British embassy and used by travellers on similar journeys to ours, driving anything from buses to bicycles. These were our first nights under canvas and we needed camping practice in a safe environment before the real thing! There is a strong camaraderie between travellers of all hues and sharing up-to-date information on hazards ahead was invaluable.

We'd been warned of the dangers of driving through Northern Kenya. Hijackers would fill the deep-tracked single-file roads with metal spikes, impossible to see in advance, leaving the vehicle beached on its sump. Forewarned, before crossing the Kaisut and Chalbi deserts into Ethiopia we stopped at Isiolo and hired two police guards. We were charged $40 US for their services, which was pretty reasonable for four days away and them hitch-hiking back. They had Enfield rifles – last used in the Boer war – which Ed made them unload before they squeezed into the back.

The roads were the worst yet encountered, but thankfully halfway across that 300-mile stretch there's an oasis and game reserve at Marsabit. Here we had three of our four spare wheels repaired. After 150 miles in six hours, by the time we reached Moyale our speedy wheel-changing would challenge the best of pit crews.

In Nairobi the incompetent British embassy staff had told us we could buy visas at the border, but we found that they could only be issued in the capital, Addis Ababa, some 600 miles to the north. We were lucky to meet a savvy Rastafarian, Tony, and with his help Ed managed to bribe a permit that would take us as far as Addis. By then it was too late for camping so we checked into an extremely grotty hotel. The loo was a seething pit of cockroaches. Sometimes it helps being a tight-arse!

At 3:00am a strange bug of the biting variety found its way under my mozzy net so I got dressed and waited for dawn. At 5:00am the wailing of the Muslim faithful started – a loud and dissonant accompaniment to our entire journey north.

We stayed in Addis a few days, sorting out visas for Sudan and Egypt and getting the Isuzu serviced. Parts of the city are beautiful but extreme poverty was everywhere. We checked into a decent hotel where Ed, using his British Airways ID card, negotiated a bargain rate.

One evening, in the nightclub under our hotel, I had to explain to one of the girls that I really wasn't interested in her services, and that she was far too young anyway. 'No problem,' she said, 'Tomorrow, I bring my mother.' Doubtless, if I'd claimed to be gay she would have volunteered her brother.

Travelling up the awesome Rift valley towards Sudan, our tyres became badly worn, and when we stopped for routine puncture repairs at a local Quickfit we were shown an effective fix. In poorer countries nothing is thrown away: inner tubes, whatever their state, are valued. The tubes are slit and compressed between a good inner tube and the tyre. Then, when a stone pierces the tyre there's a fair chance it won't penetrate through several layers of old tubing. It worked brilliantly.

After leaving Addis we stayed in the walled city of Gonder, preparing for the desert crossing into Sudan. The few signposts were all in Arabic and without Ed's GPS skills we'd still be there. Waiting for the Carnet to be stamped in Sudan, we witnessed an armed policeman viciously beating a local with a leather whip. Nobody took a blind bit of notice; it was obviously a common occurrence.

Khartoum-bound we pitched camp in remote scrubland, miles from any road. Within minutes of arriving two tribesmen appeared: wherever you go in Africa it is uncanny how the locals appear. After graphic warnings of snakes that lived in the cracked earth at the exact spot we'd chosen, they disappeared into the landscape. Swarms of locusts at dusk ensured we kept our tents sealed overnight; it was our first experience of camping in the real rough – one not to be repeated.

In ghastly Khartoum we stayed at the Blue Nile Sailing Club, where we camped on the lawn. Here we met a colourful Dutchman, Luke Reep, who had retired after selling his restaurant to make way for expansion at Schipol airport. Heading in the same direction, Luke's local knowledge helped us plan our route to Wadi Halfa. From there we would ferry up Lake Nasser to Egypt.

From Khartoum, after crossing the Bayuda desert we followed the Nile northwards, crossing at Dongola accompanied by camels and sheep. The roads were the worse yet encountered, rough enough to break our suspension. The welding needed for repairs cost 50p for two hours' work! Despite constant use of GPS we often wrong-slotted, finding ourselves in sand dunes where there should have been roads. Ed proved expert at driving out of deep sand where I'd managed to get stuck. After four days of extreme off-roading we arrived at Wadi Halfa on the banks of Lake Nasser.

In Wadi, we located Magda, recommended by his nephew at the Blue Nile Sailing Club. He was the original Mr Fixit, related to everyone from Customs officers to ferry owners. Seeing our reaction to the apology for a hotel, he invited us to stay at his house. He shared it with a bevy of sisters, cousins and aunts, all clad in traditional Muslim gear, who spent their days cooking and watching Western movies on satellite TV. We met up for men-only meals in the central courtyard and the food was awful.

From Wadi, accompanied by Luke, we took the ferry up Lake Nasser to the Aswan Dam. This 'ferry' was an open barge towed alongside a small cargo vessel, and that was home for the next three days and nights. No shower, no loo, and every few hours ear-splitting wailing when the prayer mats appeared. I had run out of rum days ago; now I ran out of books and fags. The highlight was the magnificent temples of Ramses and Nefertiti at Abu Simbel: when the Aswan dam was built in the '60s, and their original sites flooded, the temples were faithfully reconstructed on the shore of Lake Nasser. A mind-boggling engineering feat and a spectacular sight.

We thought African red tape was taxing enough, but it has nothing on Egypt. All the hand-wringing and blaming the will of Allah did little to belie the crude reality of institutional corruption.

Our problems started when the Isuzu was impounded at the ferry port in Aswan. We checked into the New Cataract hotel – very luxurious – and spent the next three days trying to get the car released. Typically, international Carnets are not accepted in Egypt and the Isuzu's release was only secured after Customs, Immigration and Traffic police had all been suitably bribed. By the time we left, Luke was apoplectic – he'd be lucky to see his Toyota again.

Whether in cars or buses, in Egypt foreigners must travel in police convoys. To avoid major roads, Ed worked out a route via the Western Desert. It was the only time that the GPS failed and we got totally lost, ending up in Luxor on the first night of the leg to Cairo. Our hotel overlooked the Nile close to where the cruise ships start their package tours. Posing as tourists, we boarded a ship and spent an enjoyable evening at their welcome drinks party. We had not reckoned on a 10:00pm departure, and narrowly escaped before the last gangplank was removed.

Up at sparrow fart start next morning, avoiding police checkpoints, we drove flat out up the Red Sea coast road, arriving in Cairo 500 miles later. There were two good things about Egypt: excellent roads and cheap diesel.

Ed's BA card came in handy when we checked into the President Hotel, where we planned the final leg. Staff at the Libyan Embassy had obviously been infected with the local culture: visas would take at least three weeks with no guarantees. So we decided to return via Jordan, Syria Turkey and Greece: a longer but more interesting route.

In marked contrast to the British embassy, the Jordanian officials couldn't have been more helpful. Waiting for paperwork we visited the Pyramids and the Sphinx. What a disappointment. The masonry is impressive enough but spoilt by both the squalor of a shanty town which goes right up to the base and by aggressive beggars. The appalling condition of Cairo's working horses and donkeys was heart-rending, the cruelty of their owners plain criminal.

Leaving Cairo, we took a tunnel under the Suez Canal and crossed the Sinai desert on the 300-mile drive to Nuweiba, the departure point for Jordan. On leaving, we explained to the Police and Customs officials that we'd been cleaned out on arrival in their lovely country and they must settle for our leftover gifts, including a gross of French letters. It was with great relief that we boarded the ferry, swearing never to return to that ghastly country.

Entry into Jordan was a doddle and we high-tailed it to Petra, famous for its lost city. We stayed at a five-star hotel, partly funded by an enthusiastic audience for my egg trick!

Leaving Jordan and entering Syria was hassle free but it was back to normal on the Syria/Turkey border. Price differentials of basic commodities between the two countries are high, and customs officials are dedicated to bagging their slice of the action. It was the busiest border of the trip and I fell out with the Carnet people, so handed negotiations over to Ed. I eased the Isuzu towards the front of the queue and two hours later Ed had

worked a miracle and the Carnet was stamped.

Leaving Turkey we ferried across the Bosporus, leaving the Word War 1 battlefields of Gallipoli behind us, into Greece. We were on the home stretch: no more visa, carnet or insurance baksheesh – pure joy.

The mountain scenery was beautiful: you don't think of Greeks skiing, but they do. I'd never appreciated either the size of Greece, or the diversity of its people, ranging from poor peasants to rich townies. Traversing this vast country was a new motorway under construction, tunnelling through mountains and crossing valleys by dramatic viaducts. It was the largest road-building project I've ever seen, funded by the dreaded EEC's more affluent members.

After crossing overnight from Igoumenitsa to Ancona, on a luxurious Greek ferry that should embarrass UK ferry operators, we drove through Italy and France, arriving in Dover just nine days after leaving Cairo. Since Johannesburg, we had been away for two months, driven for 33 days, covered 12,000 miles and used 500 gallons of diesel.

The help we had on the way from a host of memorable characters far outweighed the aggravation of the minority. I'd recommend a similar trip to anyone disenchanted with life in our politically-correct Nanny State. For anyone who'd like to do the journey in reverse, the Isuzu is waiting in the drive!

Old Windsor, March 2004. Home safely with Ed Carter.

Postscript

Since retiring I've had more offers of drives than I ever had when racing, but I've resisted the temptation. On the few occasions I've driven at track days I've found myself trying to prove I'm faster than the next guy, so I couldn't trust myself to act my age in a race. Rather than risk disappointing myself, or worse, I have not renewed my competition licence.

Creech and I still go to Le Mans, stay at Mierré and meet up with friends from the racing days. We also enjoy going to Historic Group C races, where Spice sports cars compete with Porsches, Jaguars and the like – and do rather better than I ever did!

We still go skiing every winter, holiday in Barbados, and look forward to returning to Zimbabwe when conditions allow. On summer evenings we enjoy cocktails at six on our small boat and enjoy the wildlife on the Thames – something I could never imagine a few years ago.

We don't travel as much as we used to: we find flying so much more hassle than it used to be. The days when British Airways would phone me at my office to remind me my flight was leaving shortly are long gone!

The brush with cancer in 2007 certainly focused my mind, but in mid-2008 I was given as close to an 'all clear' as the Doctors dare. I feel incredibly lucky and grateful to those who helped me pull through, and the experience has given me a new perspective on life.

Every morning I offer a small prayer of thanks; each day is more precious than it ever was before. The maxim 'Work as if you will live forever, live as if you will die tomorrow' has true meaning.

'The lucky man thinks he's clever, the clever man knows he's lucky.'

Boy, have I been lucky!

Race results

I have chosen to list my individual race results primarily by year, running the most recent events first. That means my first efforts at motor sports are discreetly hidden at the end.
– GS

I must acknowledge the detailed voluntary help of Frank de Jong and his saloon car racing resource www.touringcarracing.net in the compilation of Gordon's international results.
– JW

Le Mans 24-hours 1964–89

Year	Car	Result	Comments
1989	Spice-Ford Cosworth V8 SE 89C [C1 class]	DNF, motor failed @ 14 hours	Co-drivers: Ray Bellm/Lynn St James Last race before retiring Sponsors: Duralt, Hawaiian Tropic
1988	Spice-Ford Cosworth V8 SE88C [C2]	Class 1st; 13th oa	Co-drivers: Ray Bellm/Pierre de Thoisy 7 out of 8 Spice cars finished Sponsors: Rexona, Lucas
1987	Spice-Ford Cosworth V8 SE87C [C2]	Class 1st, 6th oa	Co-drivers: Fermin Velez/Philippe de Henning Highest C2 overall placing to date Sponsor: Dianetics (Church of Scientology)
1986	Spice-Ford Cosworth V8 SE86C [C2]	Class 6th; 19th oa	Co-drivers: Ray Bellm/Jean Michel Martin Last classified finisher, many problems! Sponsors: Canon, Listerine
1985	Spice-Tiga Cosworth V8 GC85	Class 1st; 14th oa	Co-drivers: Ray Bellm/Mark Galvin Inherited lead 4 hours from finish Sponsors: Hawaiian Tropic, Listerine, Holts & Jaeger
1984	Spice-Tiga Cosworth V8 Group C2	DNF – Crang crashed after 70 laps	Co-drivers: Ray Bellm/Neil Crang Sponsors: Waspeze, Piccolino
1982	Rondeau Ford Cosworth V8 M382 – Group C	DNF	Co-drivers: Francois Migault/Xavier Lapeyre Retired at 2:00am when leading the race Sponsors: Le Soir, Residences Malardeau
1981	Rondeau Ford Cosworth V8 M379-GTP class	Class 2nd; 3rd oa	Co-driver: Francois Migault Sponsor: Otis
1980	Rondeau Ford Cosworth V8 M379-GTP class	Class 1st; 3rd oa	Co-drivers: Jean-Michel & Philippe Martin I was also reserve driver in winning Rondeau Sponsor: Belga (Rothmans) cigarettes
1979	Dome-Ford Cosworth V8 Zero RL – Group 6 class	DNF	Co-driver: Chris Craft, who qualified us 15th… The most frightening car I have ever driven! Fuel pump failure resulted in early retirement

Year	Car	Result	Comments
1978	Charles Ivey Porsche 911 Carrera RSR – IMSA class	Class 2nd; 14th oa	Co-drivers: Larry Perkins/Jay Rulon-Miller Oldest car in the race, miraculous qualification The race included a 45-minute gearbox change
1977	De Cadenet Lola-Cosworth T380-LM – Sports 2000+ class	Class 3rd; 5th oa	Co-drivers: Chris Craft/Alain de Cadenet Qualified, but did not drive
1970	Escuderia Montjuich Ferrari 512S – Sports 5000 class	DNF	Co-drivers: Juan Fernandez/Jose Juncadella 'Hunky' crashed at White House in the wet
1964	Deep Sanderson – BMC 301 1300 Sports Prototype class	DNF	Co-driver: Chris Lawrence. Entrant: Lawrencetune Lost water early and not allowed to replenish

1988 FIA World Endurance Championship, C2 class

Date/Country	Car	Event	Result	Comments
6/3/88/Spain	Spice-Ford Cosworth V8 SE88C-C2	Jerez 800km	Class 1st; 7th oa	Co-driver: Ray Bellm More C2s than C1s
13/3/88/Spain	Spice-Ford Cosworth V8 SE88C-C2	Jarama Supersprint	Class 1sr; 7th oa	Co-driver: Ray Bellm Spice C2s finish 1–2–3
10/4/88/Italy	Spice-Ford Cosworth V8 SE88C-C2	Monza 1,000km	Class 1st; 8th oa	Co-driver: Ray Bellm Fuel tactics pay off!
8/5/88/UK	Spice-Ford Cosworth V8 SE88C-C2	Silverstone 1,000km	Class 2nd; 8th oa	Co-driver: Ray Bellm Electrical gremlin delay Spice C2s finish 1–2
12/6/88/France	Spice-Ford Cosworth V8	Le Mans 24-hours	Class 1st; 13th oa	See Le Mans results
10/7/88/Czech	Spice-Ford Cosworth V8 SE88C-C2	Czech GP (Brno)	Class 1st; 7th oa	Co-driver: Ray Bellm C2 Spices 1st to 5th
24/7/88/UK	Spice-Ford Cosworth V8 SE88C-C2	Brands Hatch 1,000km	Class 1st; 4th oa	Co-driver: Ray Bellm C2 World Champions (Team and Drivers')
3/9/88/Germany	Spice-Ford Cosworth V8 SE88C-C2	Nürburgring 1,000km	DNF	Co-driver: Ray Bellm Engine failed in 1st heat
18/9/88/Belgium	Spice-Ford Cosworth V8 SE88C-C2	Spa 1,000km	Class 2nd; 6th oa	Co-driver: Ray Bellm Spice C2s finish 1–2
9/10/88/Japan	Spice-Ford Cosworth V8	Fuji 1,000km	DNF – motor @ 4 hrs	Co-driver: Ray Bellm
20/11/88/Australia	Spice-Ford Cosworth V8 SE88C-C2	Sandown Park	Class 1st; 5th oa	Co-driver: Ray Bellm 11 C2s entered v. 7 C1s

Spice Engineering Limited won the 1988 FIA C2 World Championship for Teams, with 370 points.
Ray Bellm and Gordon Spice won the 1988 FIA C2 World Championship for Drivers, with 300 points.

1987 FIA World Sports Prototype Championship (WSPC), C2 class

Date/Country	Car	Event	Result	Comments
22/3/87/Spain	Spice-Ford Cosworth V8 SE87C-C2	Jarama Supersprint	Class 1st; 9th oa	Co-driver: Fermin Velez
29/3/87/Spain	Spice-Ford Cosworth V8 SE87C-C2	Jerez 1,000km	Class 1st; 4th oa	Co-driver: Fermin Velez Equalled team's best oa result
12/4/87/Italy	Spice-Ford Cosworth V8 SE87C-C2	Monza 1,000km	Class 1st; 7th oa	Co-driver: Fermin Velez Debut of Spice-Hart turbo
10/5/87/UK	Spice-Ford Cosworth V8 SE87C-C2	Silverstone 1,000km	Class 2nd; 7th oa	Co-driver: Fermin Velez Tyre blow out delay
14/6/87/France	Spice-Ford Cosworth V8	Le Mans 24-hours	Class 1st; 6th oa	See Le Mans results
28/6/87/Germany	Spice-Ford Cosworth V8 SE87C-C2	Nuremberg 200 miles	Class 1st; 6th oa	Co-driver: Fermin Velez
26/7/87/UK	Spice-Ford Cosworth V8 SE87C-C2	Brands Hatch 1,000km	Class 2nd; 7th oa	Co-driver: Fermin Velez Restart problems – battery
30/8/87/Germany	Spice-Ford Cosworth V8 SE87C-C2	Nürburgring 1,000km	Class 1st; 9th oa Disqualified	Co-driver: Fermin Velez Push-start penalty
13/9/87/Belgium	Spice-Ford Cosworth V8 SE87C-C2	Spa 1,000km Secures C2 World Drivers' title	Class 1st; 10th oa	Co-driver: Fermin Velez
27/9/87/Japan	Spice-Ford Cosworth V8 SE87C-C2	Fuji 1,000km	Class 1st; 8th oa Secures C2 World Team title	Co-driver: Fermin Velez

Spice Engineering Limited won the 1987 FIA C2 World Championship for Teams, with 170 points.
Fermin Velez and Gordon Spice won the 1987 FIA C2 World Championship for Drivers, with 140 points.

1986 FIA World Sports Prototype Championship (WSPC), C2 class

Date/Country	Car	Event	Result	Comments
20/4/86/Italy	Spice-Ford Cosworth V8 SE86C-C2	Monza Supersprint	Class 2nd; 14th oa 63 laps	Co-driver: Ray Bellm Debut of Pontiac Fiero
5/5/86/UK	Spice-Ford Cosworth V8 SE86C-C2	Silverstone 1,000km	Class 1st; 14th oa	Co-driver: Ray Bellm 1st win for new Spice-Fiero
31/5/86/Le Mans	Spice-Ford Cosworth V8 SE86C-C2	Le Mans 24-hours	Class 6th; 19th oa	Co-drivers: Ray Bellm/J.-M. Martin See Le Mans results
20/7/86/UK	Spice-Ford Cosworth V8 SE86C-C2	Brands Hatch 1,000km	Class 3rd; 11th oa	Co-driver: Ray Bellm Beaten by Ecosse
3/8/86/Spain	Spice-Ford Cosworth V8 SE86C-C2	Jerez Supersprint	Class 1st; 5th oa 86 laps	Co-driver: Ray Bellm Pre-event Karting accident
24/8/86/Germany	Spice-Ford Cosworth V8 SE86C-C2	Nürburgring 1,000km	Class 3rd; 7th oa	Co-driver: Ray Bellm Extremely wet, many accidents
15/9/86/Belgium	Spice-Ford Cosworth V8 SE86C-C2	Spa 1,000km	Class 2nd; 14th oa	Co-driver: Ray Bellm Beaten by Ecosse Secures C2 Drivers' title
6/10/86/Japan	Spice-Ford Cosworth V8 SE86C-C2	Fuji 1,000km	Class 2nd; 20th oa	Co-driver: Ray Bellm Punctures galore

Ray Bellm and Gordon Spice won the 1986 FIA C2 World Championship for Drivers, with 115 points.
Spice Engineering Limited second in the 1986 FIA C2 World Championship for Teams, with 68 points, 2 points behind Ecosse.

1985 World Endurance Championship for Sports Prototypes

Date/Country	Car	Event	Result	Comments
14/4/85/Italy	Spice Tiga Ford V8 Cosworth GC85-C2	Mugello 1,000km	Class 1st; 7th oa	Co-driver: Ray Bellm
12/5/85/UK	Spice Tiga Ford V8 Cosworth GC85-C2	Silverstone 1,000km	Class 2nd; 7th oa	Co-driver: Ray Bellm Ecosse won class Fuel feed problems
15/6/85/France	Spice Tiga Ford V8 Cosworth GC85-C2	Le Mans 24-hours	Class 1st; 14th oa	Co-drivers: Ray Bellm/Mark Galvin See Le Mans results
14/7/85/Germany	Spice Tiga Ford V8 Cosworth GC85-C2	Hockenheim 1,000km	Class 2nd; 9th oa	Co-driver: Ray Bellm Pitted to save fuel, and car would not restart for last lap!
11/8/85/Canada	Spice Tiga Ford V8 Cosworth GC85-C2	Mosport 1,000km	Class 1st; 5th oa	Co-driver: Ray Bellm Manfred Winklehock killed
1/9/85/Belgium	Spice Tiga Ford V8 Cosworth GC 85-C2	Spa 1,000km	Class 1st; 9th oa	Co-driver: Ray Bellm Stefan Bellof killed and race stopped after 122 laps
22/9/85/UK	Spice Tiga Ford V8 Cosworth GC85-C2	Brands Hatch 1,000km	DNF	Co-driver: Ray Bellm Suspension failed @ 12 laps

Spice Engineering won Group C2 Constructors' Championship, with 110 points.
Ray Bellm and Gordon Spice won Group C2 Drivers' Championship, with 130 points.

1984–5 Group A European Championship Touring Cars

Date/Country	Car	Event	Result	Comments
28/7/84/Belgium	Toyota Supra	Spa 24-hours	Class 1st; 5th oa	Co-drivers: Martin brothers Entrant: Hughes of Beaconsfield
7/7/85/Germany	BMW 635CSi-Juma	Nürburgring 500km	8th oa	Co-driver: Jean-Michel Martin Sponsor: Belga
26/7/85/Belgium	BMW 635CSi-Juma	Spa 24-hours	DNF	Co-drivers; Martin brothers Sponsor: Belga Inter-BMW warfare!

1984 World Endurance Championship for Sports Prototypes

Date/Country	Car	Event	Result	Comments
13/5/84/UK	Spice Tiga Ford V8 Cosworth GC84	Silverstone 1,000km	DNF – 117 laps	Co-drivers: Ray Bellm/Neil Crang New lap record
17/6/84/France	Spice Tiga Ford V8 Cosworth GC84	Le Mans 24-hours	DNF	Co-drivers: Ray Bellm/Neil Crang See Le Mans results
15/7/84/Germany	Spice-Ford Cosworth V8 Cosworth GC84	Nürburgring 1,000km	Class1st; 13th oa	Co-drivers: Ray Bellm/Neil Crang New C2 lap record!
28/7/84/UK	Spice-Ford Cosworth V8 Cosworth GC84	Brands Hatch 1,000km	Class1st; 10th oa	Co-drivers: Ray Bellm/Neil Crang New lap record
3/9/84/Belgium	Spice-Ford Cosworth V8 Cosworth GC84	Spa 1,000km	Class 1st; 9th oa	Co-drivers: Ray Bellm/Neil Crang New lap record
16/9/84/Italy	Spice-Ford Cosworth V8 Cosworth GC84	Imola 1,000km	Class 1st; 10th oa	Co-drivers: Ray Bellm/Neil Crang New lap record
2/12/84/Australia	Spice-Ford Cosworth V8 Cosworth GC84	Sandown Park (Melbourne) 1,000km	Class 1st; 10th oa	Co-driver: Neil Crang

International Sports Car Racing 1969–82

Date/Country	Car	Event	Result	Comments
16/5/82/UK	Rondeau M382 Ford Cosworth V8	Silverstone 6-hours	Class 3rd; 5th oa	Co-driver: Henri Pescarolo Otis sponsored
5/9/82/Belgium	Rondeau M382 Ford Cosworth V8	Spa 1,000km	Class 4th, 5th oa	Co-driver: Francois Migault Otis sponsored
6/5/1979/UK	Dome Zero RL Ford Cosworth V8	Silverstone 6-hours	Class 3rd; 12th oa	Co-driver: Chris Craft Built from box of bits in 5 days Never got full throttle!
12/4/70/UK	Porsche 910	Brands Hatch 1,000km	Class 3rd; 11th oa	Co-driver: Nick Gold Owner: Nick Gold
11/6/70/France	Ferrari 512S	Le Mans 24-hours	DNF	See Le Mans results
13/4/69/UK	Ford GT40 Escuderia Montjuich	Brands Hatch 6-hours	DNF	Co-driver: Jose Juncadella Clutch failed
1/6/69/Germany	Porsche 906	Nürburgring 1,000km	DNF	Owner: Nick Gold Retired at first pit stop as unable to drive following road accident
?/?/69/Spain	Ford GT40 Group 4 Escuderia Montjuich	Jarama 6-hours	Class 1st; 3rd oa	Co-driver: Jose Juncadella Spanish Championship
5/10/69/Spain	Ford GT40 Escuderia Montjuich	Barcelona 12-hours	DNF	Co-driver: Jose Juncadella Transmission failed

Tour of Britain 1973–6

Year	Car	Result	Comments
6–8/6/73	Ford Capri 3000 GXL/Wisharts	2nd oa	Sponsorship from Woolworths Beaten by James Hunt's V8 Chevrolet Camaro
12–14/7/74	3.0 Ford Capri II/Wisharts	36th (e)	Crashed at Snetterton; finished well down the order!
1–3/8/75	3.0 Ford Capri II/Wisharts	4th oa	Sponsorship from M&M Plant Hire
9–11/7//76	3.0 Ford Capri II/Wisharts	13th oa	Sponsorship from M&M Plant Hire

All with Stan Robinson as co-driver; the racing and rally stage event originally sponsored by Avon, then Texaco.

Ford Capri Racing 1973–82

International/European Championship events

Date/Country	Car/Entrant	Event	Result	Comments
23/6/73/Germany	3000 GXL/Wisharts	Nürburgring 24-hours	Class 4th; 10th oa	Co-driver: Pete Clark Big scrutineering hassles
21/7/73/Belgium	3000 GXL/Wisharts	Spa 24-hours	DNF – motor	Co-driver; John Hine
21/9/74/UK	3.0 Ford Capri GT Trio	Silverstone TT	Unclassified	Co-driver: Pete Clark
6/6/76/Belgium	3.0 Capri II/Wisharts	Spa 600km	DNF – accident	Co-driver: Pete Clark
24/7/76/Belgium	3.0 Capri II/Wisharts	Spa 24-hours	Class 1st; 5th oa	Co-driver: Pete Clark
15/5/77/UK	Capri 3.0S/GSR	Silverstone 6-hours	15th oa	Co-driver: Pete Clark
29/5/77/Germany	Capri 3.0S/GSR	Nürburgring 1,000km	Class 10th; 23rd oa	Co-driver: Pete Clark
23/7/77/Belgium	Capri 3.0S/GSR	Spa 24-hours	DNF	Crashed whilst leading!
18/9/77/UK	Capri 3.0S/GSR	Silverstone TT/UK	Class 5th; 15th oa	Co-driver: Pete Clark
8/10/77/Germany	Capri 3.0S/GSR	Nürburgring 24-hours	Not known	Co-driver: Alain Corbisier
2/4/78/Belgium	Capri 3.0S/GSR/Belga	Zolder	1st oa	Trophee Diners Club
22/7/78/Belgium	Capri 3.0S/GSR/Belga	Spa 24-hours	1st oa	Co-driver: Teddy Pilette Last long-circuit 24-hours
17/9/78/UK	Capri 3.0S/GSR	Silverstone	2nd oa	Trophee Diners Club
24/9/78/Germany	Capri 3.0S/GSR/Belga	Hockenheim	1st oa	Trophee Diners Club
8/4/79/UK	Capri 3.0S/GSR	Donington	1st oa	Non-championship race
19/5/79/France	Capri 3.0S/GSR/Belga	Paul Ricard 24-hours	2nd oa	Co-drivers: Martin brothers
21/7/79/Belgium	Capri 3.0S/GSR/Belga	Spa 24-hours	Class 5th; 5th oa	Co-driver: Alain Semoulin
16/9/79/UK	Capri 3.0S/GSR	Silverstone TT	Class 2nd; 5th oa	Co-driver: Chris Craft
13/10/79/France	Capri 3.0S/GSR	Le Mans 4-hours	1st oa	Co-driver: Alain Semoulin
20/10/79/Belgium	Capri 3.0S/GSR	Nivelles 400km	1st oa	Millennium race – big trophy!
26/7/80/Belgium	Capri III 3.0S/GSR/Belga	Spa 24-hours	Class 8th; 9th oa	Co-driver: Alain Semoulin
14/9/80/UK	Capri III 3.0S/GSR	Silverstone TT	DNF – accident	Co-driver: Andy Rouse
28/9/80/Belgium	Capri III 3.0S/GSR	Zolder	Class 2nd; 8th oa	Co-driver: Alain Semoulin
25/7/81/Belgium	Capri III 3.0S/GSR/Belga	Spa 24-hours	Class 6th; 8th oa	Co-driver: Thierry Tassin
13/9/81/UK	Capri III 3.0S/GSR	Silverstone ETCC	Class 2nd; 3rd oa	Co-driver: Andy Rouse
5/12/81/UAE	Capri III 3.0S/GSR	Dubai Grand Prix	DNF	Taken out in first corner from pole!
12/9/82/UK	Capri 2.8i injection/GSR	Silverstone ETCC	Class 10th; 13th oa	Co-driver: Andy Rouse

GS was also the 2,500 to 3,500cc class winner and third overall in the Trophee Diners Club Trans-Europe 1978. GS and his co-drivers used CC Racing Developments Capris and took three outright victories at Zolder, Spa-Francorchamps 24-hours and Hockenheim – JW

GS's Capri racing results in the UK follow. To summarise, GS won 27 races overall and was class champion in the British Touring Car Championship every year from 1975 to 1980. The highlight was seven outright victories in 11 rounds of the 1978 Championship – JW

Ford Capri Racing 1973–82: UK highlights

1982 RAC Tricentrol British Saloon Car Championship

Team sponsors Shell, *Daily Mirror*; Team-mate: Andy Rouse

Date	Car/Entrant	Event	Result	Comments
21/3/82	3.0S Ford Capri III/GSR	Silverstone/BTCC	5th oa	Andy Rouse P2. Rovers away
28/3/82	3.0S Ford Capri III/GSR	Mallory Park/BTCC	3rd oa	Jeff Allam (Rover) P1, Rouse P4
9/4/82	3.0S Ford Capri III/GSR	Oulton Park/BTCC	1st oa	Wet race. Rover P2, Rouse P3
12/4/82	3.0S Ford Capri III/GSR	Thruxton/BTCC	2nd oa	Woodman P1, Rouse P3
31/5/82	3.0S Ford Capri III/GSR	Thruxton/BTCC	3rd oa	Woodman P1, Rouse P2
13/6/82	3.0S Ford Capri III/GSR	Silverstone/BTCC	4th oa	Allam P1, Rouse P3
4/7/82	3.0S Ford Capri III/GSR	Donington/BTCC	DNF	Gear lever broke!
18/7/82	3.0S Ford Capri III/GSR	Brands Hatch (GP meeting)	2nd oa	Lovett (Rover) P1, Rouse P3
15/8/82	3.0S Ford Capri III/GSR	Donington/BTCC	3rd oa	Allam P1, Rouse P2
30/8/82	3.0S Ford Capri III/GSR	Brands Hatch/BTCC	DNF	Qualified pole. Broken crankshaft
3/10/82	3.0S Ford Capri III/GSR	Silverstone/BTCC	DNF	Shredded tyres

Final UK season for GSR/Ford Capri combination. TWR Rovers dominated the racing and the GSR Capris finished 3rd (Rouse) and 4th (GS) in class – JW

1981 RAC Tricentrol British Saloon Car Championship

Team sponsors: British Airways, *Autocar*, Kamasa. Team-mate: Philip Martin-Dye

Date	Car/Entrant	Event/Status	Result	Comments
22/3/81	3.0S Ford Capri III/GSR	Mallory Park/BTCC	DNF	Problems with new engine
29/3/81	3.0S Ford Capri III/GSR	Silverstone/BTCC	2nd oa	Won by Andy Rouse (Capri)
17/4/81	3.0S Ford Capri III/GSR	Oulton Park/BTCC	Class 1st; 2nd oa	Won by Win Percy (Mazda RX7)
20/4/81	3.0S Ford Capri III/GSR	Thruxton/BTCC	2nd oa	Won by Vince Woodman (Capri)
25/5/81	3.0S Ford Capri III/GSR	Brands Hatch/BTCC	DNS	Unable to drive – road accident
21/6/81	3.0S Ford Capri III/GSR	Silverstone/BTCC	2nd oa	Won by Peter Lovett (Rover V8)
19/7/81	3.0S Ford Capri III/GSR	Silverstone (GP meeting)	DNF	Hit spinning Woodman/Brian Muir
16/8/81	3.0S Ford Capri III/GSR	Donington/BTCC	5th oa	Beaten by 2 Rovers and Mazda RX7
20/9/81	3.0S Ford Capri III/GSR	Thruxton/BTCC	7th oa	Beaten by Rovers, Mazda and Capris
4/10/81	3.0S Ford Capri III/GSR	Silverstone/BTCC	DNF	Gearbox failure

This was the season that TWR 3.5-litre Rover V8s became dominant in the British Championship and GS suffered a nasty road accident. The Capris were desperately uprated in pursuit of the Rovers and this resulted in reliability problems. GS lost his class title, finishing fourth in the category – JW

1980 RAC Tricentrol British Saloon Car Championship

Team sponsors: *Autocar*, Valvoline. Team-mate: Andy Rouse

Date	Car/Entrant	Event/Status	Result	Comments
23/3/80	3.0S Ford Capri III/GSR	Mallory Park/BTCC-1	2nd oa	Pole position – Andy won
4/4/80	3.0S Ford Capri III/GSR	Oulton Park, Good Friday	1st oa	Close battle with team-mate
7/4/80	3.0S Ford Capri III/GSR	Thruxton Formula 2	1st oa	Fastest lap: 1m 29.84s/94.41mph
20/4/80	3.0S Ford Capri III/GSR	Silverstone International Trophy	DNF	Motor failure, lap 9
8/6/80	3.0S Ford Capri III/GSR	Silverstone/BTCC	DNF	Accident, Woodcote chicane
13/7/80	3.0S Ford Capri III/GSR	Brands Hatch/GP meeting	5th oa	Spin and off track moments
17/8/80	3.0S Ford Capri III/GSR	Mallory Park/BTCC	1st oa	Pole position
25/8/80	3.0S Ford Capri III/GSR	Brands Hatch, Aurora F1	1st oa	Fastest lap: 1m 43.5s/91.0mph
7/9/80	3.0S Ford Capri III/GSR	Thruxton, Aurora F1	1st oa	Fastest lap: 1m 30.18s GSR 1–2, Rouse 2nd
5/10/80	3.0S Ford Capri III/GSR	Silverstone Final/BTCC	1st oa	Heavy tyre wear, just made it

GS's last year as class champion, his 6th straight year ruling a ferociously fought category. GS won six races in the Capri's second most successful UK season. He finished 3rd overall in the British Championship standings, with team-mate Andy Rouse 4th – JW

1979 RAC Tricentrol British Saloon Car Championship

Team sponsors: *Autocar*, Motorcraft, Goodyear. Team-mate: Chris Craft

Date	Car/Entrant	Event/Status	Result	Comments
24/3/79	3.0S Ford Capri III/GSR	Silverstone/BTCC	1st oa	Fastest lap
13/4/79	3.0S Ford Capri III/GSR	Oulton Park/BTCC	1st oa	
16/4/79	3.0S Ford Capri III/GSR	Thruxton/BTCC	1st oa	Easter double!
28/5/79	3.0S Ford Capri III/GSR	Silverstone/BTCC	2nd oa	
24/6/79	3.0S Ford Capri III/GSR	Donington/BTCC	1st oa	Fastest lap
15/7/79	3.0S Ford Capri III/GSR	Silverstone/BTCC	1st oa	GP Meeting
12/8/79	3.0S Ford Capri III/GSR	Mallory Park/BTCC	2nd oa	
19/8/79	3.0S Ford Capri III/GSR	Donington/BTCC	4th oa	
27/8/79	3.0S Ford Capri III/GSR	Brands Hatch/BTCC	Unclassified	
9/9/79	3.0S Ford Capri III/GSR	Thruxton/BTCC	1st oa	Fastest lap
23/9/79	3.0S Ford Capri III/GSR	Snetterton/BTCC	Unclassified	
29/9/79	3.0S Ford Capri III/GSR	Oulton Park/BTCC	4th oa	Reliability problems

Class champion, 4th in overall Championship points, and six outright victories – JW

1978 RAC Tricentrol British Saloon Car Championship
Team sponsors: *Autocar*, Motorcraft, Goodyear. Team-mate: Chris Craft

Date	Car/Entrant	Event/Status	Result	Comments
19/3/78	3.0S Ford Capri III/GSR	Silverstone Trophy/BTCC	Class 2nd; 3rd oa	Soaking race, debut Goodyears
26/3/78	3.0S Ford Capri III/GSR	Oulton Park/BTCC	1st oa	Convincing win
28/3/78	3.0S Ford Capri III/GSR	Thruxton/BTCC	1st oa	Easter winning double
1/5/78	3.0S Ford Capri III/GSR	Brands Hatch/BTCC	1st oa	Wet, won by 6.4s
28/5/78	3.0S Ford Capri III/GSR	Silverstone/BTCC	1st oa	Craft makes it a GSR 1–2
25/6/78	3.0S Ford Capri III/GSR	Donington/BTCC	2nd oa	Craft win makes it GSR 1–2
2/7/78	3.0S Ford Capri III/GSR	Mallory Park/BTCC	1sr oa	Beat Walkinshaw BMW
16/7/78	3.0S Ford Capri III/GSR	Brands Hatch/BTCC	9th oa	GP Meeting. 2nd until motor cut
6/8/78*	3.0S Ford Capri III/GSR	Donington/BTCC	1st oa (DSQ)	Post race hassles
27/8/78	3.0S Ford Capri III/GSR	Brands Hatch/BTCC	2nd oa	Lap record: 1m 43.24s
10/9/78	3.0S Ford Capri III/GSR	Thruxton/BTCC	1st oa	Craft makes it a GSR 1–2 Lap record: 1m 30.31s
7/10/78	3.0S Ford Capri III/GSR	Oulton Park/BTCC	2nd oa	Beaten by BMW

*Capris excluded for technical infringement – including GSR

This was the first year GSR ran a two-car team with Chris Craft as team-mate. It was GS's most successful season, with seven outright victories and his fourth class championship title. He was fourth overall in the Championship and Capris were equal first in manufacturers' points (tied with Mini 1275GT), using new third-generation Capri 3-litre – JW

1977 RAC Tricentrol British Saloon Car Championship
Team sponsors: Spectra, Piranha, Alexander

Date	Car/Entrant	Event/Status	Result	Comments
6/3/77	3.0S Ford Capri II/GSR	Silverstone/BTCC	1st oa	Chris Craft retired late in race
20/3/77	3.0S Ford Capri II/GSR	Brands RoC/BTCC	Class 3rd; 7th oa	Start from back – gearbox
8/4/77	3.0S Ford Capri II/GSR	Oulton Park/BTCC	Class 1st; 2nd oa	Dron won by 0.45s!
11/4/77	3.0S Ford Capri II/GSR	Thruxton 200/BTCC	2nd oa	Woodman won, 7-car dice
6/6/77	3.0S Ford Capri II/GSR	Silverstone/BTCC	5th oa	Fierce race v. Walkinshaw BMW
19/6/77	3.0S Ford Capri II/GSR	Thruxton/BTCC	Unclassified	Puncture
8/7/77	3.0S Ford Capri II/GSR	Donington-eve meet/BTCC	Class 2nd; 3rd oa	Battered Capri! Rough race
16/7/77	3.0S Ford Capri II/GSR	Silverstone GP/BTCC	Class 5th; 8th oa	Another physical Capri race
7/8/77	3.0S Ford Capri II/GSR	Donington/BTCC	DNF	Propshaft failure
28/8/77	3.0S Ford Capri II/GSR	Brands Hatch/BTCC	Class 4th; 7th oa	
15/9/77	3.0S Ford Capri II/GSR	Thruxton/BTCC	Class 1st; 2nd oa	0.19s behind Dron!
16/10/77	3.0S Ford Capri II/GSR	Brands Hatch/BTCC	1st oa	Fastest lap: 1m 45.7s

This was the first year of Gordon Spice Racing (GSR). GS was class champion, 5th overall – JW

1976 Keith Prowse British Saloon Car Championship
Team sponsor: M&M Plant Hire

Date	Car/Entrant	Event/Status	Result	Comments
14/3/76	3.0 Ford Capri GT/Wisharts	Brands Hatch RoC/BTCC	1st oa	Return to racing after accident
11/4/76	3.0 Ford Capri II GT/Wisharts	Silverstone Trophy/BTCC	1st oa	
16/4/76	3.0 Ford Capri II GT/Wisharts	Oulton Park/BTCC	2nd oa	1st Walkinshaw – just!
19/4/76	3.0 Ford Capri II GT/Wisharts	Thruxton Easter F2/BTCC	2nd oa	1st Walkinshaw, again
9/5/76	3.0 Ford Capri II GT/Wisharts	Thruxton/BTCC	6th oa	Spun overtaking backmarker
31/5/76	3.0 Ford Capri II GT/Wisharts	Silverstone Club/BTCC	1st oa	Beat Walkinshaw – just!
18/7/76	3.0 Ford Capri II GT/Wisharts	Brands GP support/BTCC	DNF	Throttle cable broke on lap 1
29/8/76	3.0 Ford Capri II GT/Wisharts	Mallory Park/BTCC	3rd oa	Pole, dramatic race, motor hiccup on last lap
31/7/76	3.0 Ford Capri II GT/Wisharts	Snetterton/BTCC	1st oa	
24/10/76	3.0 Ford Capri II GT/Wisharts	Brands Hatch MoShow200/BTCC	Class 3rd; 6th oa	Physical race v. Walkinshaw!

1976 Class champion, 4th in overall Championship points, and four outright victories.

1975 Southern Organs British Saloon Car Championship
Team sponsor: M&M Plant Hire

Date	Car/Entrant	Event/Status	Result	Comments
9/3/75	3.0 Ford Capri II GT/Wisharts	Mallory Park/BTCC	Class 1st; 3rd oa	
16/3/75	3.0 Ford Capri II GT/Wisharts	Brands Hatch/BTCC	DNF	Loose wheel nuts!
28/3/75	3.0 Ford Capri II GT/Wisharts	Oulton Park	Class 1st; 4th oa	F5000 win same day
13/4/75	3.0 Ford Capri II GT/Wisharts	Silverstone/BTCC	Class 1st; 10th oa	Camaro V8s to the fore!
19/4/75	3.0 Ford Capri II GT/Wisharts	Brands Hatch/BTCC	Class 1st; 6th oa	2 x 20 lap races Record lap: 56.2s/77.61mph
10/5/75	3.0 Ford Capri II GT/Wisharts	Thruxton/BTCC	Class 1st; 7th oa	
15/6/75	3.0 Ford Capri II GT/Wisharts	Mallory Park/BTCC	Class 1st; 6th oa	
28/6/75	3.0 Ford Capri II GT/Wisharts	Snetterton/BTCC	Class 1st; 4th oa	Record lap: 1m18s/86.26mph
19/7/75	3.0 Ford Capri II GT/Wisharts	Silverstone/BTCC	DNF – half-shaft	Fastest lap: 1m 50.0s/95.95mph

NB 1975 was the last year of the American V8-engined cars. GS's F5000 accident at Mallory Park in August terminated his 1975 season, but he had already won his BTCC (2,500–3,500cc) class; Ford Capri was fourth in manufacturers' points – JW

1974

Date	Car/Entrant	Event/Status	Result	Comments
19/10/74	3.0 Ford Capri GT/Wisharts	Brands Hatch/Castrol Anniv	4th oa	British Championship

NB The 1974 season was a disaster, as development of the Wisharts-owned Plymouth Hemicuda was unsuccessful. The intention was to challenge the American V8s for overall victories, but the car was never raced.

1973

Date	Car/Entrant	Event/Status	Result	Comments
14/4/73	3.0 Ford Capri GT/Wisharts	Ingliston/Grp 1 Prod	2nd oa	Racing by price: +£1,150 class
21/4/73	3.0 Ford Capri GT/Wisharts	Snetterton/Castrol Grp 1	4th oa	National series sponsored by
22/04/73	3.0 Ford Capri GT/Wisharts	Silverstone/Castrol Grp 1	2nd oa	Castrol and Britax
5/5/73*	3.0 Ford Capri GT/Wisharts	Brands Hatch/Castrol Grp 1	1st oa	
19/5/73	3.0 Ford Capri GT/Wisharts	Silverstone/Castrol Grp 1	1st oa	
27/5/73	3.0 Ford Capri GT/Wisharts	Snetterton/Castrol Grp 1	2nd oa	
9/6/73	3.0 Ford Capri GT/Wisharts	Brands Hatch/Castrol Grp 1	2nd oa	
30/6/73	3.0 Ford Capri GT/Wisharts	Silverstone/Castrol Grp 1	2nd oa	
4/8/73	3.0 Ford Capri GT/Wisharts	Mallory Park/Britax Grp 1	6th oa	
11/8/73	3.0 Ford Capri GT/Wisharts	Croft Autodrome/Grp 1	3rd oa	
30/8/73	3.0 Ford Capri GT/Wisharts	Rufforth/Castrol Grp 1	4th oa	
13/10/73	3.0 Ford Capri GT/Wisharts	Ingliston/Grp 1 Prod	2nd oa	

*Also competed in 10-lap Shellsport Celebrity race using Ford Escort Mexicos; 3rd oa.

Formula 5000 Results, 1970–5

1975 Shellsport European Formula 5000 Championship

Entrant/sponsor: Reed Racing

Date	Car/Engine	Event/Country	Result	Comments
28/3/75	Lola T332/Fewkes Chev V8	Oulton Park Gold Cup/UK	1st – 50 laps	My first and last F5000 win!
31/3/75	Lola T332/Fewkes Chev V8	Brands Hatch/UK	DNS	Dropped valve qualifying
27/4/75	Lola T332/Fewkes Chev V8	Zolder/Belgium	7th on aggregate	4th heat 2
19/5/75	Lola T332/Fewkes Chev V8	Zandvoort/Holland	4th – 30 laps	Encouraging
27/7/75	Lola T332/Fewkes Chev V8	Snetterton/UK	DNF	Radiator holed when lying 2nd
9/8/75	Lola T332/Fewkes Chev V8	Mallory Park/UK	DNS	Testing accident terminated F5000 career

GS did not compete in F5000 in 1973–4. Chris Reed sponsored the 1975 Lola. The accident at Mallory terminated GS's season with just five out of sixteen rounds completed – JW

1972 Rothmans European Formula 5000 Championship & combined Grand Prix/F5000 events

Entrant: Gordon Spice Cash & Carry. Sponsor: Powrmatic

Date	Car/Engine	Event/Country	Result	Comments
26/3/72	Kitchmac-5.0/Smith Chev V8	Mallory Park/UK	4th	Pole position!
31/3/72	Kitchmac-5.0/Smith Chev V8	Snetterton/UK	DNF – rear suspension	Fastest lap, led race – a win lost
8/4/72	Kitchmac-5.0/Smith Chev V8	Nivelles/Belgium	7th heat 2	DNF heat 1, oil leak
22/4/72	Kitchmac-5.0/Smith Chev V8	Silverstone/UK	6th	GKN Vanwall Trophy race
29/5/72	Kitchmac-5.0/Smith Chev V8	Oulton Park/UK	DNF	Blown head gasket
24/9/72	Kitchmac-5.0/Smith Chev V8	Brands Hatch/UK	DNF	Lying P2 when electrics died

A limited season with mechanical reliability a major handicap. It was the year that GS opened his first cash & carry, which took priority over racing – JW

1971 Rothmans European Formula 5000 Championship & combined Grand Prix/F5000 events

Entrant: Gordon Spice Limited

Date	Car/Engine	Event/Country	Result	Comments
?/1/71	McLaren M10B-5.0/Chev V8	Argentine GP/Argentina	8th on aggregate	Vital prize money bonus
12/4/71	Kitchmac M10B-5.0/Chev V8	Silverstone/UK	6th	
4/7/71	Kitchmac M10B-5.0/Chev V8	Mallory Park/UK	8th	
26/9/71	Kitchmac M10B-5.0/Chev V8	Brands Hatch/UK	7th	
24/10/71	Kitchmac M10B-5.0/Chev V8	Brands Hatch/UK	4th – race stopped	Jo Siffert (BRM) killed

GS bought the ex-Howden Ganley McLaren prepared by Tony Kitchiner. It was dubbed Kitchmac after a crash in testing at Snetterton which required a major rebuild with Kitchiner modifications. Unreliability and accidents curtailed the season – JW

1970 Guards European Formula 5000 Championship

Entrant: Kitchiner Race Developments Ltd

Date	Car/Engine	Event/Country	Result	Comments
27/3/70	Kitchiner K3A/4.7 Ford V8	Oulton Park/UK	6th oa x 2	Two races, same result
30/3/70	Kitchiner K3A/4.7 Ford V8	Brands Hatch/UK	7th & DNF – 13th	Collision ended one race
5/4/70	Kitchiner K3A/4.7 Ford V8	Zolder/Belgium	9th on aggregate	8th and 10th in two heats
19/4/70	Kitchiner K3A/4.7 Ford V8	Zandvoort/Holland	6th on aggregate	5th and 7th in two heats
3/5/70	Kitchiner K3A/4.7 Ford V8	Brands Hatch/UK	12th – DNF	Oil cooler failed, 9 laps of 50
1/6/70	Kitchiner K3A/4.7 Ford V8	Mondello Park/Ireland	7th & DNF	Accident, 2nd heat
6/6/70	Kitchiner K3A/4.7 Ford V8	Silverstone/UK	14th – DNF x 2	Gear linkage and motor failures
21/6/70	Kitchiner K3A/4.7 Ford V8	Monza/Italy	4th on aggregate	3rd and 6th in two heats
28/6/70	Kitchiner K3A/4.7 Ford V8	Anderstorp/Sweden	12th on aggregate	Derrick Williams killed
12/7/70	Kitchiner K3A/4.7 Ford V8	Salzburgring/Austria	5th on aggregate	6th in both heats

The team ran out of money in July and did not complete the F5000 season – JW

BMC/British Leyland Mini racing 1965–70

1970 European Touring Car Championship

Date	Mini model	Event	Result	Comments
27/6/70	1.3 Cooper 1275 S-Arden	Silverstone Tourist Trophy	Class 8th; 18th oa	See BTCC results below

1970 RAC British National Saloon Car Championship

Entrant: Equipe Arden

Date	Mini model	Event	Result	Comments
26/4/70	1.3 Cooper 1275 S-Arden	Silverstone	Class 1st; 5th oa	Hailed a star in a private Mini, actually works/Arden!
25/5/70	1.3 Cooper 1275 S-Arden	Crystal Palace	Class 2nd; 2nd oa	
6/6/70	1.3 Cooper 1275 S-Arden	Silverstone	Class 1st; 14th oa	
5/7/70	1.3 Cooper 1275 S-Arden	Silverstone TT/BTCC	Class 3rd; 18th oa	TT meeting date
18/7/70	1.3 Cooper 1275 S-Arden	Brands Hatch (GP track)	Class 2nd; 12th oa	Beaten by Fitzpatrick's Ford
28/8/70	1.3 Cooper 1275 S-Arden	Oulton Park	Class 2nd; 10th oa	Fitzpatrick wins again
31/8/70	1.3 Cooper 1275 S-Arden	Brands Hatch	Class 2nd; 8th oa	Heat 1. Ford still wins
			Class 2nd; 10th oa	Heat 2. Ford again

1970 was the year of GS's first foray into single-seater racing, with the Kitchiner F5000 car. Hence the limited Mini season – JW

1969 RAC British National Saloon Car Championship
Team sponsors: Britax, Downton. Team-mate: Steve Neal

Date	Mini model	Event	Result	Comments
16/3/69	1.3 Mini/Cooper Car Co	Brands Hatch	Class 1st; 4th oa	Heat 1
			Class 1st; 5th oa	Heat 2
30/3/69	1.3 Mini/Cooper Car Co	Silverstone	Class 2nd; 6th oa	
4/4//69	1.3 Mini/Cooper Car Co	Snetterton	DNF	
7/4/69	1.3 Mini/Cooper Car Co	Thruxton	Class 2nd; 6th oa	
17/5/69	1.3 Mini/Cooper Car Co	Silverstone	DNF – accident	Team-mates collision. Two new bodyshells needed!
26/5/69	1.3 Mini/Cooper Car Co	Crystal Palace	1st oa	BBC televised my first ever overall win!
29/6/69	1.3 Mini/Cooper Car Co	Mallory Park	1st oa	Second smaller capacity race
12/7/69	1.3 Mini/Cooper Car Co	Croft Autodrome	7th oa	Aggregate result, two races
19/7/69	1.3 Mini/Cooper Car Co	Silverstone	Class 3rd; 7th oa	Grand Prix meeting
14/8/69	1.3 Mini/Cooper Car Co	Oulton Park	Class 5th; 14th oa	
1/9/69	1.3 Mini/Cooper Car Co	Brands Hatch	Class 5th; 11th oa	Aggregate result, two races
19/10/69	1.3 Mini/Cooper Car Co	Brands Hatch	Class 4th; 14th oa	

GS was 5th overall in the championship standings, 2nd overall in the 1,000–1,300cc class, which was won by Chris Craft's Broadspeed Escort – JW

1969 European Touring Car Championship

Date	Mini model	Event	Result	Comments
21/6/69	1.3 Cooper 1275S/Downton	Brands Hatch 6-hours	DNF	Qualified 3rd= in class; Co-driver: Steve Neal; Entrant: Britax

1968 European Touring Car Championship

Date	Mini model	Event	Result	Comments
7/7/68	1.3 Mini/Cooper Car Co	Nürburgring 6-hours	Class 5th; 14th oa	An adventure for me and Hertz
25/8/68	1.0 Mini/Equipe Arden	Zandvoort ETCC	DNF	Retired, out of fuel

1968 RAC British Saloon Car Championship

Date	Mini model	Event	Result	Comments
17/3/68	1.0 Cooper 970S/Arden	Brands Hatch	Class 3rd; 12th oa	40 laps, Arden debut, long distance!
15/4/68	1.0 Cooper 970S/Arden	Thruxton	Class 4th; 15th oa	25 laps, Easter Formula 2 meeting
27/4/68	1.0 Cooper 970S/Arden	Silverstone	Class 2nd; 13th oa	20 laps
3/6/68	1.0 Cooper 970S/Arden	Crystal Palace	DNF	Electrical problems
23/6/68	1.0 Cooper 970S/Arden	Mallory Park	DNF	Engine – low oil pressure
20/7/68	1.0 Cooper 970S/Arden	Brands Hatch	DNF	
27/7/68	1.0 Cooper 970S/Arden	Silverstone	Class 3rd; 27th oa	
10/8/68	1.0 Cooper 970S/Arden	Croft Autodrome	Class 1st; 11th oa	First class win, 40 laps
17/8/68	1.0 Cooper 970S/Arden	Oulton Park	Class 1st; 15th oa	19 laps
2/9/68	1.0 Cooper 970S/Arden	Brands Hatch	DNF	Electrics again
20/10/68	1.0 Cooper 970S/Arden	Brands Hatch	Class 2nd; 14th oa	Clinched class championship

GS won the 1,000cc class of the RAC British Saloon Car Championship with the Equipe Arden-engineered and entered Mini – JW

1967 European Touring Car Championship

Date	Mini model	Event	Result	Comments
17/9/67	1.3 Cooper S/Costello	Snetterton 500km	2nd oa	Co-driver/owner: Ken Costello

1967 BRSCC British National Saloon Car Championship

Date	Mini model	Event	Result	Comments
12/3/67	1.3 Cooper S/Downton	Brands Hatch	Class 2nd; 5th oa	Race of Champions support race
24/3/67	1.3 Cooper S/Downton	Snetterton	DNF – drive shaft	20 laps
27/3/67	1.3 Cooper S/Downton	Silverstone	Class 2nd; 12th oa	20 laps
29/4/67	1.3 Cooper S/Downton	Silverstone	Class 3rd; 5th oa	25 laps, *Daily Express* meeting
14/5/67	1.3 Cooper S/Downton	Mallory Park	Class 3rd; 3rd oa	15 laps, smaller capacity race
20/5/67	1.3 Cooper S/Downton	Silverstone	Class 6th; 16th oa	20 laps
15/7/67	1.3 Cooper S/Downton	Silverstone	Class 5th; 15th oa	20 laps, British GP meeting
28/8/67	1.3 Cooper S/Downton	Brands Hatch	DNF – accident	Tangled with Unett's Imp
16/9/67	1.3 Cooper S/Downton	Oulton Park	Class 3rd; 3rd oa	Smaller capacity race
22/10/67	1.3 Cooper S/Downton	Brands Hatch	DNF – accident	Off at Hawthorne bend

GS's last season as a privateer before landing a semi-works drive with Equipe Arden for 1968.

1966 BRSCC British National Saloon Car Championship

Date	Mini model	Event	Result	Comments
14/5/66	1.3 Cooper S/Downton	Silverstone	Class 5th; 16th oa	35 laps
30/5/66	1.3 Cooper S/Downton	Crystal Palace	2nd oa	Race for smaller two classes: split the works Coopers: surprised!
16/7/66	1.3 Cooper S/Downton	Brands Hatch	Class 3rd; 10th oa	20 laps: only works Ford and Mini ahead
29/8/66	1.3 Cooper S/Downton	Brands Hatch	Class 4th; 8th oa	20 laps
17/9/66	1.3 Cooper S/Downton	Oulton Park	5th oa	Smaller classes, 20 laps
30/10/66	1.3 Cooper S/Downton	Brands Hatch	DNF – accident	Too busy watching Jim Clark!

GS's second season as a privateer, with support from Downton Engineering, competing in the National Saloon Car Championship after opening his first car accessory shop in February 1966 – JW

1965 BRSCC British National Saloon Car Championship

Date	Mini model	Event	Result	Comments
10/7/65	1.3 Cooper S-Downton	Silverstone	Class 7th; 14th oa	British GP support race
30/8/65	1.3 Cooper S-Downton	Brands Hatch	Class 2nd; 7th oa	20 laps

GS's first season with a private Mini Cooper S competing in the National Saloon Car Championship whilst working for Downton Engineering – JW

Personal club racing, UK only, 1962–4

1964

Gordon drove Morgan +4 between March at Goodwood and 29 August at Goodwood, which then took on the new SLR aluminium body. Major meeting of the year was 11 July support race to European Grand Prix, Brands Hatch. He only did a few races and then wrote the car off at Goodwood in August – JW

1963

Date	Car	Event/Club	Result	Comments
15/4/63	Morgan +4/Lawrencetune	Brands Hatch/BRSCC	Unknown	1st race in my newly acquired Morgan 2.0-litre TR4 engine
28/4/63	Morgan +4/Lawrencetune	Snetterton/BRSCC	Unknown	Do not appear in results
5/5/63	Morgan +4/Lawrencetune	Mallory Park/BRSCC	Class 3rd	1,600–2,500cc GT cars
19/5/63	Morgan +4/Lawrencetune	Brands Hatch/BRSCC	Class 2nd	
2/6/63	Morgan +4/Lawrencetune	Goodwood/BARC	Unknown	Do not appear in results
22/6/63	Morgan +4/Lawrencetune	Goodwood/BARC	Unknown	10-lap race, 23 entries
31/8/63	Morgan +4/Lawrencetune	Oulton Park/BARC	2nd oa	Hare Trophy race
21/9/63	Morgan +4/Lawrencetune	Goodwood/BARC	Class 2nd	
6/10/63	Morgan +4/Lawrencetune	Aintree/BARC	Class 1st	GT Cars over 1,600cc, fastest lap
13/10/63	Morgan +4/Lawrencetune	Mallory Park/BRSCC	Class 1st	GT cars 1,600–2,500cc, fastest lap
26/12/63	Morgan +4/Lawrencetune	Brands Hatch/BRSCC	Class 2nd; 4th oa	Pole position, beaten by a Porsche; Dee rolled his A40 at Paddock

This was GS's first full season of club racing and a full RAC National Competition Licence was obtained after six races. From September he worked full time at Lawrencetune Engines Ltd – JW

1962

Date	Car	Event	Result	Comments
23/4/62	MG TF	Goodwood	DNF	Head gasket
7/7/62	MG TF/Derrington	Goodwood 5-lap handicap	DNS	Engine failure in qualifying
26/8/62	MG TF/Derrington	Brands Hatch	DNF	Overheating
1/9/62	MG TF/Derrington	Goodwood 5-lap handicap	DNS	Engine failure again
22/9/62	MG TF/Derrington	Goodwood 5-lap handicap	DNS	Not one signature all season

GS's first season's results say it all! The objective was to obtain five signatures on his provisional RAC Competition Licence in order to upgrade to a full licence. The car was sold in October 1962! – JW

Index